MY KOREA:
FORTY YEARS WITHOUT A HORSEHAIR HAT

Kevin O'Rourke

My Korea:

Forty Years Without a Horsehair Hat

By

KEVIN O'ROURKE

RENAISSANCE BOOKS

MY KOREA: FORTY YEARS WITHOUT A HORSEHAIR HAT

First published 2013 by
RENNAISANCE BOOKS
PO Box 219
Folkestone
Kent CT20 2WP

Renaissance Books is an imprint of Global Books Ltd

ISBN 978-1-898823-09-4

British Library Cataloguing in Publication Data
A CIP catalogue entry for this book is available
from the British Library

Set in Bembo 12 on 13pt by Dataworks, Chennai, India
Printed in England by TJ International Ltd, Padstow, Cornwall

For the Columbans – Eighty Years in Korea

CONTENTS

CONTENTS

CONTENTS

ACKNOWLEDGEMENTS

MOST OF THE poems in this volume appeared previously in various collections: *Tilting the Jar, Spilling the Moon* (Dedalus, 1993); *Singing Like a Cricket, Hooting Like an Owl* (Cornell East Asia Program,1995); *Mirrored Minds: A Thousand Years of Korean Verse* (Eastward Books, 2001; *The Book of Korean* Shijo (Harvard, 2002); *A* Shijo *Poet at the Court of King Sonjo* (Kegan Paul, 2005); *A Hundred Love Poems from Old Korea* (Global Oriental, 2005); *The Book of Korean Poetry: Songs of Shilla and Koryŏ* (Iowa University Press, 2006); *Poems of a Wanderer: Selected Poems of Sŏ Chŏngju* (Dedalus, 1995); *Looking for the Cow* (Dedalus, 1999); *The Music of What Happens* (Universal, 1992). The Sŏ Kiwŏn stories appeared previously in *Koreana* and in the *Marok Biographies* (Jimoondang, 2001).

ACKNOWLEDGMENTS

INTRODUCTION

THIS BOOK IS not an autobiography; I shudder at the thought for I am a private man. Nor is it a novel though much of the material is presented in story form; for I am not the flamboyant novel-writing type either. It is something in between, what I call, rightly or wrongly, a miscellany. It aims not so much at simple as symbolic truth, a kind of correlative to forty years of cross-cultural experience.

I came to Korea in 1964. I came from an Ireland that was one of the poorest countries in Europe; outside toilets and houses without running water or electricity were still fairly common. I remember the marvel of the tilley lamp when I visited my aunt's house in what we termed 'the country', and my cousin, still visibly excited by the mystery of electricity, following me up and down the stairs to turn off switches I had extravagantly turned on. And I remember a confrere on Korea's East Coast telling me that a tilley lamp was a better reading light than any bulb. I remember the first oranges and pears in the shops after the war and the excitement of gum bubbles big as a football exploding in my face. I remember the adventure of crossing Glangevlin on the way to Bundoran. The talk for days before the trip was about the state of the road and the thickness of the fog on top of the mountain. Bundoran was a magic place for kids in the nineteen forties and early fifties. The Horse Pool, the Priests' Pool, the Nuns' Pool, the caves, the cliff walks, Shane House and the Green Barn are engraved indelibly in my memory. The Imperial Hotel and Shell House represented modernity and elegance. We didn't dare dream of the august heights of the Central or the Great Northern.

Despite great changes in the forties, fifties, and early sixties, Ireland was still a backwater when I left in 1964. I did not realize this for a long time because 1960s Ireland was a paradise compared to 1960s Korea. In the intervening fifty years, Ireland has been transformed by the Celtic tiger and retransformed by the collapse of same; and Korea has moved from being a medieval land of total insignificance in world terms to being a highly developed modern country and a major player in world economics. Even the wildest extravagances of the Celtic tiger pale in comparison with Korea's development in the last fifty years. And I have seen it all happen. In 1964, Seoul was a city of three million people with three bridges over the Han and one ten-storey building in the heart of the city, the New Korea Hotel – it's still there, beside City Hall. I have lost count of the number of bridges over the Han, and Seoul's skyline is like Manhattan's. Kangnam was paddy-fields as was the entire city beyond Suyuri, going north, and T'apshimni, going east. People have even begun to speak of Seoul as a beautiful city, citing Namsan, Sajik Park, Inwangsan, the Pukhak Skyway, and Lee Myungbak's redeveloped Ch'onggyech'on as visible proof.

Parts of Tŏksu Palace, the widening of Chongno and the construction of Pagoda Park may have been the brainchild of a Lisburn man, John McLeavy Brown, Chief Commissioner of the Korean Customs and Financial Adviser to Kojong, but most of what happened here is rooted in 1500 years of cultural history and in the Korean character that grew therein. I seek in this book an imaginative correlative for my experience of Korea. It is a poet's account, what the heart has taught, and it should be interpreted as literature not history, philosophy or sociology. Much of the account is true; much is half true. Some of the characters are real; others are amalgams of several characters; still others are products of the imagination. Most of the stories have some basis in fact, but they have been altered and expanded, not just to protect privacy, although that was sometimes a concern, but also to contribute to the creation of an imaginative version of fifteen hundred years of assimilated history and culture.

The account features neither plot line nor sequential time. The text is peppered with my own poems, stories and essays, and with poems and stories from the Korean. Much of what I know of the Korean cultural experience came courtesy of the poems of Sŏ Chŏngju, a great poet who should have won the Nobel Prize. His name dots the pages of this book. A bantam cock of a man, his raucous voice still rings in my ears. He gave me an imaginative entry into Korean history and culture for which I am eternally grateful. Most Koreans approach history and culture as exercises in sociology. Their accounts are framed in an abstract idiom that misses the heart of the matter. Opinions tend to be a rehash of the opinions of professors fifty years ago. Sŏ Chŏngju's stories of old Korea are different, primarily because they are not shackled by fixed notions of people and events. They are pure poetry, the best introduction I know to Korea's cultural mother lode. I use the poems freely, combining them with narrative and exposition in an attempt to present living in Korea as a process of growth in cultural exchange. During forty-plus years trying to take in and interpret an intense personal and public experience, my quest has always been for understanding, for what the people of Shilla called 'the light of heaven'. Most of my missionary colleagues came here to teach. I figured early on that there were more than enough of them for the task. For my part, I found there was much more to learn than to teach.

Korea is home to me. When I go to Rosslare in Ireland, I'm on my holidays. I arrive with a contented grin. When I get back to Inch'ŏn Airport, I'm home. I heave a contented sigh and look forward to the pleasures of living in my Seoul apartment again after months of being pampered by my family in Ireland.

Loving Korea does not blind me to certain grating aspects of the Korean experience. Sŏ Chŏngju (1915–2000) writes:

In this land, at this moment in time, someone of our race is doing a shameful deed, selling short his being human. What of it! One extra-cleansing bath, one meticulous assuaging of the heart and again we can stand tall between earth and sky, for we are possessors of a tradition of great pride, something to be supremely grateful for: we are the people whose country gets the first seep of morning light.

If you think Korea is beyond the shameful deed, think again. Korea has had more than her share of soiled moments. If you think Japan is uniquely the land of the rising sun, think again; Korea also lays claim to the first light of the sun. And if you think selling humanity short is anything less than a universal sin, think again. Northern Ireland, Vietnam, Iraq and Afghanistan are tips of the iceberg, historical symbols of the inhumanity of man.

Sŏ Chŏngju had a keen awareness of modern man's penchant for the shameful deed, but he also had a great ability to see the beauty of old Korea.

Dolmens

The people of old Chosŏn were too pure-hearted to commit any of those ugly, seedy sins that bring pain to the world after death, so when they breathed their last and crossed into eternity, they had no bitter remorse, no teeth-grinding rancour. Eternal life in the role of Immortals and nymphs, however, was so interminably protracted that sheer excess of boredom sometimes brought an itch, and when this happened, they would ask the most beautiful among the nymphs to scratch the itchy spot.

Mago was famous as the nymph who best scratched the itchy spot. As a consequence of her fame, even Chinese Immortals in later ages pleaded their cases with her.

This is why those old dolmens from Tan'gun Chosŏn – beds with ceilings that dot the northern frontier – have always been called Mago Houses.

Sŏ Chŏngju (1915–2000)

Some people see only what they want to see. I see the ugly as well as the beautiful. Living the spirit of the *Tao Te Ching* is not easy. I have great difficulty in seeing the ugly as a dirty window that can be cleaned with a rub of a cloth. Manil-sa, a nondescript temple in the south built on an incredibly beautiful site, is a paradigm of the mysterious turns that the beautiful takes in Korea:

Manil-sa

The king's seal teeters in air;
mountain tops are geese in flight.
This is a magic place, made for monk things.
The temple site is perfect
though nothing that stands there is old
except the stone stele inscribed with
the names of Yi Sŏnggye and the founding monk.
A blue plastic can spoils
the mountain god's shrine.
Why seek out the ugly?
Does not the beautiful suffice?
Vision is never just black and white.
Ugly and beautiful are sides of a coin;
they need each other to get the balance right.

If you want to see Korea's traditional beauty, you must go to the temples. At the same time be aware that few man-made artefacts in Korea, including temple buildings, are very old. Wars, fires, and the elements have seen to that. And those ugly plastic cans are everywhere.

The awareness of Korea's natural beauty is a fairly recent phenomenon. In the nineteenth century when Korea was still a hermit kingdom, the tops of mountains and headlands were denuded, and the countryside, at least what was visible from the sea, was deliberately made ugly in order to discourage interest on the part of foreign devils. From the beginning of vehicular traffic at the end of the nineteenth century, until Park

Chunghee began the modern hardtop road system in the late '60s, the country was permanently shrouded in a layer of dust. In 1964, there were a hundred kilometres of paved roads in the entire country: Seoul to Osan, Hongch'ŏn to Inje, and part of the Seoul to Ch'unch'ŏn road. A recent Hwang Sŏg'yŏng novel notes that there was hardtop in Yŏngdŭngp'o. I was not aware of this. In the '60s and '70s, buses and trucks roared along country roads filling the air and lungs with grit. It was a lot of fun getting where you wanted to go, but you arrived with dust embedded in every pore. Natural beauty was not a typical topic of discussion. Modernization brought roads, and roads ended that all-pervasive cloud of dust, except, that is, for the Gobi Desert dust storms, loaded with various types of insidious Chinese goo that continue to bedevil us every year.

Modernization inevitably brought destruction in its wake. Most of the interesting parts of downtown Seoul have disappeared. In the '60s and '70s the area around City Hall had lovely winding alleyways dotted with teahouses and drinking establishments where artists and writers held court. You could walk into a tearoom and meet Kim Tongni or Sŏ Chŏngju or any one of a dozen of the most important men in the arts. The greats sported their fame; they didn't feel the need to hide behind the veil of anonymity.

Kim Sŭngok's 'Seoul 1964, Winter' was the cult story of the decade; it proclaimed a new post-war existentialism, very exciting and very avant-garde, which sent me looking for the scratch on the door of the toilet in the Yŏngbo Building in Chongno 2 ka, the street lights that weren't working in Pyŏnghwa market, and the dark windows in the Hwashin Department Store. I hate what the City has done to the area between the old Hwashin and Kwanghwamun, and what it has done to all of Mu'gyodong and the area at the back of City Hall; and I regret the gutting of one of the last bastions of old Seoul, Sajikdong, between the old Naija Hotel and Independence Gate. There is much talk of the glories of Pukch'on, a village of hanok houses in Chongno, but much of Pukch'on has already suffered the indignity of developers' bulldozers. North Ahyŏndong, Wang-shimni, Tongŭimun, Chŏngnyangni and Kirŭmdong are all being remade. When these new town projects are complete, hardly a stone of old Seoul will be intact. The cultural loss is colossal, but Seoul's heart beats on.

Loss

I grieve with you
in grieving over the past:
the felling of a world tree,
leaves scattered
who knows where.
Yet the tree lives on,
a shredded jigsaw
carved on
memory's bone.

Until recently Korea didn't really care about such cultural loss. More significantly her people rarely raised a word of objection. In the last few years, the newspapers have featured a spate of articles calling for conservation in Wangshimni, Tongŭimun, Kirŭmdong and other new town centres. The call for conservation comes too late for the road along the Han to Ch'unch'ŏn, and the road by the P'aldang Dam to Yangdŏg'wŏn and Hongch'ŏn, which have been defaced by ugly *kalbi* houses, love hotels, and cafes. The same fate has befallen the road north to Kŭmhwa through Ildong and Idong, a scenario that has been repeated throughout the country wherever new roads to tourist destinations have been made. High-rise apartments have turned the village of Masŏk into an eyesore; it was once one of the most beautiful village landscapes in the world. And I shudder to think of what's been done to Tonamdong, that lovely old residential area in Seoul. The light of the sun has been denied forever to its residents. If you want to know what the old Tonam Market was like, you have to have been there or read Pak Wansŏ. Thank God for one or two people with sensibility who regret the sacking of the lovely old in favour of the biscuit tin new. And thank God for those who have preserved the old beauty in those alleys near An'guktong Rotary, across the road from the entrance to Insadong, with their lovely *hanok* houses, wine bars, and teahouses.

The area is a rarity in modern Seoul; indeed very few people even knew it was there until four or five years ago when the boom in restaurants, cafes, wine bars, and small boutiques began to pick up speed. I remember Sŏr'aksan when it was pure magic. If you stood below the temple and looked up, the mountain soared above you on all sides. One gigantic parking lot destroyed the landscape; space replaced mystery. There's a temple near Songch'u, with a bell tower from the seventeenth century and a main worship hall that looks even older. An elephant painting, and other abstract paintings on themes I haven't seen elsewhere, adorn the outside walls of the main worship hall. The paintings are on plain timber, none of the usual red and green *tanch'ŏng* colouring. It's a beautiful building but spoiled by the new buildings and the modern granite Mireuk on the hill behind. The Korea I know and love has always mixed liberal doses of the ugly with the beautiful. I'm not sure how such exquisite taste can be combined with such appalling lack of taste. Hundreds of temples throughout the country attest to this. Until recently no one seemed to notice or care. When Pak Wansŏ mourned the removal of a hill in her village, she was the exception. One can only hope that the movement for conservation will gain momentum and salvage something from the indiscriminate destruction.

1

KOREA IN THE 1960s

YOU REALLY HAD to see Korea in the sixties to know what it was like. Korea time was the conceptual axis on which the culture turned. Modernization and the need for quick decisions have done away with this lovely, lazy, exasperating way of life. If you couldn't do something today, there was always tomorrow, or the next day, or next week. If you know some Korean, ask yourself when was the last time you heard the word *kŭlp'i* – two days after tomorrow! Sŏ Chŏngju describes this old-time world:

Two Ascetics Meet on Sosŭl Mountain

Kwan'gi lived in his grass hut on the southern peak of Sosŭl Mountain, Tosŏng lived in a cave on the northern side; they were close friends and often travelled the intervening ten *li* to visit each other. Their arrangements to meet were not according to our rigid norms of year, month, day and hour, but were based on a much more refined standard. When the fresh breeze blew from the north, not too strong and not too weak, and the leaves on the trees leaned to the south, Tosŏng in the north followed that breeze toward Kwan'gi on the southern peak, and Kwan'gi, refreshed by the breeze, would come out to meet him. And when the wind blew fair in the other direction, and the leaves on the trees leaned toward the north, Kwan'gi on the southern peak set out to visit Tosŏng on the northern peak, and Tosŏng,

seeing how the breeze blew, would come out to meet his friend.
Can't you hear the Immortals laugh?

Sŏ Chŏngju (1915–2000)

Arriving in Korea is etched in my memory like a scene from a
Somerset Maugham story. Ireland in the 1960s understood the
Tosŏng-Kwan'gi notion of time; my group was a month late
getting here. Frank McGann, complete with straw hat and cigar,
met us at Kimpo airport and gave us our first introduction to
the land of the morning calm. Frank was an old hand – he had
been here since Japanese times; in fact he had been under house
arrest in Hongch'ŏn during the Pacific War. Grannies' eyes light
up with delight to this day when they recall Frank handing out
American candy to kids in Hongch'ŏn. We drove from Kimp'o
to Columban Headquarters in Tonamdong by a long tortuous
route, some of which was paved, more of it unpaved, all of it full of
potholes, diversions and various minor discomforts. I remember
soldiers and military hardware everywhere. Very little of Korea's
extraordinary five-thousand-year cultural tradition appeared to
the eye: there were no laughing Immortals, no beautiful temples.
We didn't see South Gate that day, and Kwanghwamun Gate
had not yet been rebuilt. The taste of a vague unease was like
grit under our teeth. Seoul was ugly. There is no other word for
it. Ramshackle and ugly: narrow streets, building sprawled on
building, house jammed on house; one false rub of the jeep on
low slung eaves and you could take most of the block with you.
A jeep once swiped a hundred yards of houses in Songjŏngni
in Chŏlla. And I was there the night a brand new Toyota land
cruiser knocked a retaining wall in Soyangno in Ch'unch'ŏn
sending chicken feathers flying two storeys down. The New
Korea Hotel, a ten storey *highrise*, towered over the downtown
area. The tram tracks on Chongno were painful to drive across.
There were not too many vehicles around: the taxis were mostly
the old *shibal* variety, rebuilt war surplus Russian jeeps. The first
Datsun Bluebirds had just been introduced and were destined

to dominate. Apart from these, there was a profusion of *hapsǔng* minibuses and the rather limited tram system.

No one said anything, but there was visible relief as we swung through the huge Chinese gates that guarded the Tonamdong compound of the Columban Fathers. I learned much later that the property had been a geisha house, hence the lovely Japanese garden. The North Koreans requisitioned the house during the Korean War, and they left behind an upright piano, which in subsequent years was the occasion of so much celebration that a parsimonious superior decided to sell it.

We were met on the steps.

'Welcome to Korea, lads. School begins tomorrow at one o'clock.'

It wasn't exactly what we had in mind, but *Roma locuta est*, and anyway it was nice to be here.

2

THE COLUMBANS

THE COLUMBANS ARE a society of missionaries, founded in Ireland in 1916, with home houses in Australia, Britain, Ireland, New Zealand and the US. In recent years we have ordained quite a few Columbans from our mission territories and they are the hope of the future. Our founding vision was to work in evangelization among the Chinese, but we were forced by circumstances to branch out in East Asia and South America. In the 1920s and 1930s, we were a suspicious lot to the British authorities. Documents recently released by the British government show that British diplomats in the Far East viewed us with singular suspicion: they saw us as an organization of Sinn Feiners, bent on the destruction of British institutions. It makes amusing reading today. The last Columban priest in China was expelled in 1953. Anticipating what was coming, the society expanded into the Philippines, Burma, Japan and Korea. In the 1960s, prompted by a call from the Pope, the Columbans moved into South America.

In 1964 I came to Korea as a Columban.

Salute

At eighteen I joined the army.
At twenty-four I was commissioned.
I came to this foreign place,
which I learned to love as I love my life.

I gave it my best years
and I was rewarded with love and affection.
Eighty years have passed.
The bells of jubilee ring out.
My spirit rests under mounded grass.
For the remnant it's time to go;
a bleak prospect, I suppose.
Weeds cover the yards of home;
pigeons nest among broken tiles.
But behind the cathedral in Ch'unch'ŏn,
on the hill in Hongch'ŏn,
in the dead fields of Seoul –
friends' forever beds –
in Chŏlla and in Chejudo
something Christlike lives.
May it ever be so!

By any standards, the Columbans were an extraordinary group of men, especially those I call the men of old, who were mostly in their fifties or older when I got here in 1964. I look back now at these giant men, the lives they lived, the isolation and loneliness of their parishes, the Spartan conditions they endured, and I marvel at their strength. In my time in Kangwŏn Province, the most northerly part of South Korea, I never saw one of the old hands buy a new chair, or lay a new strip of carpet. Anything that was new came from younger men. In fact, the man who installed a flush toilet in his house – the first in a priest's house in the province – was almost excommunicated by the bishop for his wilful extravagance!

There are plenty of Korean priests now and quite a few Korean Columbans. Our role in Korea has changed greatly.

The men of old are gone. I mourn their passing:

The Men of Old

Giant men, they lived giant lives
though on something less than giant scale.

Over a cocktail I've heard them marvel
at the old French missionaries,
the guts, the endurance, the faith.
The French lack substance to me,
but these men are real; many of them I knew,
and those I didn't are mythically mine,
warp and woof of the Columban thing
with which I identify.
I marvel at these earthen vessels:
lovely, misshapen, bulgy presences,
each a unique firing in the master kiln.
Moulded from the first earth,
they stand in stark contrast
to our peas in a pod times.
Theirs was a harsh theology:
the flesh the enemy, the battle bitter.
Yet the harshness of the moral view
was tempered by a humanity that shone
like the finest glaze, warm, familiar, true.
Selfless, crucified men,
they were their own Heaven and Hell:
only the innocent could be so.

Monsignor McPolin, a tall, thinking, iron man, was first ruler of the roost in 1933. He taught patrology in Dalgan Park, the Columban seminary in Ireland, when I was a student. Bishop Quinlan, old tyrant, leader of the Columban advance from Chŏlla to the northern province of Kangwŏn, was wise as an owl; he was loved, feared, and admired. His priests entertained him with salmon-trout, bananas, marmalade and bus loads of flattery and fuss; I always thought a tumbler of whiskey would have done as much. Harold Henry was the flamboyant bishop of Kwangju, the southern diocese, which was the first Columban territory in Korea. He was known in Dalgan Park as the Lucky Strike bishop because he invariably had a pack in his top pocket. Not the greatest of card players, his favourite gambit was to jump to three-no-trumps, which said much about his style and personality. Brian Geraghty, a Galway man, big in heart and deed, felt that salvation would be inevitable if he got the people to sit on seats rather than on the floor. P. Dawson, with his Sŏ Chŏngju style corncrake voice and infectious laugh, was a snooker player of real quality. He was famous for shouting sandpaper defiance at his Japanese jailors: he'd wash in no Jap water, he cried.

Pat was sentenced to five years imprisonment for spying and saying inappropriate things about the emperor. Of the second charge he was undoubtedly guilty. When he got to jail, he was asked 'Are you a bishop?' The query sought the reason for his five-year sentence whereas his two companions, T.D. Ryan and Jerome Sweeney, got three. The simple answer was that Pat's offensive remarks about the emperor probably rated a fifteen year sentence! Within the prison he wasn't any different. Assigned to clean the latrines, he always did the chore to the tune of the Japanese national anthem! Pat Dawson's real claim to fame was that he put innumerable Korean kids through school. I remember walking with him in Myŏngdong the last time he came back before he died – he was in his eighties. It took two hours to walk from the Midopa Department Store to Myŏngdong Cathedral. People ran out of every alley, fell to their knees and cried 'Shinbunim! Shinbunim! (Father, Father!)' tears gushing from their eyes. Daw, as we called him affectionately, was enormously embarrassed. I was humbled. I knew I was looking at a great missionary who would only be remembered by the people he had helped. Daw spoke panmal, low form, children's language. Cardinal Kim had a story about Bishop Quinlan telling a minister of state that he'd be talking panmal because that was all he knew and for the minister not to take offence but to talk panmal in return. I never knew Bishop Quinlan use panmal to adults. I think the cardinal was mixing him up with someone else. It could have been any one of half a dozen others. Our collective language skills were not great. In a famous speech, one of our more colourful parish priests lumped together the governor of the province, the city mayor and the county chief under the generous heading of *yŏrŏgaji yangban* (assorted gentry)! T.D. Ryan, a laughing Buddha priest, was skilled in all the wily ways. He was noted for keeping a special section in his notebook titled 'Words not to be remembered.'

Next, the martyrs, a special group, I know them only by repute: Tony Collier shielded his catechist from a bullet in Ch'unch'ŏn. Tony died but the catechist lived. Paddy Reilly, betrayed by his hairy arms, was shot to keep an accountant's books straight – there weren't supposed to be any foreigners north of Mukho, a town on the East Coast. The communists made sure Paddy didn't disturb the bookkeeping. Jim Maginn sent a boy to get a battery for his Zenith radio in Samch'ŏk and was apprehended as a result. Frank Canavan, of Death March fame, died just before he was due to be freed. He had his final wish: Christmas dinner in heaven. Monsignor Brennan, Tom Cusack, and Jack O'Brien, were part of the holocaust inventory in Taejŏn; their remains were never found.

Bishop Quinlan, Phil Crosbie and Frank Canavan were the three Columbans on the Death March. Phil Crosbie tells the story in *Three Winters Cold*, and it is a gripping read. It was translated into Korean in 2004. Philip Deane, a journalist, who also experienced the Death March tells his story in *I Was a Captive* (1953). Deane gave a talk in Dalgan Park some years ago. He told of a day in North Korea when George Blake, the famous (or infamous) triple agent (British, Russian, and Israeli) came in from the yard where a North Korean captain had just shot an ailing American soldier. Blake, who was reputedly a good linguist, began to curse in a dozen languages. He cursed God, the world, the war, the cruelty of men. Bishop Quinlan put his arms around him and said gently, 'That's enough, that's enough, George! If I had had a son, I'd have wanted you to be him.' Then he turned to Philip Deane and said, 'Sorry, Philip, you'd have had to be content to be number two.' It's a Zen moment in the history of the Columbans, pure poetry.

There were so many characters: Pat Deery, who built the cathedral in Wŏnju, renowned for imprecating his love of the bishop; Frank Woods, a hugely popular foxhole chaplain and hunter supreme; anyone fool enough to shoot the lead goose – and there often was one – risked the scorn of this intrepid priest.

Tom Kane, a noted wit and contributor to the word hoard, coined many of the popular Konglish expressions in use among us; the roll of the tongue, he said, controlled the dice of language.

And finally, a vessel from a later firing, the most cultivated man of all, Dick Delaney.

Sanctity

He was a saint; a brilliant man
buried in the back of beyond.
He had no attachment to material things.
He loved his general factotum,
he loved Jesus and he loved a shot.
His only other concession to this world
was his insistence on a cigar
to ease his morning business out.

Dick was one of the best read men I've ever known. He spent his life in a mouldy Cleary's suit, puffing the odd cigar, deep in his beloved books. A Korean priest once said, 'There was only one priest ever in P'ungsuwŏn.' It was a magnificent tribute, one I never heard given to another missionary, especially since the parish was one of the oldest in the country and had produced more priests than any other parish. Dick was dearly loved. The fact that he only had fifty Korean words in his vocabulary was irrelevant. He radiated the light of heaven wherever he went and everyone felt its warmth. He is clearly out of season in this company because he came later in life after a career as a professor in Dalgan. The men who knew him there said he was a boring prof, but when he talked about a book he liked over a few whiskies, he was wonderful. On reflection, it was only when Dick came on a visit to Sŏngshim College in Ch'unch'ŏn that he had an audience for his inner world. I include him because he epitomized what was best in the earlier giants. More than once he lost his month's maintenance in a poker game and smiled.

Spring Scents

Spring scents fade:
the glory of these men too
is a diminished thing, a memory
fast fading in the hearts of a few.
I record the names
of these priests of Melchizedek.
I record them for the succeeding
generations of Columbans,
lest we forget.
And I record them for the succeeding
generations of the people they served,
lest they forget.

And there were so many great stories. One of my favourite stories describes two men storming into Hoengsŏng at the outbreak of the war in 1950:

Wisdom

The commies are coming,
the commies are coming!
We'll stay, we'll stay
for Christ and glory!
Bejazus we won't.
We're getting our butts in gear;
we're getting to hell out of here.
Fourteen chickens wrapped
the front axle of the jeep as it pulled into Hoengsŏng.
Funny how a bottle of whiskey and a friend
could dull even the most imminent threat.

The Hoengsŏng incumbent refused to budge. 'First things first,' he said, 'there's a bottle to be drunk: then we're off.' Seoul fell before they left. They had to find an alternative road south, which they duly did.

Then there was Pat MacGowan, alone in the records for keeping a cardinal out. This was the result of a failure in communication between Pat and Paul Ch'oe, a Seoul priest who enjoyed our company. Pat's Korean wasn't great. He spent most of his language study time trying to figure out the accusative case. This wasn't much help because Korean doesn't have cases. Anyway, the result was that the cardinal was kept waiting in the yard. Paul Ch'oe did not believe it was a mistake, but it was. Mistakes like this were easy because Pat guarded his sitting room and kitchen like the Bastille.

Hunting was a very popular winter sport. There were stringent rules on guns, which were supposed to be kept in the local police station for reasons of national security. The ordinances were not always strictly observed. There are many stories about warming up jeeps to go duck and goose hunting on a winter's night, fortifying body and soul with a good modicum of the warming brew, putting on numerous layers of clothes as insulation against temperatures that sometimes went to ten or fifteen below Fahrenheit, going back for a little more of the warming brew, and ending up switching the engines off at two in the morning, too tipsy to risk taking a gun anywhere. One of my favourite hunting stories had to do with a casual jeep trip on the East Coast on a cold January day. Hunting was far from everyone's minds, but the guns were always at the ready at this time of year. Suddenly a pheasant struts by the side of the road. Already saliva is dripping. A roast pheasant was a luxury addition to the stark diet of the time. The jeep eased to a halt. One man said — one man always seemed to say — 'Leave this to me!' He readied himself, took aim, fired. 'The bastard ducked!' he cried in dismay.

Smart Bird

The doleful enunciation
that the pheasant ducked

on a wintry day on the East Coast
always elicited delighted chuckles
from padres pleased by any bird
smart enough to cheat an arbitrary fate
and mush the plans of the parish priest
for an elegant evening plate,
but it was the corroborating speech
from the marksman in the front seat
that invariably brought down the house.

The magnanimity of judgment of the second marksman, who undoubtedly thought he should have taken the shot himself and was quite certain he would not have missed, was nothing short of extraordinary. We were not quite as confident of his abilities.

These first fruits men had a wonderful rugged individuality. They were all characters, in the sense we once understood that word in rural Ireland, when every town and village had its population of 'characters.' A few drank more than was good for them. It wasn't easy not to drink too much in the Korea of the time. In 1964 a bottle of Chivas Regal in the Foreigners Commissary in Seoul (a government sales outlet designed to get badly needed greenbacks) was three dollars, and a bottle of French wine was one dollar. Coke and Seven-Up were a dollar a can. You couldn't afford NOT to drink the alcohol, and you certainly couldn't afford to drink the Seven-Up and coke. A lady at the checkout in the commissary once spoke disapprovingly to one of our men when he bought a few cans of Wall's sausages, a pound of butter and a case of scotch for his month's provisions.

'Oh, Father!' she cried.

'Lady,' he replied. 'There's more nourishment in my basket than yours.'

The men were generous to a fault, spending any extra money on people in need. School fees, hospital charges, and house rentals were the main headings of their expenditures. They were constantly on the road, ferrying people in and out of hospital, arranging for treatment, even surgery – harelip surgery in particular – and very often paying for it. And when they came into Seoul to unwind, I remember nights when they literally took the roof off the Columban central house. The atmosphere at the snooker shoot-outs was both hilarious and electrical, and the standard of the snooker had to be seen to be believed. These men were larger than life, the most giving, exciting men I've known in my life. On top of their selflessness, they had, to a man, an extraordinary sense of camaraderie. To pass a man's house was the unforgivable sin. They entertained you with the best they had and for as long as you cared to stay. The parishes were isolated, lonely places. In the '60s we went for a week several times a year to the East Coast. Sometimes we didn't get past Kansŏng, the first parish at the northern end of the coast. But the full trip would require stops in Kansŏng, Sokch'o, Yangyang, Chumunjin and Kangnŭng. If you took the train from Seoul or Wŏnju to Kangnŭng, an overnight trip, then Kangnŭng, Mukho, and Samch'ŏk were *de rigueur* stops. You could get away with not going down to Uljin because it was so far and the road was so bad. Usually, the incumbent came up to Samch'ŏk when he heard we had arrived.

24 S was the name of the military road from Wŏnt'ong (outside Injae) to Sokch'o, the forerunner of the present highway that runs past Paekdam-sa, the temple where Chun Duhwan chose to meditate on his past. In the old days only military vehicles were allowed to use this road, but sometimes we were able to persuade the soldiers to let us through. The regular road north to Kansŏng had two one-way sections, and if you were unlucky enough to meet a convoy or two, you could be there all day. 24 S took hours off the trip, but the last few hundred metres to the top of the pass were hair-raising. The jeep, growling in low-low, would slide inexorably across the loose shale towards a drop of at least a thousand feet on the driver's side. At the top of the pass, a granny invariably came out of the bushes with a basketful of American beer, Budweiser usually. We never figured out how she got up there, but she was as grateful a sight as the flowers in May and invariably we bought the entire basket.

I remember the East Coast road as the worst in the country. Huge iron trucks loaded with raw ore bound for Japan ploughed up and down several times a day. The washboard was gut-shaking, and you could get lost in the potholes. After Park Chunghee hard-topped the entrance to Sŏr'ak, Harley-Davidson enthusiasts would truck their bikes down from Wŏnju and Seoul and take off, three abreast, like bats out of hell, along the new road. Farmers beware! The road was barely ten feet wide. If the motorcycle road hogs travelled the southern route through Taegwallyong Pass and Kangnŭng on their way to Sŏr'ak, they might be tempted by a culinary delight advertised as 'Nude Dog' which was served in a food stand at the top of the pass. The term is so succinct, so much more exciting than Hot-dog-hold-the-bun!

My first visit to the East Coast was in the summer of 1965. We had just finished language school and were going on a holiday before reporting for duty in Ch'unch'ŏn. We hired an ancient *hapsŭng*, which broke down repeatedly. I remember half the engine on newspapers somewhere near Hoengsŏng. How the driver ever got it together again was a source of amazement. He turned the key and the engine fired. We took off again, broke down again. More newspapers, more genius. Back on the road again. It was late by the time we got to Kansŏng where we spent the night. The parish priest prided himself on his skill in making martinis. He always made them in the kettle. The recipe was simple. He poured in a bottle of gin and followed it with two teaspoons of martini. Add ice, shake like hell, pop in a few olives or cocktail onions. They were wonderful.

Next day we went on to Sokch'o. The priest's house in Sokch'o was the only house in Kangwŏn Province that you could say was beautiful. The beauty, I should add, was all on the outside. The location was wonderful; the house was perched on a height overlooking the sea, with a lovely bay window on the sea side. House and church were reputed to have tank tracks in the walls, courtesy of the American army who helped with the construction. Both buildings were whitewashed. A Cinderella house in an anything but Cinderella world. The house featured Bishop Quinlan's usual back-of-an-envelope, multi-door design; a central living room with doors off it to every room in the house. The frugal nature of the previous incumbent had resulted in a paint job of the interior that had to be seen to be believed. Walls and ceiling were diarrhoea green, and I remember the woodwork as an awful brimsy brown. The paint was American army paint, guaranteed to be rust proof, damp proof, and virtually indestructible, which made it irresistible to the pastor, a practical man for whom colour was a very minor consideration. The new parish priest, a lamb of a man affectionately known as Frankie Ferocious, had done nothing about the décor. He probably wasn't even aware that it was offensive. But some of his guests were very offended. Over a few cocktails and an endless succession of beers, they announced that something would have to be done. First thing in the morning, runners were sent to the market to buy paint and replenish the beer. Work began. It was hot thirsty work. More beer than paint was poured. By early afternoon, the eager workers, no longer quite so eager, declared a holiday. The project continued sporadically throughout the week. By Friday, half the ceiling was done and most of the walls. There was a problem. Danny Chi was due to be consecrated bishop of Wŏnju next day, and the leaders of the paint gang, after much theological toing and froing, had decided to go to the celebration even though they lacked the appropriate wedding garments. The ceiling was left unfinished in the style of Naeso-sa Temple in North Chŏlla. I'm afraid none of the painters had any idea of the Naeso-sa story, with its wonderful symbolism of the beautifully incomplete. Sŏ Chŏngju tells the story:

Painting the Great Worship Hall in Naeso-sa

Painting the Great Worship Hall in Naeso-sa entailed man power, bird power, and tiger power; and even that was not sufficient so that it remains unfinished today. On the West side, along the top of the inner wall, a master sits in meditation. Take a look at the mind-blowing incompleteness of the unpainted blank space beside the master. That's what I want to talk about.

When the Great Worship Hall was built and the search was on for a master painter, a nameless wanderer came from the west in the twilight of the day and accepted the painter's task. After painting the outside, he moved within the shrine, locked the door securely from within and cried:

'Let no one dare enter this place until I have completed my task.'

But in the mundane world and in the temple, it is the foolhardy that cause the trouble. Thus, one foolhardy monk, unable to control his curiosity, stole over, bored a hole in the paper window and peered within. The wandering master was nowhere to be seen. Instead a lovely bird fluttered in flight across the ceiling, brush gripped in its beak. It dipped the brush in a dye that came from its body, thus painting the shrine, beautifully, beautifully. But at the sound of the intruder, the bird cried in bitter dismay and fell flat to the floor where it stretched four paws listlessly out: bird had become tiger.

'Tiger Monk, Tiger Monk, rise!' The monks called on the tiger in their local dialect, just as they would call a fellow monk, but the tiger did not move. All they could do was wish the tiger reanimation in the next life. With this in mind, they called the temple Naeso-sa, meaning resuscitation in the future. Across the centuries the monks go up morning and evening to bow and bow again toward the blank unpainted spot.

Two of the men involved in the aborted paint job took the wrong train in Samch'ŏk on the Saturday morning and ended up in Pusan, where they went AWOL for three weeks! The house in Sokch'o has been remodelled and extended several times since. Little of the old magic remains and there is no need to bow to the blank spot on the ceiling.

A lot of water ran under the collective Korean cultural bridge between Tan'gun's legendary founding myth and the momentous arrival of the Columbans in 1933. Tan'gun's place is secure; I'm not so sure about the Columbans. Their memory, of course, will remain in the hearts of the friends they made and the people they served, but if the past is any guide to the future, you can be pretty sure that the great Korean collective memory will swallow their contribution without a gurgle. Of the foreigners who left a mark on Korean society, Hamel's name is probably best known. I stress the name bit because apart from his name most folks know very little about him. Among the knowledgeable unknowledgeable, some say Hamel and his crew were responsible for the red tint in Korean hair; others cry, 'Nonsense! The red tint came from washing the hair with beer.' Take your pick. I have no idea when the red tint first came to the fore, or when beer was first made in Korea, but I can assure you that the beer in the '60s would turn more than your hair red. You see the odd photograph of Paul Georg von Molendorff, dressed in court clothes, but he's not much more than an image any more. Molendorff served as director of the maritime customs and as deputy foreign minister to King Kojong.

No one remembers the Irishman John MacLeavy Brown, another director of the maritime customs and Kojong's chief financial adviser, although his name adorns a plaque in Pagoda Park. William Franklin Sands' book *At the Court of Korea* is an intriguing account of Korea's people and institutions around 1900, a must read for anyone interested in colonial Korea, but man and book are long forgotten despite the reprint by RAS in the eighties. Horace Allen, missionary and diplomat, introduced Western medicine to Korea. He was physician to the court and a confidante of Emperor Kojong. Korea has made little effort to ensure that the memory of these foreigners survives. The Protestant missionaries fare only marginally better. Yonsei University preserves the Underwood name, but Gale, Trollope and the other prominent Protestant missionaries are mostly names in history books, known to historians and literature buffs but for practical purposes forgotten. Francesca Rhee, Syngman Rhee's wife, is well remembered, but I doubt if very many Koreans (or foreigners) know her maiden name. When I tried to write an obituary for Phil Crosbie, who had been on the Death March with Bishop Quinlan, one of the big Seoul English language dailies refused to print it on the grounds that no one would know him.

I suppose the tendency to forget is part of the loss of *inshim*, the natural benevolence on which Koreans traditionally pride themselves. *Inshim* has been in steady decline over the last forty years, part of the fabric, I believe, of rapid industrial development. I've noticed the same thing in Ireland. The loss of *inshim* resides in a fundamental intolerance, an obsession with my rights and an insensitivity to yours. Money takes over; traditional values die. In the old days Korean folks were always very helpful; they smiled all the time. The immigration office was not yet the most dreaded office in the land. In fact, you never had to go there in person. I was once top of the most wanted list in Korea for failing to renew my residence permit, a designation I maintained for six months. I was living in Ch'unch'ŏn at the time, and Mukho was the port of entry for Kangwŏn Province, which meant that papers for renewal of residence filed in the provincial office in Ch'unch'ŏn had to be sent to Mukho to be processed. My residence permit lay in the bottom of an official's drawer in Ch'unch'ŏn for six months. The residence thing was so relaxed that it didn't even occur to me to go and pick up the permit until someone – enjoying himself enormously, I should add – told me I was listed with hoodlums anonymous on the walls of Mukho Immigration Office under the title Most Wanted. I was threatened with jail at first, but eventually I was exonerated and my good name was restored. The O'Rourkes of Breifne were respectable again. My only regret was that the official in Ch'unch'ŏn lost his job. His offence seemed small enough.

On another occasion I was called in to the local office to vouch for the identity and good standing of the parish priest. The parish priest was a ten-years-in-the-orient veteran, a man who prided himself on his considerable experience and who regarded curates as useless baggage imposed by bishops on long suffering, hard working pastors. He did not appreciate this kind of public demeaning, especially as he knew the curate would have the story all over the diocese in a matter of days and all over the country within the week. I think he would gladly have gone to jail rather than be exposed to the ordeal. You will appreciate that I savoured the occasion to the full and was very slow to commit myself to any declaration of recognition much less approval.

There is a hilarious story from Japanese times about a foreigner who went into a ranking bureaucrat's office in Kangnŭng city administration. Without looking up from his voluminous sheaf of papers, the official asked, though not directing the question at anyone in particular – to formally note the presence of the foreigner would have been an unspeakable indignity – 'And what brought the long nosed *nom* here today?'

The reply was equally acerbic.

'The long-nosed *nom* came to see the short-nosed *nom*.'

Note how this knowledgeable foreigner kept his reply in the non-personal third person. History, fortunately, recounts no more of the details of the incident.

In the '60s and '70s police smiled and waved at minor and sometimes major traffic goofs. When you didn't know any other way home, it was normal to ask the traffic policeman to reverse the traffic on a one-way street, and invariably he obliged. The police on occasion drove us home after curfew when there was no other way of getting there. Parking lot attendants put up with everyone's mistakes. Public anger was relatively unknown. The arrival of the cap and whistle as symbols of authority put an end to all this serenity. The cap and whistle brigade do not take prisoners.

President Chun Duhwan's name is not exactly synonymous with accepted notions of freedom, but in 1982 he ordered the lifting of curfew restrictions (midnight to 4.00 am), which were first imposed by American occupation troops in 1945. I recall the curfew with affection. On weekends, we liked to go downtown to one of the new *saeng maekchu* (draught beer) houses in Myŏngdong (the OB Cabin was very popular) as an antidote to the drudgery of formal language learning, and at the same time as a forum to practise what we had learned at school in the previous week. Myŏngdong was always referred to by its Irish equivalent, the town of the lights. 'Let's go down to Baile na Soilse and quaff a few schooners,' was all the spur that was necessary to get us moving. These were the days of tramcars, old battered *shibal* taxis and the ubiquitous *hapsŭng* minibuses. *Shibal* taxis and Blubirds were relatively difficult to catch at night.

The *hapsŭng* was the most readily available form of transport, but there were difficulties. To catch the last *hapsŭng* – I can still hear the ringing of the *hapsŭng* girl's nasal cry in my inner ear: 'Chong-no, Hae-wha-dong, Sam-sŏn-gyo, Ton-am-dong, Mi-a-ri, Su-yu-ri' – meant rushing the last pint, a dire deed to anyone of Irish sensibility. I don't know that we always tried very hard because four foreigners piling onto the last *hapsŭng* were liable to cause a lot of confusion. Our bum expanse was considerably larger than the local variety and the *hapsŭngs* had not been built with us in mind. As a result we often missed that fatal encounter with the last *hapsŭng* and were forced to seek alternative routes home. People were invariably very kind. Taxis rushing home stopped to help us, private citizens often gave us lifts, and at times, as noted already, the police were kind enough to escort us home. But inevitably there were the nights when fate was not so kind and we had to walk the last stretch home. I don't ever recall, however, having to hoof it further than from Shinsŏldong to Tonamdong, a thirty minute walk.

I remember vividly the last frantic rush of cars at 11.50 and the eerie silence that descended on the city at 12.05. It was now curfew time and the city was dotted with police and military barriers. Getting through the barriers was always exciting. Invariably when challenged, 'Where you go?' we replied, 'Ŭijŏngbu.' And invariably the policeman or soldier said 'Okay, you go.' We lived close to Tonamdong Intersection and there was always a barrier there. One night when challenged with the invariable

'Where you go?', one of the group gave the standard answer, 'We go Ŭijŏngbu,' though our house was only fifty metres away and the guard must have known it. However, when the guard saw us turn for home, he made an unexpected response. He said, 'You no go there Ŭijŏngbu,' whereupon one of the group said, 'Ah, the trouble with you, sir, is you only know one road to Ŭijŏngbu!' The witty response became a catch phrase for those who think they have explored every avenue in dealing with a problem and are now in a position to offer a neat solution, a sure recipe for disaster in Korea. As one astute man used to say about Korean politics: 'When you have studied the matter inside out, examined all the possibilities and come to a reasonable conclusion, the only thing you can be certain of is that you've got the wrong answer.' Two plus two was never four in Korea.

3

LEARNING THE ROPES

OVER THE FIRST FEW MONTHS we were given an introduction to Korean mores. Our pastoral counsellor talked from his own personal experience. Like most of the early missionaries he was colonial in his mindset, which meant that whereas he had no great affection for the Japanese, he thought they were a necessary evil and an inevitable part of Korean economic development. Many foreigners were tarred with the *ch'inil* (pro-Japanese) brush because of attitudes like this. He also had negative attitudes about Korean abilities to do things the way he thought they should be done. He felt the screw was never given the last turn, equipment was inherently flawed, bits and pieces inevitably fell off. He didn't know it, but he was also pointing out the flaws of Japanese merchandise in the first years of Japan's industrial development. Learning is a long process. Korea was at stage one while Japan had moved on to stage two. Our counsellor had forgotten Japan's stage one.

Along with a colonial mindset, the older missionaries had a flawed view of the Confucian legacy, which I believe came, in part at least, from the early French missionaries and Dallet's book on the Korean church. Dallet never set foot in Korea. He compiled his book on the basis of letters sent home to Paris by the French missionaries. The book is amazing for the wealth of information it contains on Korean institutions and mores. The shorter English version should be compulsory reading for those who don't read French but who aspire to live long-term in Korea. Dallet reached some wrong conclusions, inevitably so, I suppose, since he was relying on second-hand information. One of the areas where Dallet got it wrong was in dealing with the Confucian tradition. Korea in the 1800s had a large population of dispossessed *yangban* who for one reason or another could not get posts in the bureaucracy. To work was beneath their dignity, but they retained the right to complain and criticize. They were a constant drain on society and a thorn in the side of the developing church whose appeal, despite *yangban* beginnings, was egalitarian. The Catholic church tended to attract the more disadvantaged people in society: *chung'in* (a middle group between *yangban* and commoner), commoners, *kisaeng,* butchers, and so on. Dallet made the mistake of judging the great Confucian tradition by the attitudes and actions of a disgruntled, dispossessed minority. Gale and Allen shared this jaundiced view. Our counsellor had inherited Dallet's view of Confucian culture, but he had a great sense of humour and a bottomless well of fun stories, and he regaled us with all his skills. The general advice he gave, and sage advice it proved to be, could be summarized in three propositions. Don't try to be more Korean than the Koreans. Make friends rather than enemies because in Korea friends and enemies tend to be for life. And if you have some extra money, give it, don't lend it. Money lending is destructive of human relations.

Trying to be more Korean than the Koreans was not a problem in the '60s and '70s. We lived distinctly Western lives, in Western space, speaking a lot of English. Our lifestyle was probably an inevitable condition for survival, physically and spiritually, but it was also the prime source of our language problems. We never learned the language of the kitchen. The Korean church was so welcoming and our sense of camaraderie was so strong that feelings of not-belonging were only experienced by a minority. However, I am aware now that the sense of being an outsider was a feature of the experience of some young expats in the '80s and '90s who didn't have the luxury of a church support community. They desperately wanted to be accepted;

not-belonging was an enormous source of pain. Today, too, young ex-pats tell me about feelings of alienation in alleyways, subway cars, stores, work places and rented accommodation. I am shocked by stories of abuse and resentment that are totally outside my experience.

Our counsellor's injunction to make friends not enemies was so true it hurt. Many of my friends today have been friends for forty years. Solidarity in friendship is what makes the Korean experience so special.

The third proposition was not a problem for me. My total resources when I arrived in Seoul came to about $500, and by the end of the year, the experienced poker players had tucked it safely in their inside pockets. In all modesty I should add that I got it back with interest over the next ten years.

Purity of heart and generosity of spirit were the virtues that defined the Korean experience. Of course, it wasn't all plain sailing. *Yokshim* (greed, desire) constantly tries to ensnare even the most innocent heart.

Evening on the Mountain: Song to the Moon in the Well

A mountain monk coveted the moon;
he drew water, a whole jar full;
but when he reached his temple, he discovered
that tilting the jar meant spilling the moon.

Yi Kyubo (1168–1241)

Most of us spilled a little moonlight every day, but despite the depredations of *yokshim* on foreigner and Korean alike, the overflowing heart, Korea's gemstone since Shilla and Koryŏ, is my abiding memory of the early years, and as Sŏ Chŏngju notes, green celadon is its perfect symbol:

Good Times in Koryŏ

Tenth month of the third year
of the reign of Sukchong:
glorious day; not a prisoner on Koryŏ soil,

jails utterly empty.
Sunrays blossomed in that emptiness
like yellow chrysanthemums,
sunrays wherein Tan'gun's smile was etched,
a smile that opened again the village of the gods.
Green celadon, coloured and fired
in the village of the gods.
Cloud-crane patterned, cloud-crane patterned,
Koryŏ pale green celadon.

Sŏ Chŏngju (1915–2000)

I discovered very early that Korea gets in the blood. If you are going to leave, you better get out before the five-year limit. Otherwise in your heart you will never be able to leave. I have known many who stayed too long, and when eventually they left, they were more or less unhappy in situations outside Korea. This was true of diplomats and business people as well as missionaries.

In the Blood

If you wonder why Korea is in the blood,
look to the heart, to friends that endure,
to loyalty green as pine and bamboo,
to flowers that bloom in the snow.

4

CULTURAL ADAPTATION

NEW IN KOREA? Feeling the strain? You are much better off than we were. At least you can read Dr Crane's *Korean Patterns* (1967). Beg, borrow or steal it. It tells you how the Korean mind works and the areas in which a foreigner must be particularly careful. Insightfully, Crane begins not with relationships, which would be the obvious place to start, but with *kibun*. There is no English word for *kibun*, but when you have been in Korea for a while, you'll know all about it. *Kibun* controls everything. With good *kibun*, you feel good; with bad *kibun*, you feel bad. By the time you motor through the gradations of good, better and best, not to mention bad, worse and worst, you'll know a lot about *kibun*. For one thing, you'll know that it's not just a matter of *your kibun*; the other person's *kibun* is important too. That's lesson number one.

Directions

Kibun controls the show.
Rationalize afterwards, if you must.
Don't shirk the bill, though.
Consequences never go.

And read Yi Munyŏl's *Our Twisted Hero*. This book gives the psychology of relationships and consequently of power in Korea. Ultimately, it is an allegory on power, said to be like *The Lord of the Flies* but really very different. It is an allegory about the abuse of power during the era of the generals in the '80s, but the way relationships work here shows how they have worked throughout history at all levels of Korean society, from government to hospitals and schools, from crooks to bishops.

Ŏm Sŏkdae, monitor of the sixth grade in an elementary school, rules his class with an iron fist. A sinister, shadowy figure, he terrorizes his classmates into abject submission, reducing them to cringing, fawning pawns. He beats them, takes their money, uses them to cheat on exams, collects 'dues', sells preferment and in general insists on being treated as a king. The story is told from the point of view of a transfer student from Seoul who challenges Sŏkdae's dictatorship. A long, lonely struggle ensues, which ends in the capitulation of the Seoul boy. However, in capitulation, the Seoul boy discovers a new side to Sŏkdae's corrupt regime: he begins to taste the sweets of special favour and power. The Seoul boy becomes Sŏkdae's reluctant lieutenant.

A new teacher takes over the class and is suspicious of Sŏkdae. An investigation reveals that Sŏkdae has been cheating on his exams. The teacher gives him a severe beating, humiliating him in front of the class. The boys who had supported Sŏkdae so loyally now turn on him like snakes. The Seoul boy is the only exception.

After Sŏkdae's departure, the long process of restoring democratic procedures in the class begins. Boys are elected to positions of responsibility and just as quickly deposed; some groups act recklessly, some groups do not act at all. In the end, after much pain and soul searching dignity is restored to all.

Our Twisted Hero shows the boys under extreme pressure: how they react to power and against power, and how their parents and teachers react. Everything here is grist to the mill. The story is extremely well constructed, expertly told, and the characterization is excellent. The only weakness in the story is a rather debatable ending, which sees the hero carted off in handcuffs many years after the main action has concluded. The truth is that in Korea Sŏkdae types succeed. The end was probably dictated by concern over critical reaction to the moral implications of the theme. Despite this flaw, *Our Twisted Hero* is a considerable achievement. Published first by Mineumsa in Seoul in 1988 just before the Olympics, subsequently Hyperion brought it out in New York in 2001. You will read it in a couple of hours and be rewarded by an enhanced understanding of the power systems that operate in government, business, schools, hospitals, church and elsewhere.

And read Richard Rutt's *Virtuous Women*. It's a rotten title but a great book. *Virtuous Women* will introduce you not only to the delights of classical Korean literature but also to the intricacies of the search for inner illumination, which in Korea is the distinguishing mark of the cultivated man. The heart of the book is Rutt's reworking of Gale's translation of *The Nine Cloud Dream,* the only *great* novel in Korean classical literature. A symbolic narrative, it gives you an early entry into the world of personal cultivation and Korean Zen, two ideas that are sides of a coin. I use the term Zen here in the broad sense of inner illumination and insight, what the Koreans call *yoyu* or largess of spirit. Without *yoyu* and insight you won't understand much of what happens to you in Korea. As a bonus, the volume carries a lyrical translation of a *p'ansori* (folk opera) version of Chosŏn's great love story *Ch'unhyang ka* (Song of Ch'unhyang), guaranteed to change your feelings about the stolidness of Confucian culture.

Hŏsaeng's Tale by Pak Chiwŏn (1737–1805), a noted Shirhak (Practical Learning) scholar and the finest prose stylist of his age, is another must read, especially if you belong to the business world. *Hŏsaeng's Tale* maps out the basic strategies for making money in Korea. Copyright considerations prevent me from giving you the texts of *Our Twisted Hero* and *The Nine Cloud Dream,* but *Hŏsaeng's Tale* is not burdened by such restrictions. Saengwŏn was the Mr title given to someone who passed the minor civil service examination. Mr Hŏ sounded unbelievably stuffy and

Hŏ Saengwŏn unbelievably awkward. I avoided the problem by calling the hero Hŏsaeng.

HŎSAENG'S TALE

Hŏsaeng lived in Mukchok Village. The village well was at the top of Namsan valley where an ancient ginko pointed at the sky; the wicker gate of Hŏsaeng's house, invariably open, faced the gingko. The house was more hut than anything else, a two-room straw affair that had virtually been blown away by wind and rain. Hŏsaeng blithely ignored the ravishes of wind and rain; all he ever wanted was to recite the classics. Meanwhile, his wife, courtesy of her needlework, managed – with great difficulty – to keep food in their mouths. Today she was very hungry.

'What use is all your reading?' she cried tearfully. 'You're never going to take the state examination.'

'I haven't completed my studies yet,' Hŏsaeng said with a laugh.

'Can't you work at a trade?' she asked.

'How can I?' he replied. 'I never learned a trade.'

'Can't you start a business?'

'How can I?' he said. 'I don't have the capital to start a business.'

She was really angry now. 'How can I, how can I? Is that it? Words, words! Is that all you have from all your reading?' she shouted. 'How can I work at a trade? How can I start a business? Maybe my honourable husband could be a thief?'

Hŏsaeng closed his book and got abruptly to his feet. 'Such a pity,' he said. 'I gave myself ten years to complete my reading; I've only had seven....'

Hŏsaeng disappeared out the door. He knew no one in the town, so he paraded up and down Chongno and eventually buttonholed a passerby.

'Who's the richest man in Hanyang?' he asked. Hanyang was an old name for Seoul.

'Mr Pyŏn!' the passerby said.

Hŏsaeng quickly searched out Pyŏn's house.

'I'm a poor man,' Hŏsaeng said, bowing politely to Pyŏn. 'I have no money,' he continued, getting straight to the point, 'but I have an idea worth trying out. Will you lend me 10,000 nyang?'

'Certainly,' Pyŏn said, and he handed over the money on the spot.

Hŏsaeng left without even saying thanks. Tattered belt, missing tassel, crooked heels, shabby coat, battered hat, runny nose – to the eyes of Pyŏn's sons and the hangers-on that filled the house the stranger looked like a beggar. They couldn't make sense of what had happened.

'Do you know that man?' they asked when Hŏsaeng left the room.

'No, not at all,' Pyŏn said.

'You throw 10,000 nyang to someone you've never seen in your life. You don't even ask his name. What's going on?'

'You wouldn't understand. A man coming to borrow usually wears his heart on his sleeve. He protests his reliability but has servility written across his face. And he keeps repeating himself. This man's appearance was shabby, but he spoke simply. He had pride in his eyes, no trace of shame in his face; he was obviously a man who would be content without material possessions. A man like that who says he has a plan wouldn't be contemplating something small. And anyway I wanted to test him. If I wasn't going to give him the money, I might ask his name, but I didn't see much point in asking when I'd already decided to give him the money.'

Hŏsaeng did not go home. Cash in hand he headed straight for Ansŏng. Ansŏng is the crossroads between Kyŏnggi and Ch'ungch'ŏng, the town where the three southern provinces come together. He got himself a place to stay and began buying all the fruit in the locality: dates, chestnuts, persimmons, pears, apricots, tangerines, citrons, everything. To those willing to sell he paid the going price; to those not so willing to sell he paid double the going price. And he stored all his produce. Soon he had all the fruit in the countryside and the gentry discovered they could not hold a feast or offer a ritual sacrifice. So the merchants came back to Hŏsaeng, and the fruit they sold at double the price they now bought back at ten times the price.

Hŏsaeng heaved a deep sigh. The sad state of the country is pretty obvious when 10,000 nyang can control the fruit market.

Hŏsaeng took knives, hoes, and dry goods to Cheju Island where he bought all the horsehair he could get.

'Soon,' he said, 'no one will be able to cover their topknots.'

Sure enough, before very long horsehair hats were ten times the price. Hŏsaeng made a million nyang from his horsehair trading.

One day Hŏsaeng met an old sailor. 'Do you know of an uninhabited island,' he asked, 'where a man might live?'

'Yes,' the boatman said. I know of such an island. We got caught once in high winds and rough seas and sailed due west for four days. Eventually we came to an island. It's about halfway between Samun and Changgi. Trees and flowers in profusion; fruits and berries everywhere; wild animals in flocks; fish without fear of men.

Hŏsaeng was delighted. 'If you take me there,' he said, 'we can both be rich.'

The boatman agreed to take him.

And so it was that on a day when the wind blew fair, the two men rode the wind southeast until they reached the island. Hŏsaeng climbed to the top of a high rock and surveyed the scene.

'The island is so small,' he said with palpable disappointment, 'it's hard to know what to do. But the soil is fertile, and the water is good. I suppose I can live the life of a rich old man.'

'But who will we live with?' the boatman said. 'There's no one here.'

'People gather wherever virtue raises its head,' Hŏsaeng answered. 'It's the lack of virtue not people that worries me.'

Pyŏnsan at the time was teeming with robbers. The authorities recruited soldiers from all over the country to round up the robbers, but the robbers were not easy to capture. The robbers, of course, could not live normal lives. They were forced to hide in remote places, and they were often hungry. Their situation was dire.

Hŏsaeng went to the robbers' mountain camp and tried to win over their leader.

'If a thousand men steal a thousand nyang, how much is that a head?'

'One *nyang* a head.'

'Have you all got wives?'

'No.'

'Have you land, dry fields or wet?'

'No.'

The robbers laughed at the incongruity of the questions. 'If a man had land, wife and children, would he choose the bitter life of a robber?' they asked.

'So why don't you get wives, build houses, buy oxen, and cultivate the land?' Hŏsaeng asked. 'You wouldn't have to suffer the indignity of being called dirty thieves,' he said. 'You'd have the pleasures of married life. You could go around without fear of capture. You'd be rich in spirit.'

The robbers were in total agreement. 'Of course,' they said, 'we want that kind of life. We just don't have the money.'

'Thieves worried about money?' Hŏsaeng said. 'That's a good one! All right, I'll give you the money. Come to the shore tomorrow. You'll see boats with red flags; they're loaded with money. Take as much as you want.'

Hŏsaeng gave his pledge and left. The robbers laughed. They said he was crazy.

Next day the robbers went down to the shore. Sure enough, Hŏsaeng was waiting there with 300,000 nyang. They were all amazed.

'General,' they said, bowing deeply, 'we await your command.'

'Good,' Hŏsaeng said. 'Take as much money as you can.'

The robbers fell on the bags, fighting with one another to get at the money first. It was purely an exercise in greed; not even the strongest among them was able to carry 100 nyang.

'I feel sorry for you lot,' Hŏsaeng said. 'You're not much good as thieves, hardly able to carry off 100 nyang; and there's no point in trying to be respectable because your names are on the thieves roll. There's just no way out for you. Take 100 nyang each and come back with wives and oxen. We'll see how good you are then.'

The robbers agreed and scattered, each with a moneybag on his shoulder.

Meanwhile Hŏsaeng prepared a year's provisions for two thousand people. Then he waited. The robbers returned to a man. On the appointed day, he got them all on board ship and sailed to the uninhabited island. Peace reigned in the mainland; Hŏsaeng had cleaned out all the robbers.

The robbers hewed wood and built houses in their new island home; they wove bamboo and made animal folds. The land was so fertile that the hundred grains grew vigorously. In a single year the fields produced the grain of three years; each stalk had nine ears. The robbers stored a three-year supply of grain, loaded the rest on boats and sold it in Changgi Island, a Japanese territory where the crops had repeatedly failed. They netted 1,000,000 nyang in silver from the relief they provided.

'My little experiment is over,' Hŏsaeng said with a sigh.

Hŏsaeng gathered together his two thousand men and women. 'When I brought you here,' he said, 'I thought to make you all rich first and then to set up a new literary and administrative culture. But the land area is small and the signs of virtue shallow. I must leave this place. I advise you to put spoons in the right hands of your newborn; first from the womb should eat first.'

Hŏsaeng burned the boats. '*You* can't leave,' he said, and *outsiders* can't come.' Then he threw 500,000 nyang into the sea. 'If the sea dries up,' he said, 'someone will take it. 1,000,000 nyang is more money than this place can handle. What would a tiny island do with such a huge sum?' he said. Then he took all those who could read and write and put them on his ship. 'The roots of evil must be removed from the island,' he said.

Hŏsaeng travelled all over the country, helping the poor and the weak. Finally, 100,000 nyang in silver remained. 'With this,' he declared, 'I will repay Pyŏn.'

Hŏsaeng went to see Pyŏn.

'Do you remember me?' he asked.

Pyŏn was somewhat taken aback.

'You don't look any better now than you did then,' he said. 'Did you lose the 10,000 nyang?'

Hŏsaeng laughed.

'Well-oiled faces belong to wealthy people like you,' he said. 'Does 100,000 nyang give knowledge of the Way?' he said as he handed over 100,000 nyang. 'It is to my eternal shame,' Hŏsaeng continued, 'that I borrowed 10,000 nyang from you. I gave up my reading because of a morning's hunger.'

Pyŏn got to his feet in amazement, bowed and refused the money. He would accept, he declared, ten percent interest.

'Do you think I'm a hawker?' cried a very angry Hŏsaeng. He brushed past Pyŏn's restraining arm and left.

Pyŏn followed discreetly. From a distance he saw Hŏsaeng disappear into a small, dilapidated straw hut at the foot of Namsan. He noticed an old granny doing her washing at the well and went across to talk to her.

'Who owns that tiny straw hut?' Pyŏn asked.

'It belongs to Master Hŏ,' she answered. 'The master was always content to study; he lived a life of poverty. Then one day he walked out the wicker gate and he hasn't been back in five years. His wife lives alone now. She observes the day he left as a day of ritual offering.'

Pyŏn knew now that the man's name was Hŏ. He sighed and turned back.

Next day, Pyŏn gathered up the money and went to Hŏsaeng's house to return it, but Hŏsaeng would not accept it.

'If I wanted to be rich, would I throw away 1,000,000 nyang and take 100,000? But if you insist on supporting me, that's fine. Come and see me from time to time. Make sure our grain bin isn't empty; see to it that we have clothes to wear. I'll be content with that. I don't want the burden of material possessions.

Pyŏn tried everything to get Hŏsaeng to change his mind, but it was no use. From then on, when grain or clothes were needed, Pyŏn came in person and helped out. Hŏsaeng accepted his help gladly unless he brought too much, in which case he would frown and say, 'Are you trying to ruin me?' But if Pyŏn brought a jar of wine, Hŏsaeng was always very pleased. They would drink until they were drunk.

In the course of a few years, a strong bond of fine feeling grew between the two men. One day Pyŏn quietly asked Hŏsaeng how he had managed to make 1,000,000 nyang in five years. Hŏsaeng told him.

'It's easy,' he said. 'Chosŏn boats don't ply the seas; Chosŏn carts don't travel the roads. Commodities in this country begin and end their lives in the same place. 1,000 nyang is not a lot of money; it's not enough to get a monopoly on any item. But break it into ten 100 nyang units and you can now buy ten items. Small items are easily handled. Lose on one and make on the other nine. That's the normal principle of profit; that's what hucksters do. With 10,000 nyang, however, you can easily have a monopoly on one item. The principle is to get a corner on the market. Fill carts, load boats. If it's a village, buy the whole village. Catch everything in one tight net. Of the ten thousand species of fish in the sea, get a monopoly on one. Of the ten thousand medicinal herbs and plants used by physicians, get a monopoly on one. When a commodity is concentrated in the hands of one man, the hucksters soon run out of supplies. This, of course, is bad for the people. If the authorities ever made use of my methods, it would be disastrous for the country.'

'How did you know I'd give you the money?'

'Anyone with 10,000 nyang would have lent me the money; you weren't my only hope. I believed in my ability to make 1,000,000. Fate, of course, is in the hands of Heaven, so I had no way of knowing whether you would give me the money or not. But the man who listened to me was fated to be a lucky man because Heaven, not me, was in control of whether he got richer. So why not lend me the money? When money is lent, the money takes over: it creates its own success. Were it up to me personally, who knows whether I would have succeeded or failed?

Pyŏn changed the subject. 'These days,' he said, 'The scholar-officials are intent on wiping out the disgrace they suffered in Namhansan Fortress at the hands of the barbarians. Isn't it time for high-minded scholars to stand up and be counted? A man of your talent, why bury yourself here?'

'A-ha! Men have buried themselves throughout history. What about Cho Songgi? He proved himself an excellent envoy when he was sent to the enemy, but he died an old pauper. And what about the hermit Yu Hyŏngwŏn? He could have procured the provisions for the army, but he spent his time idling by the rugged sea. Those in authority will know all about these cases. I'm a man who knows how to buy and sell. The money I made was enough to buy the heads of nine kings, but I threw it into the sea and came home because there was nowhere to use it in this country.'

Pyŏn sighed and went away.

Pyŏn had been on friendly terms for some time with Yi Wan, a minister of state. Yi Wan was a special adviser to the king and he wondered if Pyŏn knew any man of talent who might serve the king. Pyŏn told him Hŏsaeng's story.

'Amazing,' the minister exclaimed. 'Can it be true? What did you say his name was?'

'I've been acquainted with the man for three years, Minister, but I still don't know his given name.'

'He's obviously an extraordinary man. Let's go to see him.'

That night Minister Yi sent his soldiers away and set out on foot with Pyŏn for Hŏsaeng's house. Pyŏn told the minister to wait at the gate and went in alone to tell Hŏsaeng the background of the minister's visit. Hŏsaeng acted as if he hadn't heard. 'Let's have the wine you brought,' he said and they proceeded to enjoy the wine. Pyŏn kept mentioning the minister's mission. He was embarrassed because Hŏsaeng kept the minister waiting outside. For a long time Hŏsaeng made no response, but eventually, late into the night, he allowed the minister to come in. However, he didn't get up to greet him. The minister was a bit nonplussed at first. He began to explain why he had come. He said he was looking for capable people in the government. Hŏsaeng cut him off with a wave of the hand.

'The night is short,' Hŏsaeng said. 'Too much talk. It's boring. What did you say your official post was?'

'I'm a minister of state.'

'Well then, you have the trust of the country. I recommend Waryong, Reclining Dragon, a man comparable in brilliance to Chuko Liang. Can you get the king to visit him three times in his straw hut and issue a formal invitation to service?'

Minister Yi bowed his head in thought for some time.

'That would be difficult,' he said. 'Can I hear a second proposal?'

'The word second is not in my vocabulary,' Hŏsaeng said, looking away from the minister but at the same time unable to resist the minister's question.

'Many of the descendents of the Ming lords thought Chosŏn owed them something, so they took refuge in this country, wandering around without much purpose. Would you ask the court to have the royal household give their daughters in marriage to these émigrés? And can you plunder the households of Kim Ryu and Chang Yu and use their possessions to set these émigrés up with material possessions?'

Minister Yi bowed his head in thought for a long time.

'That would be difficult,' he said

'Difficult, difficult, everything's difficult!' Hŏsaeng cried. 'So what *can* you do? Here's something really easy. Can you do this?'

'I'm willing to listen,' the minister said.

'Before espousing any great cause under Heaven, it is necessary to conspire with the great heroes under Heaven. If you want to attack a country, you must send secret agents first. Otherwise you won't succeed. The Manchus are now the lords of Heaven. They don't have very cordial relations with the Chinese, but they trust us completely. Of course, Chosŏn was the first nation to bow to their dominion. Tang and Yuan of old accepted our children as students and promoted them in the civil service. The Manchus will do likewise. And if we ask them, they won't forbid our merchants entry. They will accede to our requests because they will see our efforts as motivated by friendliness. So pick your young men. Cut their hair. Dress them in barbarian clothes. The scholars among them can take the examination for foreigners. The peasants can cross the Yangzi; operate as merchants, gather information on the state of the land and conspire with local heroes to turn the world upside down. Thus we can wash away our national disgrace. And if you cannot find a suitable candidate for emperor among the descendants of the Ming, get the great chieftains under Heaven to recommend a candidate. If you succeed, you will have played a master's role in setting up a great nation; if you fail, you will at least retain your status as elder uncles of the emperor of the land of the white gulls.'

Hŏsaeng finished his long harangue.

Minister Yi said, 'The scholar-officials are most fastidious about decorum. They're not going to cut their hair and wear barbarian dress.'

Hŏsaeng was angry again.

'Who are these self-styled scholar officials,' he said chidingly. 'Born in a barbarian land, they boast of scholar-official status. What could be more foolish? The white clothes they wear is the dress of merchants. They wear their hair up, gimlet style, aping the manners of the southern barbarians. What's all this decorum talk? Fan Uch'i thought nothing of his hair when it came to repaying his enemies. King Wuling didn't think it shameful to wear barbarian dress when it was a matter of making the nation strong. You want to have revenge on your enemies, you say, but you make a big deal of your hair. In a time that calls for galloping on horseback, brandishing swords, throwing spears, drawing bows, and casting stones, you insist on wide sleeves and decorum! I made you three proposals. You're not willing to do any of them and yet you call yourself a trustworthy servant of the king. Is this the model of a trustworthy servant? A man like you should have his head chopped off!'

Hŏsaeng groped for a sword to run the minister through. A frightened Minister Yi got quickly to his feet, dashed out the back door and took to his heels.

Minister Yi returned next day. The house was empty; Hŏsaeng was gone.

5

IN AT THE DEEP END

James Scarth Gale writes:

Compared with the Western world, with its indescribable hubbub, Korea is a land of the most reposeful silence. There are no harsh pavements over which horses are tugging their lives out, no jostling of carts or dray-wagons, no hateful clamour that forbids quiet conversation, but a repose that is inherent and eternally restful. The rattling of the ironing sticks is not nerve racking, but rather serves as a soporific to put all the world asleep. Apart from this one hears nothing but the few calls and echoes of human voices. What a delightfully quiet land is Korea! In the very heart of its great city Seoul, you might experiment at midday in the latest methods of rest-cure and have all the world to help you. (*Korea in Transition*, p. 17)

Can you believe it? Korea the land of repose! The amp and loudspeaker put paid to that many years ago. Seoul is a clamourous, noisy place, and with countless millions milling in the streets, there's no way you can avoid them. In addition to being constantly deafened, you'll be pushed up and down stairs, squeezed into corridors and elevators, elbowed, shoved, shouted at, made fun of, and, depending on your general levels of sensitivity, more or less aggravated, irritated, peeved and annoyed. Once out on the street, you are Crane's mythical Mr Everyman Non-person, (more about this later), noticed by everyone but seen by no one. You will feel constantly that you are coming out of a football match and being pushed into a bullfight. It's surprising how much physical contact there is in a culture where touching is – or at least used to be – rude!

So how to deal with people? Until someone knows you, you don't exist. Going up or down the stairs, students will push you out of the way, but if they are *your* students, they will stand back and bow. Introductions are extremely important. So get those name cards and put your titles down. It helps people break the ice in relating to you. People need to know how big a deal you are. Knowing whether the person you are meeting is older or younger is pivotal in starting the relationship. If older, then you are a little more formal, he/she a little less formal. The opposite pertains if you are older. It may take a little jockeying around to establish the basic information without rudely asking the other party their age. But it can be done. You will find that you are much more reluctant to ask someone's age than most Koreans.

Very few foreigners are aware that in the old days it was impolite to say 'Good morning, Professor Kim.' The name in Korea had a sacred aura like the name of Yahweh in the Old Testament; it was not to be used if at all possible. Only rude foreign devils were capable of such boorish exposure of a man's name. Western influence has changed this, but the relics remain. To this day you say 'Good morning Professor, Good morning President, Good morning Chairman, Good morning Sister.' You do not add the person's name.

Everyone in Korea has an appropriate title. Unfortunately, the foreigner often is not too sure what it is. The Columbans had a seminarian on overseas training who worked in a parish in Wŏnju. What to call him was a big problem. Eventually the problem was solved when someone hit on the layman title. From then on he was known as Layman X. Figuring the intricacies of titles is enormously complex, well beyond the ability of most of us. What we need is safe practice. Over the last twenty years the culture of the *ajŏsshi-ajumŏni* title has changed enormously.

Nowadays everyone seems to be either *ajŏsshi or ajumŏni*. In the apartment yard, I'm normally addressed as *ajŏsshi* or *harabŏji*. *Harabŏji* and *halmŏni* are okay, but a foreigner should be careful about using *ajŏsshi* or *ajumŏni*. Err always on the side of safety. Giving someone a little extra rank doesn't hurt. The worst that will be said of you is that you are very polite. *Sŏnsaengnim* is almost always appropriate. Your doctor, your dentist and your teacher can always be called *sŏnsaengnim*. A nurse is called *kanhowŏnnim*. Your housekeeper should be addressed by name – Miss Lee, Miss Kim. When you get to know her well you can call her *ajuma* or *ajumŏni*, but don't do it in front of non-family members. Your kids will call her *ajuma* or *ajumŏni* very quickly, but they too should use her name in front of outsiders.

Never call the waitress *agasshi*. You will save yourself some pain if you note her name when she first approaches your table. But if you don't know her name – Miss Lee, Miss Kim, Miss Park – call out '*Yŏgiyo!*' to attract her attention, Similarly the waiter should be Mr Kim, Mr Park and so on (*chibaenim* perhaps if he's a head waiter), not *ajŏsshi*. Young people who know each other well address each other by name, Myŏngja *sshi*, Kimun *sshi*; the girls often call an older boy *op'a*, an older girl *ŏni*. If you know students well, you can use their names, but be careful. In the office avoid Kim *sshi* (*sshi* translates as seed); Kim *sŏnsaeng* is better; there's no need for *nim* between equals. Miss Kim and Kim *yang* are widely used. When cordial relations exist, it's always permissible to refer to someone slightly older as *hyŏngnim*. Don't call your taxi driver *ajŏsshi*; call him *kisanim*. Don't call the man who comes to fix the sink, fridge or computer *ajŏsshi* even though you hear Koreans use this title; better call him *kisanim* or don't use any title. Most people in my apartment complex call the guards in the yard *ajŏsshi*. I don't call them anything, but if circumstances force me to make a choice, I call them *kyŏngbiwŏnnim*. Many Koreans smile at this, but the guards don't think any the worse of me. Never call a woman *samonim*. It's polite all right, but they don't like it. We used to use *pu'inkkesŏ* or perhaps Kim *yŏsa* if we knew the woman's name, but I don't hear either of these too much anymore. And never refer to your wife as *yŏsa* or *pu'in*. It's a certain giggle causer. When talking to equals, she is *chip saram,* or *anae,* or *ajumŏni*; she's *ch'ŏ* when talking to people that outrank you. The wife refers to her husband as *namp'yŏn* or uses his name, Mr Kim, Mr Cho. In direct address the husband calls his wife *yŏbo,* the wife calls her husband *yŏbo* or *chagi.* In the old days she referred to him as *pakkat yangban* (outside master) or *sŏbangnim.* Nowadays these appellations raise a smile. The general principle is, if you don't know the appropriate title, use *sŏnsaengnim,* and if *sŏnsaengnim* feels awkward, don't use any title. Finally, be aware that when polite people start calling you *ŏrŭshin,* you are already on the slippery slope to old age.

Social standing is critical in interpersonal relationships. There are only two class categories anymore: *yangban* and *sangnom.* *Yangban* is an honorific term for the nobility; *sangnom* is so bad that no one admits to belonging to this class. Now, of course, there are all sorts of *yangban*: the real *yangban* who traces his bloodlines in family registers (*hojŏk*) to mid-Chosŏn and earlier; and the manufactured *yangban* who created a family registry with a little bribery and general skullduggery and thus raised the family escutcheon from *sangnom* to *yangban.* I've been told that 10% of the population was *yangban* at the end of Chosŏn, but that by the time the country got through the Japanese occupation, there were none left! This, of course, is a Korean gentleman poking fun at prized traditional institutions. You should be aware that while it is always permissible for Koreans to belittle Korea, it is never permissible for foreigners to do so. There are five or six family names that are *sangnom,* but I have no intention of listing them here because that sort of information is offensive. Suffice it to say I've noticed over the years that a lot of my foreign friends have *sangnom* Korean names, probably given by a Korean mentor with a sardonic sense of humour. Most of these friends are blissfully unaware, or pretend to be, of the joke they carry on their name cards. What's in a name? According to Dr Crane foreigners are *sangnom* anyway!

You will appreciate then that a thorough grounding in the *yangban* concept is *de rigueur* for aspiring long-term residents. The definitive text, *The Yangban's Tale*, was written by Pak Chiwŏn (1737–1805), the indefatigable Chosŏn dynasty *Shirhak* (Practical Learning) scholar. Again copyright restrictions do not pertain.

THE *YANGBAN'S* TALE

A *yangban* lived in Chŏngsŏn in Kangwŏn Province. A man of most benevolent disposition, he loved reading the classics. Whenever a new county magistrate was appointed, it was customary for the new appointee to seek out the *yangban* and express his warmest feelings of respect. However, such was the poverty of the *yangban's* household that he had borrowed 100 bags of rice from the government granary over the last number of years, a state of affairs that greatly angered the inspector when he came to town on an official inspection and examined the accounts of the government granary.

'What son-of-a-bitch of a *yangban* has depleted the army grain?' he shouted and he ordered the arrest of the *yangban*.

When the county magistrate got the official arrest order, he was filled with pity for the *yangban*. But what could he do! The *yangban* had no means of repaying the debt. The magistrate was caught in an impossible situation. He couldn't put the *yangban* in jail; and he couldn't disobey the order of a superior.

The *yangban* in his desperate plight was reduced to tears. He wept day and night but unfortunately failed to come up with a plan.

The *yangban's* wife cried out in frustration:

'You've spent your life sitting there reading and now there's no way of repaying the debt. *Yangban, yangban!* I'm sick of rotten *yangban*. The title is rubbish!'

A rich man lived in the village, and when the story of the *yangban's* misfortune was noised abroad, the rich man had a serious discussion with the members of his household.

'No matter how poor a *yangban* is, he's always respected and honoured. No matter how much money I make, I'm always despised. I'm not let ride a horse. If I meet a *yangban*, I must tremble and grovel. I bow, I scrape, I crawl. It's a dirty life. Now the local *yangban* has a huge problem. He's caught; he has no way of repaying the government grain. So why shouldn't I buy his title and be a *yangban* myself?'

As soon as the rich man had the agreement of his household, he went to see the *yangban* and offered to repay the government grain. The *yangban* was delighted. True to his word, the rich man went to the government office and repaid the debt.

The shocked magistrate, not sure what this was all about, went to see the *yangban*. The *yangban*, dressed in hat and knee breeches, fell to the ground in fear and trembling. He couldn't even look at the magistrate, and he kept referring to himself in the low form as 'Your servant, your servant.' More shocked than ever, the magistrate helped the *yangban* to his feet.

'What does all this mean? Why on earth are you doing this?'

The *yangban* was even more overwhelmed. He fell to his knees again, kowtowed and said, 'A thousand pardons. Your servant has sold his *yangban* title and repaid the grain debt. From now on, the rich man on the other side of the street is the *yangban*. Your servant can no longer behave with the arrogance of the past.'

The magistrate was filled with wonder by all he heard.

'This rich man is truly a wise man, a *yangban*. No meanness in the accumulation of wealth: a man of righteousness. Takes the urgency of another man's predicament as his own: a man of benevolence. Hates the low, loves the high: there's wisdom here. This man is truly a *yangban*. At the same time if people sell the *yangban* title by private agreement, without a proper deed, there'll surely be lawsuits in time to come. This transaction will only be accepted if I call the people of the village together, appoint witnesses, and draw up a proper deed. I'll sign the deed in my capacity as magistrate.'

So spoke the magistrate.

Accordingly the magistrate called all the ranking men in the town to a meeting. He also called the farmers, artisans and small traders. He sat the rich man on the right of the dais in the place of honour, and he put the *yangban* in the courtyard. Then he drew up the deed and read it aloud.

'This deed is drawn up on such-and-such a day in the ninth month of the tenth year of the reign of Ch'ienlung.

The *yangban* title has been sold to repay a debt in government rice; the price is 100 bags of rice.

There are several divisions of *yangban*. There is the scholar *sŏnbi*; there is the official who participates in government; there is the man of virtue known as *kunja* or wise man. The *muban* (military nobility) stand to the west; the *munban* (civil service nobility) stand to the east. Hence the *yang* or double branch of the nobility. You must choose from among these divisions.

Henceforth, you must perpetrate no base deed. You must imitate the men of old and respect their will. You must rise at the fifth watch, light a candle and sit with your eyes trained on the tip of your nose, knees bent, heels supporting your buttocks. You must recite fluently from *The Writings of Tung-la*, and your voice must sound like a gourd sliding across ice. You must endure the pangs of hunger, put up with cold and never let the word "poor" pass your lips. You must grit your teeth, tap the back of your head with your fist and with a gentle cough swallow your saliva. You must clean your official hat with your sleeve, but the dusting movement must be as smooth as water waves. When you wash your hands, you must clench your fist and refrain from scrubbing. When you rinse your mouth, make sure there is no offensive odour. Call your servants with a long, easy drawl; walk slowly, drag your feet. In copying from the *True Treasure of Classical Literature* and the *Anthology of Tang Poetry*, make sure you use tiny sesame seed lettering, a hundred characters to the line. Don't soil your hands with money; never ask the price of rice. No matter how hot it is, you mustn't take off your thick *pŏsŏn* socks. Don't eat with your topknot uncovered. When you eat, don't begin with the soup, and don't gulp your food. Don't work your chopsticks like pestles and don't eat raw leek. When you drink wine, don't slurp on your beard; when you smoke don't suck in your cheeks. No matter how angry you are, don't beat your wife; no matter how vexing affairs may be, don't throw dishes. Don't hit the children with your fist. Don't call a servant a rotten so-and-so. When you're annoyed by an ox or a horse, don't curse the owner. Don't warm your hands over a brazier. When you speak, don't let your spittle fly. Don't butcher beef or eat it. Don't gamble. If any of the hundred provisions are at odds with appropriate *yangban* decorum, you must bring this deed to the government office and have it corrected.'

His Lordship the magistrate of Chŏngsŏn affixed his signature to the deed; the chief clerk and the inspector signed as well. The usher then took out the seals and attached them here and there across the deed. The sound of the seals rang out like the beat of a big drum; the seals on the deed were like the stars in the sky. When the local headmen had all read the deed, the rich man, visibly discountenanced, thought for a while and said, 'Is this what a *yangban* is? I always heard a *yangban* was like one of the Immortals. If this is all there's to it, it's not very attractive. Can't you correct it, give the rank a little more substance?'

Whereupon the magistrate wrote a new deed.

'When Heaven created our people, it made four divisions. Of these four divisions, the most prestigious was the *sŏnbi* scholar; the *sŏnbi* was *yangban* and there was nothing better. He had neither to farm nor engage in trade. With a little learning, he could advance in the civil service. At worst, he had the rank of *chinsa*. The red certificate of the civil service is no more than two feet long, but it holds a hundred things. It is the *sŏnbi's* money bag. If a *chinsa* gets his first appointment at thirty, every other post in the bureaucracy is open to him. His sideburns can grow white sitting under a sunshade; his stomach can swell to a chorus of "yeas" from his servants. In his room he can seat a *kisaeng* beside him; he can breed cranes in the trees in his garden. An impoverished *sŏnbi*, resident in the country, can do as he pleases. He can take a neighbour's ox and plough his own fields first; he can call the villagers to weed his fields first. No one can curse him for behaving thus; no one can express resentment, not even a man who is hauled in and has lye stuck under his nose, not even if he is strung up by the topknot in punishment.'

The rich man took the deed, stuck out his tongue and said, 'Stop, please! This is unbelievable! Are you trying to turn me into a thief?'

The rich man covered his head with his hands and took to his heels. Until the day he died, he never mentioned the word *yangban* again.

RAMIFICATIONS OF THE *YANGBAN'S* TALE

You now understand the sublime importance and unimportance of the *yangban* concept, as well as the niceties of the class system in Korea. You will have perceived that the *sŏnbi* scholar class is best of all; that the farmer is reasonably respectable; that the artisan is a step lower; and that the merchant ranks last of the four. Of course, a few doghouse professions have not been mentioned, notably, *kisaeng*, monk, *mudang* (shaman), slave and butcher. The butcher is the bottom of the barrel, but even here there are gradations: the beef butcher is superior to the pork butcher, who in turn outranks the dog butcher. So if someone calls you a dog butchering son-of-a-bitch, you'll know that you have given great offence. Ex-pat merchant types should not feel too unhappy. At least you are not listed among the doghouse professions, although in Confucian terms you are not much better.

At the beginning of Chosŏn, the king stood on top of the social pyramid. The nation was composed of king and people (*paeksŏng*). The people, with the exception of the slave class, were *yangmin* (the *yang* character meaning good). A *yangmin* who passed the *kwagŏ* civil service examination became *yangban* upon taking up an official appointment. The *yang* character in *yangban* is different from the *yang* character in *yangmin*. *Yangban* means the two services, civil and military; *yangmin* simply means the good people. The term *yangban* was restricted to those in public office. Gradually *yangban* began to think of themselves as a separate class. To a *yangban*, everyone else was *sangmin*, meaning ordinary people, which included peasants and merchants. As time went on, however, *sangmin* became *sangnom*, and the *sangnom* label is very definitely pejorative. In late Chosŏn, landlords among the *yangmin* – self-styled *sŏnbi* (literati) – began to adopt the *yangban* style of living. Gradually the families of literati and office holders called themselves *yangban* and did not marry *sangmin* (ordinary people). This in turn served as a spur to wealthy *sangmin* to doctor their family registers so that they appeared to be *yangban*. Public office did not follow automatically from claiming *yangban* status. One had to pass the *kwagŏ* civil service exam AND take an official post. Even then, those who took the exam often encountered discrimination in the kind of post that was available to them, particularly so in the case of people from the north and the west.

The *yangban / sangnom* distinction is part of Korean folk history. When a *yangban* drank from Yŏngwŏl's '*Chuch'ŏn*' (Wine Spring), he got refined rice wine, but *makkŏlli* was as much as a *sangnom* could squeeze out of it. An irate *sangnom* borrowed a *yangban* cloak and horsehair hat and approached the spring with new confidence, but all he got was *makkŏlli*. In his rage he blocked the spring with a huge stone and the well dried up.

The Yangban's Tale doesn't mention two further grades in the status system of old Korea, *chung'in* and *so'ol*. Although these classifications are no longer really relevant, I suspect they could still be dragged out at marriage negotiation time. *Chung'in* do not appear as a discrete class until the sixteenth century. They took the *chapkwa* (miscellaneous) civil service exam. Many grew quite wealthy from contacts with the Chinese, which enabled them to build commercial connections. I have also read somewhere that they took the regular *mun'gwa* exam too. One way or the other, they had restricted opportunities for promotion. *Chung'in* ranked between *yangban* and commoner; they were the secretaries, translators, interpreters, accountants, geographers, scientists and doctors in the administrative system. They worked in technically demanding positions that *yangban* would not take. They were the brains of the bureaucracy, did all the work and were rewarded with small stipends and smaller respect. *Sŏ'ol* was the term for a child of a *yangban* and *kisaeng,* or a *yangban* and his concubine. Like the *chung'in,* the *sŏ'ol* was precluded from rising very high in the bureaucracy. At least this was the case until the Hideyoshi Wars. After Hideyoshi and the subsequent Manchu Invasion, Korea endured a terrible bout of national depression. The intellectuals looked for a new code to re-establish the national dignity. Part of the effort led to a rejection of Chinese influence in art and writing. Why should we imitate great masters from the past, the radicals cried? In the changes that ensued, the *sŏ'ol* found themselves being promoted to ranking positions in the bureaucracy. To the end *chung'in* were denied much promotion, but with their brains and skills they emerged in the 1800s as a very wealthy class. *Chung'in* students were among the first to study abroad, mostly because *yangban* would not allow their beloved sons to mingle with barbarians. A number of these *chung'in* intellectuals played prominent roles in the Enlightenment period. *Chung'in* were also first to wear the dirty label of Japanese collaborator. Chosŏn had discriminated against them for hundreds of years; one can understand why they jumped at the chance to increase their personal wealth under the Japanese.

CONCLUSIONS FROM THE STUDY OF THE *YANGBAN* CONCEPT

What are the lessons to be drawn from studying the *yangban* concept? First, it behoves you to treat everyone, on every occasion, as *yangban*, and to hope that sometimes, at least, you will be treated as *yangban* in return. This is quite a lot to hope for since, as Dr Crane points out, the foreigner begins as *sangnom*.

The great key to cultural accommodation is the realization that in Korea all the people are Korean. Korean culture excludes; it is *paet'ajŏgida* as the Korean language puts it. In addition to the basic meaning of excluding or exclusive the term has the additional meaning of cliquish. Cliques of one kind or another control everything and have done so since time immemorial. Examples abound: Yi Sŏnggye and the founding of the Chosŏn dynasty; Sejo's usurpation of Tanjong's throne; the factional squabbles in mid-Chosŏn and the purges that claimed countless lives; Taewŏn'gun's henchmen; Queen Min's inner circle; the various groups that curried favour with the Chinese, the Japanese, the Americans, the British, the French, the Russians and the Germans; the in-groups around Syngman Rhee, Chang Myun, and Park Chunghee; the insiders in the administrations of General Chun and General No; the henchmen of Kim Youngsam, Kim Daejung and Noh Moohyun; the in-groups in both government and civilian organizations and in the great *chebŏl* companies; the gurus in schools, hospitals and church organizations. Cliques are the arbiters of power. The foreigner just does not belong. Without malice, he is simply discounted. That's one reason he finds it so difficult to do business here. The rules of exclusion hit him at every corner. He is constantly treated as if he has no feelings. Things are said at meetings that ignore his presence. I remember meetings with the chancellor of my school many years ago when I was foolish enough to say I disagreed with the august man's view. There would be a stunned silence, followed by comments from various professors to the effect that I was a foreigner and didn't understand. Often a well-meaning professor would beg forgiveness on the grounds that my Korean was very poor, oblivious of the fact that his defence of the chancellor involved insulting me. Then the chancellor would say, 'No, no I like people to say what they think,' and the uneasy professors would turn to me and say in chorus – as if I hadn't understood what the chancellor said – 'You may freely express your views.' I always left these meetings giggling.

Another example of Korea's excluding culture, which you may have noticed – how could you miss it? – is how very rare it is for an elderly foreigner to be offered a seat on the subway. It's a matter of not being seen with the eyes of the spirit as opposed to the eyes of the flesh. Whenever I am offered a seat, it is invariably by a man who thinks I am much older than him and in much worse shape, while I am smilingly convinced of the opposite. The truth is we could both use the seat.

New Year's Day: Year of the Dog

Whenever I see a white-haired old man with a stick,
I say to myself: 'When I'm old, I won't go out.'
What a laugh! Already I'm sixty-three;
old men offer me their seats on the train;
they think I'm in worse shape than them.
The indignity of growing old defies definition;
it's the old Chinese shrimp thing in reverse:
sweet head, tail full of shit.

After a poem by Yi Chehyŏn (1287–1367)

When *yangban* talk occurs around me, I quickly point out that the O'Rourkes were kings of Breifne, which makes me royal stock (*wangshil*). Rourke, I always add, is a Viking word meaning the good king. People are always enormously impressed even if they laugh themselves silly at my insufferable foreign arrogance and impertinence. I always hasten to point out that the family came down a few pegs over the generations, not that I really believe this, but I know that a dust of humility is always good. My approach doesn't get me much recognition, but it puts a quick end to *yangban* talk.

It's important not to be too constrained in your ideas about the *yangban* system because the tradition takes some interesting twists. Many Koreans would be appalled to find out that King Yŏngjo's mother was a maid in the royal kitchens. Her duties were to look after the water for the morning ablutions of the court ladies, an onerous duty, no doubt, given that court ladies tended to be a testy lot. But Yŏngjo's mum rose from the ignominy of her station to become the bearer of the king's son, a future king himself. Yŏngjo ascended the throne after Kyŏngjong's brief reign, which ended in an allergic reaction to pickled crab – poisoned, no doubt. There are those who hint that elements close to Yŏngjo were responsible. As you might surmise, Yŏngjo had a bit of a complex about his parentage.

Kojong's first son, Prince Wanhwa, was born to a *chung'in* palace woman. Taewŏn'gun, delighted by the mother's lack of rank, which translated as an utter absence of indebtedness to ranking others, wanted to appoint the child crown prince. He even discussed the matter with Queen Dowager Cho. The prince died in childhood, ostensibly from measles, but there are lingering doubts about malicious intent.

In recent years my titular Dow Jones has taken a dip. I used to be *shinbunim, kyosunim, sŏnsaengnim*, but these days *ajŏsshi* or *haraboji* is as much standing as I get. There was a guard in my apartment complex many years ago who seemed intent on cutting my pretensions to rank. When I parked my car in a way that outraged his finer sensibilities – and I seemed to do this regularly – he ya-yad me forthwith. Now I don't like being ya-yad; ya-yaing is doggie talk to me, so I ignored him. Of course, no one likes being ignored. Inevitably the guard let me have both barrels. Now while I sympathize with a cruel fate that forced him to deal with an obtuse long-nosed fool, I did so wish he wouldn't raise his voice. Next to being ya-yad, I hate this most. He shouted; I got mad, venom-quiet mad. He screamed about regulations; I asked about etiquette; did he know the meaning of white? He snarled about rules; I pointed out all the other cars blatantly in violation of his rules. I reminded him that his job was to make my life as ruffle-free as possible. He looked at me as if I had two heads. I played my final card: I proclaimed that I pay his salary. There was a moment of hair-on-end shock, of stunned disbelief. Our altercation stuttered to an eerie conclusion. He walked away in total disgust, his only other option being murder, and presumably the elusive sage still disapproved of violence.

I'm not too sure what my loss of status is all about, because I think I've gained greatly in dignity in the intervening years.

Yeats says that men improve with the years. In the case of the great poet, 'De mortuis nihil nisi bonum' is the guiding principle, and when the time comes, I would hope for such treatment myself. At any rate, I now have a nice salt and pepper mop of hair in place of the original nondescript mousy brown. And while I'm not a natty dresser, I'm certainly not the slob I was as a young man. And in addition to a doctorate in Korean literature, and an honoris causa doctorate from NUI in Ireland, I have published more than twenty books, some in prestigious US university presses, I had a poetry column in the Korea Times for many years and subsequently in the Korea Herald, and I travel free on the subway because I'm an honorary citizen of Seoul. Not bad for a *sangnom*. Of course, none of this does me much good. Only those who know me well give me a title, and to tell the truth I'd prefer if people who know me didn't use a title. For the rest, I'm *harabŏji* or *ajŏsshi*. I have been called much worse. An angry motorcycle policeman once called me a *shipp'al shang nomsaekki*, a phrase I'd rather not translate, but believe me it's pretty bad. I don't even know what my offence was, but I think it involved an illegal U turn at a time when U turns were part of the daily diet. How times change! We once bet our driver $20 he wouldn't do a figure of eight around the policeman at the center of Kwanghwamun intersection. The nice policeman laughed and waved. If you tried this in the US or Ireland today, you would get a huge fine and maybe even a month in jail.

A little reading poked large holes in my ideas on status. I was shocked, for example, to discover that the monk was *sangnom*, and that for hundreds of years monks were barred from entering Seoul. It was actually the Japanese who permitted them to come back to the capital. The priest could not reasonably expect to fare much better in status politics, but I never knew one who thought for a moment that he might be *sangnom*. While priests always seemed to be treated with great courtesy, my reading introduced me to stories where the priest *nom* was a recurring character and the *yasujaengi* was very bad news indeed.

Chungnom is a common appellation for a monk; and *shibunom* is not as rare as most priests think. At the end of the nineteenth century when missionaries were banned from entering the country, some of them adopted the guise of mourners. They were clad in white and wore veils over their faces. It worked great until they went to rural villages. The village dogs were not fooled by mourning garb. The butter-cheese smell of a foreign *sangnom* was unmistakable; the dogs duly went berserk. Not to worry. Clergy, whatever their status, have always managed to move in the higher echelons of society.

Yangban sometimes had surprising ideas about what constituted decorum. When Ch'ae Chaegong, prime minister to Chŏngjo, was holding a meeting with his ministers in the *sarang*-reception of his house, he was mortified to hear what sounded like someone urinating loudly in the brass chamber pot. Upon investigation he discovered his mother sitting on the pot in the next room, urinating to her heart's content. 'You mustn't do that, mother,' the prime minister said, 'when I'm holding a meeting with my ministers.' To which the redoubtable lady was said to reply, 'My undercarriage produced a prime minister in its time. Is something as inconsequential as a pee now to be denied?'

The bottom line is that anyone with plenty of money is *yangban* nowadays. And the foreigner's *sangnom* status is really marrowbone talk, only of consequence when he is unknown or when there's trouble in the air. On the surface, where so much of Korea's interrelating takes place, the foreigner will usually be treated as *yangban* unless he is foolish enough to antagonize everyone. *Yangban* status for a foreigner is a sort of pseudo designation that breaks down under stress. And when it breaks down, look out!

6

THE CULTURAL EXPERIENCE:
WHERE TO BEGIN

回

FOR TOURISTS, Korea begins with It'aewŏn and Insadong; for cognoscenti, Korea begins with a man rather than a place: Tan'gun is the great initiator. And no one tells the Tan'gun story better than Sŏ Chŏngju.

The Tan'gun Myth

Long, long ago, on the brightest of bright mornings, God looked carefully over every corner of this rugged world. Mind and eyes were clear and vigilant; one son only, the beloved Hwan'ung, stood at His side.

'My beloved son,' said God the Father, 'choose the land where you would wish to live and rule.'

Hwan'ung the Son considered the world with critical eye – mountains, plains, rivers and seas, all the wondrous weave of creation. He compared, considered, considered, compared: nowhere could he find a land to match the magic of Chosŏn.

'The land of Chosŏn seems particularly fine,' said Hwan'ung the Son, whereupon God the Father asked, 'Why?' To which the Son replied with a smile: 'It is the land where the morning sun first rises, first shines: everything is clear, majestic, bright. It is a world that fills my heart with longing: everything is vivid, fresh as if laid in lovely flowers. Wherever the eye goes, there are fine mountains, limpid streams – no other land is quite like it.'

And as God's most beloved son, Hwan'ung, accompanied by the host of spirits that arbiter wind, rain, clouds, food, clothes, and livelihood, was about to descend on T'aebaek Mountain in the land of Chosŏn, God the Father gently tugged his sleeve, put his lips close to his ear and in low tones bestowed upon him the following secret advice.

'When you live on Earth for a while, you will discover that earthlings, unlike our practice here in Heaven, are accustomed to take several wives and they call a child born of a concubine illegitimate. Thus, some day a muttering half-wit mob may emerge to defeat in arms the most heaven-like of your descendents. They may even demand a change in your genealogical records: they may call you the illegitimate son of Heaven and their ancestors the legitimate heirs. Though such a time come, my beloved son, inform the successive generations that they must always preserve with quiet dignity the majesty of a people whose land opens first to the sun.'

There are two exquisitely important messages here for anyone with plans to stay a while in Korea. Firstly, you must realize that Korea is the most beautiful country in the world. And secondly – that is, if you want to survive in the most beautiful country in the world – you need to learn the *sago pangshik* (life view) of the earthlings who live there.

Sage advice indeed. You won't be here very long before you discover that Korean earthlings love to make rules about how people should comport themselves. The impulse, I believe, comes from *yangban* consciousness, which begins in the pursuit of personal freedom and ends in denying everyone else their freedom, thus clouding the light of heaven.

Sŏ Chŏngju continues the story:

God's most beloved son, Hwan'ung, descended to the quietest spot on T'aebaek Mountain and sat in the shade of a huge juniper, evergreen, soothingly fragrant, where he gave serious thought to the kind of life he would provide the people of this land.

And when he had considered the problem up and down and sideways and had consulted all his feelings, he decided on a strategy: 'Yes,' he said, 'a hundred is better than ten, a thousand is better than a hundred, ten thousand is better than a thousand. Ah,' he went on, 'but this is niggardly thinking. Life in heaven is without end; the life of this people should also be without end. Whether they die young or old in the flesh, they shall live in the knowledge that the life of the heart is without end, carried forward from generation to generation. Made in the image of God, my father, they will know there is no ending.'

Further reflection, however, revealed to Hwan'ung two things that might impede the heart of the people from continuing majestically from age to age like the heart of Heaven: firstly, the well-born use of strength by the base-born, which is the way of the fierce tiger; and secondly, the tendency of the courageous but foolish to screw up everything they do, which is the way of the bear.

Some more lessons. To inherit the heart of heaven, you must be brave as a tiger and foolish as a bear. The tiger ingredient urges you to *yangban* consciousness and power; the bear ingredient ensures that you screw things up anyway. A perfect recipe for black comedy!

Sŏ Chŏngju continues:

And so Hwan'ung decided that if he were to rear sons and daughters who would continue the life of the heart forever, he would have to begin with the girl who was to be his wife: he would have to root out all immaturity. He chose a girl foolish as a bear and a girl with the disposition of a tiger.

'You are not fit to look directly on the light,' he said, and he thrust them into a very dark place.

'Endure, endure,' he said. 'To be able to endure whatever bitter acrid trouble comes your way is to be fully human, a quality to be passed on to the thousand generations. I shall divide between you some of the bitterest mugwort and some of the most acrid garlic. This is all you will eat. Have courage. The one who endures to the end I will take as my wife.'

The fierce tiger girl and the foolish bear girl, each confident of her ability, having gotten from Hwan'ung, God's most beloved son, the mugwort and garlic with which to sustain herself, contended in the black cave to see who could endure her trial best. Of course the nitwit tiger girl lost. The fool of a bear made a better pretence of endurance than the predator tiger: thus the bear girl, in her foolish way, bore up well on the diet of bitter mugwort and hot garlic, while the fickle tiger, in a sudden fit of craziness, born of feelings of superiority, ran off to matters extraneous.

Thus in the battle between *yangban* pretentiousness and native foolishness, you are advised to put your money on foolishness. In the West it is called the idea of being fools for God's sake, which is, of course, the missionary ideal.

Sŏ Chŏngju concludes the story:

The bear girl, who had proved herself able to endure the bitter and the hot, showed herself capable of preserving inwardly the heart of Heaven, forever, without end, and thus was chosen as Hwan'ung's wife.

When Hwan'ung saw the foolish bear girl emerge with a cultivated heart, he realized that it would be good to fill her heart with the never ending heart of Heaven. This he did. Subsequently, the stately mien of the girl fired the heart of Hwan'ung, and from the intimacy that ensued, the bear girl bore a child – Tan'gul by name, Tan'gun in modern parlance.

In old, old Korean tan'gul meant 'heaven', a name that suggests man should always strive to be heaven minded. Since the injunction is to be heaven minded, living as tan'gul (Tan'gun) meant age unlimited. If you ask why Tan'gun's age was first set at 1908, the answer is that this is an aggregate number: it includes Tan'gun's age in the flesh, plus the cumulative age of all his descendants who ruled in his name. If the plan was to highlight the intensity of the line, then the count should be through the generations.

There you have it: the birth and history of the nation, the *yangban* compulsion in individuals and institutions to make rules that alienate people, and the light (heart) of Heaven as the central value in Tan'gun's Korea.

Figure in the Distance *(hanshi)*

At first I wondered
if the figure
on the distant sands
were a white heron,
but to the sound
of piping on the wind
the vast expanse of sky and river
faded into evening.

Chŏng Chak (1533–1603)

7

THE CONFUCIAN MONOLITH

THE SADAEBU RULING elite who helped Yi Sŏnggye found the new dynasty in 1392 resolutely promoted Confucian ideology while relentlessly striving to root out Buddhist ideology. This introduced an overwhelming moral emphasis in the conduct of state and human affairs. From the time of the military coup in 1170, poets, with few exceptions, were *sadaebu (sa – sŏnbi,* scholar; *taebu –* administrator; hence *sadaebu –* scholar-adminis-trator), a pattern that was maintained until the eighteenth century. For the *sadaebu* elite, anything that smacked of passion was frowned upon. Soon poetry began to display the symptoms of a profound dissociation of sensibility from which it suffered for a long time. One hundred and fifty years into the new dynasty, prominent thinkers like Yi T'oegye regarded passion as vulgar. T'oegye associated passion with *hŭng,* the buzz of excitement that accompanies the apprehension of beauty, and *hŭng,* he felt, lowered the barriers of control essential in the life of a wise man. Children, in T'oegye's view, should not be exposed to the vagaries of *hŭng.* The wonderful Koryŏ *kayo,* replete with pris-tine *hŭng,* were subjected to the nip of the censor's scissors; and to this day, musicians playing Chosŏn dynasty court music wear deadpan faces. The effects of the dissociation of sensibility expe-rienced in Chosŏn society were enormous. The new ortho-doxy inculcated a way of life that eschewed passion. Reason was the supreme faculty; imagination (also feeling and sensation) was suspect. The emergence of a rigid moralism was inevitable.

It affected every aspect of life, and continues to do so to the present day. The only way to obviate this uncompromising moralism was through a life of inner illumination, as practised by literati like Sŏ Kŏjŏng, who refused to be stifled by the strictures of Neo-Confucianism.

A tradition doesn't establish itself in a day. The roots of Confucian ideology were already in place in Koryŏ, and the process by which Chŏng Tojŏn's ideology imbedded itself in Korean *yangban* consciousness was presumably slow. History provides innumerable examples of people and events that do not observe strict Confucian norms. Yulgok's mother, for example, was not a typical Confucian housewife, and the burial arrangements for Yulgok's family are not according to strict Confucian etiquette. Yulgok's wife has the first position, then Yulgok himself, followed by Yulgok's brother and wife, then Yulgok's parents. Men and women are buried together, not at all the norm in Confucian burial arrangements. And *shijo* – Korea's short song genre – attests to unexpected departures from the norms of Confucian ethics. We will see examples later. So we must be careful about jumping to conclusions on the rigidity of life in the early part of the dynasty. I suspect that there was much more freedom in the interpretation of Confucian norms in early Chosŏn than in the period after Hideyoshi.

Personal cultivation was the heart of Confucianism. Chŏng Kŭgin (1401–1481), an official in early Chosŏn, composed 'Sangch'un kok' (Song in Praise of Spring), a *kasa* extolling the wisdom of the man who shuns the world and buries himself in nature. It may not be clear from the English, but 'Sangch'un kok' is full of Chinese cliché phrases, which are indicative of the direction in which Confucian ideology began to move fairly early in Chosŏn.

Song in Praise of Spring (kasa)

You who are buried in the dust of the world,
what do you think of my life?
Have I the elegance of the men of old?

Many a man in this world is my equal;
immured in hills and woods could I be ignorant of joy?
My thatched hut faces blue waters;
in the thick of pine and bamboo,
I am master of wind and moon.[1]
Winter is over; a new spring is here.
Peach and apricot bloom in the setting sun;
willows and fragrant grasses green in the fine rain.
Cut with the knife, or drawn with the brush,
the creator's art is tremendous.
Birds sing in the woods;
informed by the energy of spring,
every note beguiles.

I am one with my world; one with joy.
I close the brushwood gate;
I sit in the pavilion; I stroll and recite:
mountain days, quiet, alone.
No one knows the flavour of leisure; I am on my own.

Neighbours, we'll go sightseeing.
Stroll today on green grass; tomorrow take the ritual bath;[2]
gather wild greens in the morning; go fishing in the evening;
strain mature wine with a fibre cloth;
cut flower sprays to count our cups.
We cross the blue waters, propelled by flower breezes.
Fragrance fills our cups, petals fall on our coats.
If the wine jar empties, let me know.

I take the boy to get some wine:
elder – stick in hand; boy – wine on back.
I recite as I stroll; sit on the bank of the stream,
wash my cup in clear water, fill it to the brim.

---

[1] Reference to Su Dongpo's 'Red Cliff'.
[2] Reference in the Analects to a ritual bath. See Waley's translation 2.25.

I cast my eyes on blue waters; peach blossoms flow by.
The peach paradise must be near.[3] Is that it over there?
I walk the sliver path between the pines; azaleas fill my arms;
I hurry to the top of the peak, sit among the clouds.
Ten thousand villages stand in view.
Mist and evening light make broidered silk.
Yesterday's dark fields are filled with the light of spring.

Fame and honour shun me; riches and wealth shun me.
What friends have I but clear wind and bright moon?
I eat from my lunchbox, drink from my gourd;
    no time for foolishness.
I would not be averse to a hundred years of this joy.

Chŏng Kŭgin (1401–1481)

THREE ANECDOTES

If you are squeamish, don't read these three anecdotes. They are included here because they are stories – however ugly – of personal cultivation. They also show the enormous cultural differences between East and West in what can be discussed in polite conversation without offending propriety.

Confucius and his disciples wandered all day through the mountains until they came to a miserable hut. An old woman prepared soup which the master ate with relish. The disciples were very hungry, but they did not touch the soup because they saw discharge from the old woman's nose fall in as she prepared it. The disciples thought only of the impurities in the soup; Confucius thought of the human warmth displayed by the old woman in looking after her guests.

---

[3]   The Peach Paradise refers to the utopia discovered by the fisherman in the 'Preface to the Peach Blossom Spring' by Tao Yuanming (365–427). The fisherman announces his discovery on his return to the world, but he is unable to find the Peach Paradise again.

Confucius sat down with his disciples and listened to them cut down to size the men of the world. Subsequently Confucius took his disciples to the market. He wanted to buy a calf, but before agreeing to buy, he discussed the calf's pedigree: father, grandfather, great grandfather and so on. The disciples were unanimous in their view that there was no necessity to go into such detail about the blood lines of a base-born animal.

'Well, when you fellows get together, you do a lot of talking about the blood lines of men; why make a big deal out of me going into the pedigree of the calf?'

The disciples realized that Confucius was reprimanding them for their shallowness.

Confucius walked at the head of his band of disciples. At the edge of the forest they saw a man defecating, pants down, backside bare. Confucius called the man over and reprimanded him severely for doing something so uncouth in the full view of passersby. A few days later, Confucius was once again at the head of his band of disciples when they saw a man defecating in the middle of the road. Confucius ignored the man and continued on his way. After a while one of the disciples asked, 'Master, a few days ago you reprimanded the man defecating at the edge of the forest. Today you see a man with bared backside defecating in the middle of the road and you pass by without a word. Why?'

'Reprimands are reserved for people,' Confucius replied. 'There's no point in reprimanding an animal!'

The mountain may be high (shijo)

The mountain may be high,
but it is still below heaven.
Climb and climb again; everyone can reach the summit.
Only he
who never climbs insists the mountain is high.

Yang Saŏn (1517–84)

Two Bulls

Prime Minister Hwang Hŭi (1363–1452) watched an old farmer ploughing with two bulls, one yellow and the other black.

'Which bull is best?' Hwang Hŭi shouted. The farmer interrupted his ploughing to come over and talk. After glancing about, he whispered that the black one was probably the better of the two. Hwang Hŭi was curious about the farmer's diffidence.

'Why do you talk so carefully about such a trivial matter?' he asked.

The farmer replied, 'Animals are not any different from humans: they shouldn't be criticized in their hearing. It might hurt their pride.'

This was the gentle side of the Confucian tradition.

After a poem by Sŏ Chŏngju (1915–2000)

Pear Painting (hanshi)

The old tree trunk is a jumble of knots;
the cool fragrance tells me it's a pear.
Wrapped in last night's frost and snow,
a branch has managed to bloom.

Yi Tal (1539–1612)

She's Right, You're Right

When Hwang Hŭi was prime minister, a slave voiced a grievance. She explained her position and asserted the rightness of her case.

The prime minister agreed with her.

'You're right,' he said.

A second slave came in and explained her position. 'You're right, too,' the prime minister said.

'You can't answer like that – she's right, you're right,' Hwang Hŭi's wife exclaimed. 'Judgment must be made on principle.'

'Yes indeed,' the prime minister said. 'I do believe you're right.'

Sŏ Chŏngju (1915–2000)

Spring Day *(hanshi)*

There's gold in the willows;
the jade glint has gone from the plum.
New water in the tiny pond is greener than moss.
Spring joy or spring turmoil – which is greater?
    The swallows haven't come; the flowers haven't bloomed.

Sŏ Kŏjŏng (1420–1488)

YULGOK AND T'OEGYE

Yulgok and T'oegye were outstanding Chosŏn dynasty philosophers. Stories abound about who was the greater. One such story takes the sleeping habits of the two distinguished gentlemen as the arbiter of greatness. Yulgok's supporters were delighted when the master slept in a dark room; he was quiet as a baby. T'oegye's followers were dismayed to find their master sleeping in a brightly lit noisy room. They were forced to admit defeat. Next day when they told T'oegye of their great shame, he rebuked them in the severest terms. 'You fools,' he cried, 'have you not heard of the thunderbolts of heaven and earth?'

Yulgok fathered only one child, a girl. T'oegye had numerous progeny.

T'oegye's portrait adorns the 1,000 wŏn note; Yulgok's portrait adorns the 5,000 won note. To'egye's followers went to the Bank of Korea to have the matter out with the authorities. Why was their master on the lesser note? The bank president replied, 'But we see the 1,000 wŏn note so much more often!'

Even ignorant men seek perfection *(shijo)*

Even ignorant men seek perfection;
Perhaps the way is easy.

67

Not even wise men can be perfect; perhaps the way is difficult.
Easy or difficult,
between the two, I do not feel the advance of age.

Yi Hwang (1501–1570)

This is the final poem in *The Twelve Songs of Tosan*, which is a short compendium of the Confucian Way.

SONGGANG (PINE RIVER) CHŎNG CH'OL

Songgang Chŏng Ch'ŏl was a brilliant if rather controversial official. In a career punctuated by periods of voluntary retirement, dismissal and exile, his friends consistently said nice things about him while his enemies – and he had many – excoriated him.

Here is the Chŏng Ch'ŏl loved and admired by his friends:

Autumn Night *(hanshi)*

I listened to the rustle of falling leaves
and thought it was the sound of forlorn rain.
I called for the lad to look outside.
He said: moonlight is hanging on the trees.

And here is the Chŏng Ch'ŏl, 'prickly pink in wine' who was excoriated by his enemies.

YULGOK AND SONGGANG

Songgang Chŏng Ch'ŏl, requested Yulgok (Chestnut Grove) Yi I, to rebuke the Eastern Faction member, Kim Hyowŏn, allegedly a small minded good-for-nothing. Yulgok smiled gently but voiced no agreement.

Back home, Sŏ Chŏngju tells us, Songgang composed a poem on what he felt had been a refusal. Here is the poem with Sŏ Chŏngju's comment:

If a man's will is as unshakeable as a mountain,
why keep returning like a river?

The river was indeed a river, a rather turbulent river,
prickly pink in wine, providing no place for Yulgok's smile to shine.

HUNMIN KA

Chŏng Chŏl's *Hunmin ka,* a *shijo* series of moral admonitions
for the common people, is inferior poetry but a primer of Confucian moral attitudes. 'Puŭi moja' is typical of the series.

Puŭi moja – Father's Honour; Mother's Affection (shijo)

My father gave me birth,
my mother sustenance.
Without father and mother, would I have life?
How can I
repay a favour that is boundless as Heaven?

KOSAN YUN SŎNDO (1587–1671)

Kosan Yun Sŏndo is my favourite Confucian worthy, not
because *The Fisherman's Calendar* is the supreme achievement in
the *shijo* form, but because he managed to do very little, politically or otherwise, that he didn't want to do. And that is some
achievement in Korea or anywhere else.

As soon as Yun Sŏndo heard about the Manchu Invasion, he
rushed to Kanghwa only to find that Kanghwa had fallen and
the king had flown to Namhansan Fortress. Yun Sŏndo returned
south without paying his respects to the king, a flagrant breach
of etiquette. Back in Haenam he learned that the king had sur-
rendered to the Ch'ing and was back in Seoul to negotiate peace
terms. Yun Sŏndo was so disappointed with this turn of events
that he decided to sail to Cheju and live in retirement. On the
way his ship dropped anchor at Pogildo, a small island some
twelve kilometres off the tip of Haenam, which became his personal Peach Garden Paradise. He lived in Pogildo in retirement
and spent his time in leisurely pursuits and in projects to beautify the environment. His enemies charged him with a breach
of due decorum in failing to pay his respects to the king on that

fateful trip to Kanghwa, and they used the supposed frivolity of his lifestyle on Pogildo at a time of national calamity to show his untrustworthy nature.

Yun Sŏndo's life revolved around his study. He awoke in the morning with the cock, drank a tonic prescription for purifying the blood, combed his hair, washed himself – even the sequence is intriguing – dressed neatly and proceeded to the first formal task of the day: teaching the children. After breakfast he got on his cart-palanquin-buggy, and, taking his musicians along, went to one or other of his villas to divert himself. He describes the mood:

Lazy I am (shijo)

Lazy I am:
Heaven knows this well.
Of all the many affairs of men not one has Heaven
　　entrusted to me.
Mine it is
to watch over rivers and mountains,
　　for this demands no rival struggle.

Sometimes he took a bamboo cane and walked along the banks of the Nangyŏn'gye, where he liked to sing, and if the weather was good, invariably he went all the way to Seyŏnjŏng, which was his favourite pavilion. It was customary on these trips to have the servants prepare wine and side-dishes in abundance, which were transported in a small cart. If the party was going all the way to Seyŏnjŏng, there was a rest stop at Chŏngsong'am. Yun Sŏndo always brought the children along. At the lake he lined the girls up in a small boat so that he might look at their brilliant dress-clothes and lovely faces reflected in the water while he sang from *The Fisherman's Calendar*. Sometimes he did not bother with the boat but went straight to the pavilion where he had the musicians play for him. Sometimes he divided the performers between East Terrace and West Terrace and had them face each other and dance, or he chose someone particularly adept to climb Oksuam (Jade Water Rock) and dance there with long sleeves fluttering in the wind so that he might enjoy the reflection in the water. Sometimes he went to the fishing hole, where he liked to throw out a line. Sometimes he dug lotus roots. His joy was in the delights of the day, and he did not return home till the sun was declining. He never missed this daily schedule unless he was unwell.

This picture of a typical day in the life of the old master comes as a surprise to those of us who expect Confucian scholars to be dark, frugal chewers of mountain greens, men who are aloof, staid, and predictable in their responses. Chŏng Pyŏng'uk, one of the first incisive commentators on modern Korean culture, makes the point that what distinguished Yun Sŏndo was his ability to break from the austere traditional mould, to be not just a scholar and honest bureaucrat but also a free man. The Confucian gentleman was traditionally distinguished by the pleasure he took in self-cultivation and *p'ungnyu* (flying wind) elegance.

Yun Sŏndo had more than his share of the slings and arrows of outrageous fortune. He spent twice as much time in exile as in government service, but it would appear that when he had it good, he had it very good indeed. Even in his sixties his abiding hope in the inevitability of spring, political and otherwise, allowed him to rise above the worst of winter, which was some achievement in such politically parlous times.

Has the worst of winter passed? *(shijo)*

Has the worst of winter passed;
where is the snow wind?
Spring's breath shimmers across a thousand, ten thousand
   mountains.
I'll open my door
at dawn and look at the light in the sky.

ŎBUSASHI SA (THE FISHERMAN'S CALENDAR)

The ideal of the wise man in nature suffuses the *shijo* tradition. Yun Sŏndo's *Ŏbusashi sa* (The Fisherman's Calendar) is its finest embodiment. *Ŏbusashi sa* is a cycle of forty *shijo* describing the four seasons in one of Yun Sŏndo's favourite retreats. The fisherman is a time-honoured symbol of the wise man who lives simply in nature. The reader, while experiencing the day-to-day life of the idyllic fisherman through the four seasons, constantly feels the tensions between the concepts of retreat in nature and public service in the court, and the tensions inherent in the efforts of a Confucian gentleman to work out his own confusions. The tensions between inner illumination and public service are rarely discussed in Korea, but they are essential for an understanding of the spirit and practice of the Confucian ethos.

The refrain, *Chigukch'ong, chigukch'ong*, represents the winding of the anchor chain; *ŏsawa* is the rhythm of the oars.

SPRING

1. Mist lifts on the stream in front,
    sunlight illumines the mountain behind.
    Push away, push away!
    The night tide is almost out; soon the morning tide
       will be coming in.
    Chigukch'ong, chigukch'ong, ŏsawa!
    Flowers
    in profusion adorn the river village; distant hues are best.

2. The day is hot;
    fish jump in the water.
    Weigh anchor, weigh anchor!
    Seagulls in twos and threes fly back and forth.
    Chigukch'ong, chigukch'ong, ŏsawa!
    My fishing pole
    is ready; did I put the *makkŏlli* jar on board?

3. An east wind springs up;
    waves get up a lovely swell.
    Hoist the sail, hoist the sail!
    I leave East Lake behind, move on through to West Lake.
    Chigukch'ong, chigukch'ong, ŏsawa!

The mountain
in front passes by, giving way to the mountain behind.

4. Is that the cuckoo singing?
Is that the willow grove greening?
Row the boat, row the boat!
A few fisher houses glimmer in and out of the haze.
Chigukch'ong, chigukch'ong, ŏsawa!
Shoaling fish
flash in a clear deep pool.

5. The reference here is to the song that concludes *The Fisherman*,
ascribed to the Chinese poet, Qu Yuan (ca.300 B.C.)

Gentle sunlight bathes the water;
the waves are like oil.
Row the boat, row the boat!
Should I cast the net; my fishing pole might be better?
Chigukch'ong, chigukch'ong, ŏsawa!
The song of the fisherman
stirs my heart; I forget all about the fish.

6. The offices referred to here are prime minister, minister of the
right, and minister of the left.

The evening sun slants in the sky;
enough, it's time to go home.
Lower the sail, lower the sail!
Willows and flowers are new at every bend.
Chigukch'ong, chigukch'ong, ŏsawa!
Shall I look
with envy on the three highest offices in the land
or think of the affairs of men?

7. There are echoes here of a famous Chinese poem, *Chuan zi he
shang shi* ascribed to Qu Yuan, which describes a fisherman who
has no luck fishing but settles for a boatload of moonlight.

I long to walk on fragrant grasses,
to pick orchids and gromwells, too.

Heave to, heave to!
What have I loaded in my tiny leaf-like boat?
Chigukch'ong, chigukch'ong, ŏsawa!
On the way out,
I was alone; on the way back, I have the moon.

8. The Peach Paradise refers to the utopia discovered by the
   fisherman in the 'Preface to the Peach Blossom Spring' by Tao
   Yuanming (365–427). The fisherman announces his discovery on
   his return to the world, but he is unable to find the Peach Paradise
   again.

   Tipsy, I stretch out;
   what if I drift through the fast water?
   Tie up, tie up!
   Petals drift by in the water; the Peach Paradise must be near.
   Chigukch'ong, chigukch'ong, ŏsawa!
   How well hidden
   from the red dust of the world of men!

9. I hang up my fishing line,
   look at the moon through the rush-awning window.
   Drop anchor, drop anchor!
   Has night fallen already? The cuckoo's call is limpid on the air.
   Chigukch'ong, chigukch'ong, ŏsawa!
   Excitement
   unabated, I forget where I'm going.

10. Will there be no tomorrow;
    how long till the spring night sets?
    Beach the boat, beach the boat!
    My fishing pole is my walking stick as I head for the
        brushwood gate.
    Chigukch'ong, chigukch'ong, ŏsawa!
    Days like this
    are a fisherman's life.

SUMMER

1. Protracted rain comes to an end;
   the stream begins to clear.
   Push away, push away!
   I put my fishing pole on my shoulder; excitement grips me deep.
   Chigukch'ong, chigukch'ong, ŏsawa!
   Who painted
   these layered mountain peaks in the mist tinted river?

2. Wrap my rice in lotus leaves;
   don't bother preparing side-dishes.
   Weigh anchor, weigh anchor!
   I have my bamboo rain-hat on; what did I do with my
      sedge rain-cape?
   Chigukch'ong, chigukch'ong, ŏsawa!
   White gull,
   so very impassive, are you following me or am I following you?

3. Wind rises in the pondweed;
   it's cool at the rush-awning window.
   Hoist the sail, hoist the sail!
   Are summer winds steady? Let the boat drift where it will.
   Chigukch'ong, chigukch'ong, ŏsawa!
   North bank,
   south river; it's all the same to me.

4. The muddy water reference is to the song that concludes 'The
   Fisherman', ascribed to Qu Yuan: When the Canglang's waters are
   clear,/ I can wash my hat strings in them; when the Canglang's
   waters are muddy,/ I can wash my feet in them. The admonition
   is to seek official preferment when times are good, and to retire
   gracefully when times are bad. The middle section refers to Fu
   Cha of Wu who was so angry at the suicide of his servant Wu
   Yuan that he had the body put in a sack and thrown into the Wu
   river. The final section refers to Qu Yuan again. A minister in the
   kingdom of Chu, he was banished for objecting to official policy.
   Distressed, he committed suicide. The idea here is that the poet

might catch Qu Yuan's soul in a fish. The poem is a meditation on loyalty.

> So what if I wash my feet
> in muddy water?
> Row the boat, row the boat!
> I would go to the river Wu; how sad the stormy waves
>   of a thousand years.
> *Chigukch'ong, chigukch'ong, ŏsawa!*
> I would go
> to the river Chu, but I might catch a fish with a human soul.

5. The inference here is that one should give the best fishing place to an old man just as the people of Lei gave Emperor Shun the best place in ancient times.

> In the thick shade of the willow grove,
> a mossy spot catches my eye.
> Row the boat, row the boat!
> When I reach the bridge, I'll assign no blame
>   in the fishermen's wrangling.
> *Chigukch'ong, chigukch'ong, ŏsawa!*
> If I meet
> the crane-haired old man, I'll follow the example of *Lei Lake*.

6. Excitement grips me deep;
    I had no idea day was fading fast.
    Lower the sail, lower the sail!
    Beating time on the mast, I sing boat songs.
    Chigukch'ong, chigukch'ong, ŏsawa!
    Who knows
    the old world graces embedded in these songs?

7. The first section appears to be a loose translation of a poem by the Tang poet Li Shangyin (812–858).

> The evening sun is grand,
> but twilight is close at hand.

Heave to, heave to!
The path that winds across the cliff slopes down beneath the pines.
Chigukch'ong, chigukch'ong, ŏsawa!
The song of the oriole
studs the green grove.

8. The mosquitoes are small minded men who seek only personal gain, while the blowflies are even more despicable types who ruin a man by slander. The final comment would seem to be tongue in cheek while the poet battles with the various insects that trouble him. Sang Hongyang of Han was a wily economics expert who made a large personal fortune while working for his country.

I'll spread my nets on the sand,
lie down under the rush-awning and rest.
Tie up, tie up!
The mosquitoes are a pest; are the blowflies any better?
Chigukch'ong, chigukch'ong, ŏsawa!
My only fear
is that the wily rogue of Han, Sang Hongyang, may be listening in.

9. The middle section quotes a phrase from the Tang poet Wei Yingwu (737–ca.792): *crossing – fields – crosswise – boat.* However, the sense of the phrase seems to be a boat tied to the ferry landing strangely defying the current by sitting crosswise in the water. The final section also incorporates a phrase from the same Wei Yingwu poem: *river – edge – hidden – plant/grass.*

Who can tell how wind and waves will change
in the course of the night?
Drop anchor, drop anchor!
Who was it said 'the boat tied at the ferry cuts across the current'?
Chigukch'ong, chigukch'ong, ŏsawa!
The hidden
plants by the river's edge are truly lovely.

10. I look up at my snail-shell hut;
   white clouds are all around.
   Beach the boat, beach the boat!
   I climb the stony path, bulrush fan sideways in my hand.
   Chigukch'ong, chigukch'ong, ŏsawa!
   You ask
   if a fisherman's life is leisurely; well, this is what I do.

AUTUMN

1. How unspoiled the life of the fisherman,
   away from the outside world!
   Push away, push away!
   Laugh not at an old fisherman; he's part of every painting.
   Chigukch'ong, chigukch'ong, ŏsawa!
   Seasonal pleasures
   are all fine; but the autumn river is best of all.

2. Autumn comes to the river village;
   the fish grow fat.
   Weigh anchor, weigh anchor!
   Leisurely hours spent on broad waters.
   Chigukch'ong, chigukch'ong, ŏsawa!
   I look back
   on the world of men: the farther off the better.

3. White clouds get up;
   tree branches rustle.
   Hoist the sail, hoist the sail!
   Off to West Lake on the full tide, on the ebb tide to East Lake.
   Chigukch'ong, chigukch'ong, ŏsawa!
   Redshank
   blooms in the pondweed: it's a joy to see it everywhere.

4. Out there where the wild geese fly
   I see peaks I've never seen before.
   Row the boat, row the boat!
   I fish a bit, but it's the mood that really intoxicates.
   Chigukch'ong, chigukch'ong, ŏsawa!
   The evening sun,
   dazzlingly bright, gold broiders a thousand peaks.

5. How many fine silver-jade fish
   have I caught?
   Row the boat, row the boat!
   I'll make a reed fire, select the best for broiling;
   Chigukch'ong, chigukch'ong, ŏsawa!
   I'll tilt the crock jar
   and fill the gourd dipper full.

6. Wind blowing gently athwart,
   the billowing sail brings me back.
   Lower the sail, lower the sail!
   Darkness deepens in the sky; pure pleasure remains.
   Chigukch'ong, chigukch'ong, ŏsawa!
   I never tire of
   red-tinted trees and clear water.

7. The image in the first section is presumably taken from Su Dongpo's
   'Red Cliff', which describes moonlight settling on the river like
   dewdrops. The Phoenix Pavilion is a reference to the royal palace
   where the poet would wish to send the pure moonlight. Legend
   tells of the white hare that grinds medicinal powders on the moon.

   White dewdrops angle over the river;
   the bright moon has risen.
   Heave to, heave to!
   Phoenix Pavilion is far away; to whom shall I give this pure light?
   Chigukch'ong, chigukch'ong, ŏsawa!
   To a noble guest
   I'll feed the medicine the jade rabbit grinds.

8. Xu You washed his ears in the river when the emperor suggested giving him the throne. The west wind dust is a reference to the dust of the outside world.

   Are heaven and earth different?
   What place is this now?
   Tie up, tie up!
   West wind dust doesn't reach this far; no need to fan it away.
   Chigukch'ong, chigukch'ong, ŏsawa!
   I've heard
   nothing; no need to wash my ears.

9. Frost falls on my clothes;
   I do not feel cold.
   Drop anchor, drop anchor!
   My fishing boat is cramped; is the fleeting world any bigger?
   Chigukch'ong, chigukch'ong, ŏsawa!
   Tomorrow
   will be like this, as will the day after.

10. I'll go to my stone hut among the pines
    and watch the moon at dawn.
    Beach the boat, beach the boat!
    But how can I find the leaf-strewn path through these deserted
        hills?
    Chigukch'ong, chigukch'ong, ŏsawa!
    White clouds
    follow me; my hermit clothes weigh me down.

WINTER

1. Winter sunlight falls thick
   after the clouds have cleared.
   Push away, push away!
   Ice binds heaven and earth, yet the sea remains unchanged;
   Chigukch'ong, chigukch'ong, ŏsawa!
   billow after billow,
   rolls of silk unfurled.

2. Are line and pole in proper order;
   has the boat been sealed with bamboo?
   Weigh anchor, weigh anchor!
   They say nets freeze on Xiao Lake and the Xiang River.
   Chigukch'ong, chigukch'ong, ŏsawa!
   There's no better place
   for fishing now.

3. The fish have left the shallows,
   gone to deeper pools.
   Hoist the sail, hoist the sail!
   Let's head for the fishing grounds while the weather holds fine.
   Chigukch'ong, chigukch'ong, ŏsawa!
   Fat fish bite,
   they say, when the bait is right.

4. When the snow cleared last night
   the whole world had changed.
   Row the boat, row the boat!
   A sea of glass in front, jade mountain folds behind.
   Chigukch'ong, chigukch'ong, ŏsawa!
   Is this where the Immortals live,
   where the Buddha lives? It cannot be the world of men.

5. Oblivious of net and pole
   I tap the lip of the boat.
   Row the boat, row the boat!
   How often have I pondered going back across the river?
   Chigukch'ong, chigukch'ong, ŏsawa!
   Those unpredictable
   strong gusts, will they blow or not?

6. Li Su of Tang released flocks of ducks and geese to conceal the
   movement of his troops, thus gaining victory in a battle with
   Wu Yuanji. The 'shame of the trees' refers to the fears of the

retreating troops of Fu Jian after a shattering defeat in 383: they were afraid that the enemy was concealed behind every tree.

Crows fly off to roost;
quite a few have passed me by?
Lower the sail, lower the sail!
The road ahead darkens; snow falls in the fading light.
Chigukch'ong, chigukch'ong, ŏsawa!
Who will attack
Oya Lake, and wash away the shame of the trees?

7. Red cliffs and green rock faces
   surround me like a painted screen.
   Heave to, heave to!
   What matter whether or not I've caught big-mouthed
       fine-scaled fish?
   Chigukch'ong, chigukch'ong, ŏsawa!
   I sit in my sedge cape and hat,
   heart quickening in my solitary boat.

8. How valiant that solitary pine
   standing on the bank!
   Tie up, tie up!
   Do not find fault with murky clouds; they block out the world.
   Chigukch'ong, chigukch'ong, ŏsawa!
   Do not tire of
   roaring waves; they blot out the dust and clamour.

9. Yan Ziling retired from the court of Emperor Guangwu; dressed in sheepskin he spent his life fishing the Qili River. Jiang Taigong fled from the tyranny of the Shang king, Zhou, and spent ten years fishing. King Wen discovered him on the banks of the Wei and brought him back as chief counsellor.

   It's been said from of old
   that the sage lives in seclusion.
   Drop anchor, drop anchor!

Who was it that wore the sheepskin and fished the Qili River?
Chigukch'ong, chigukch'ong, ŏsawa!
What of the man
who fished for ten years, counting the time on his fingers?

10. Ah! the day comes to a close
it's time to eat and rest.
Beach the boat, beach the boat!
Red petals tint the snow-filmed road as I walk merrily home.
Chigukch'ong, chigukch'ong, ŏsawa!
Till the snow moon
crosses West Peak, I'll keep my pine window aslant.

STRUTTING THEIR STUFF

Keep an open mind when you are discussing Korean Confucianism. The most surprising things can colour *yangban* decorum. Many commentators said that Yi Chŏngbo (1693–1766) couldn't have written this *shijo*. The facts, however, are indisputable.

I'll never forget the boy *(shijo)*

I'll never forget the boy
who slept here last night.
He could be the son of a tile-maker the way clay yields to his touch,
or the scion of a mole the way he burrows and thrusts, or
perhaps the stripling of a seaman the way the oar answers his
pulse. His first experience, he avows, a claim that raises certain
doubts.
I've had my share before
and I assume I'll have some more, but the memory of that
boy last night is a pleasure I shall always store.

Yi Chŏngbo (1693–1766)

The Chosŏn dynasty was purportedly a man's world. Women were subservient, meant to be neither seen nor heard. This may not be the whole story, Kim Sujang (1690–?) tells us:

Look at that girl in blouse and patterned skirt (shijo)

Look at that girl in blouse and patterned skirt,
Her face prettily powdered, her hair as yet unpinned.
Yesterday she deceived me and now she's off to deceive another,
Fresh-cut flowers
held firmly in her hand, hips swinging lightly as the sun goes down.

Kim Sujang (1690–?)

Cock and dog are symbols of faithfulness and punctuality. Eighteenth century mores may not have been quite as strict as some would have us believe.

Of flying birds and beasts that crawl (shijo)

Of flying birds and beasts that crawl,
cock and dog are marked out for a fall.
For when within the green gauze screen my love lies sleeping on
my breast, the cock cries loud and raucous and routs him from
his rest. And when he comes to the outer gate, the dog makes
such a snapping, barking flurry that my love must take his leave,
departing in a hurry.
Poultry-peddlers, dog-meat-mongers,
when next you cry outside my gate, you'll get that cock and dog
trussed tightly for the plate.

Anonymous

Here is a song of innocence and experience that would warm the cockles of William Blake's heart. How much of the story do we have in this highly ironical poem?

It is the third watch (shijo)

It is the third watch. The girl in the bridal bedroom is so gentle,
so beautiful, I look and look again; I can't believe my eyes.
Sixteen years old, peach blossom complexion, golden hairpin,
white ramie skirt, bright eyes agleam in playful glance, lips
half-parted in a smile. My love! My own true love!

Need I say aught
of the silver in her voice and the wonder of her under the quilt?

Anonymous

Song of Right and Wrong *(hanshi)*

When it came to discerning right from wrong, Kim Sakkat
(1807–1863), the rainhat poet, usually managed to throw the
cat among the pigeons. What would T'oegye or Yulgok make
of his moral principles? Would Hwang Hŭi have a problem?
In East Asian lore, right and wrong are sides of a coin, inseparable parts of a single reality.

Year by year, the years go, inevitably they go.
Day by day, the days come, inexorably they come.
The years go and the months come in a flurry of come and go,
genesis of time in Heaven, of human affairs on earth.

That right is right and wrong is wrong is not indubitably right;
that right is wrong and wrong is right is not indubitably wrong;
that right is wrong and wrong is right is just conceivably right;
that right is right and wrong is wrong is both right and wrong.

Kim Sakkat (1807–1863)

Korean Confucianism became more and more scarred by formalism as the dynasty unfolded. Sŏ Kiwŏn's witty satire on Ma
Chun, a conscientious official, highlights the niceties and confusions of the Confucian tradition, encapsulating what it had
become by the end of the nineteenth century. Conscientious
official was a rank in Chosŏn that gave temporary *yangban* status, which could be lost in the succeeding generations of the
family by failure to procure public office.

THE MAROK BIOGRAPHIES: MA CHUN'S TALE

Ma Chun was the eldest son in a line that went back to a conscientious official. His sixth ancestor was given the honourable
title; subsequently his great-great-grandfather served as vice-
minister, and his great-grandfather had been a county magistrate. His ancestors maintained the proud family escutcheon as
best they could. In his grandfather's generation, however, the
family fortunes wavered badly: his grandfather managed to pass
the civil service examination at the *chinsa* level but failed to
get an official post; and most recently, his father had fallen in
rank to *saengwŏn*, a level that threatened the family with being
dropped completely from the ranks of the nobility. There were,
of course, many reasons for this slide in the family fortunes.
To stay in the ranks of the nobility, the family had to serve in
public office for three successive generations. *Chinsa* was not
an official post. It behoved Ma Chun, as the ranking grandson, to serve at least as a county magistrate; otherwise the Ma
family was finished both as conscientious officials and as nobility. Thus, from Ma Chun's earliest years, his father's expectations
of his son – the third generation of only sons – were enough to
bring tears to the eye. The father, thrilled when his son finished
the Thousand Character Primer at the age of seven, sent him
to a fairly well-known Confucian scholar uncle in Ch'ŏngju
and had him study there until marriage some ten years later.
Indeed had family circumstances permitted, he would have
gotten his son private tuition from a renowned scholar in the
capital. Ma Chun's name read backwards – Chunma – means
swift horse. No such pun was intended when naming the child
originally, but the father secretly hoped for the day when his
son would gallop. And if completing the Thousand Character
Primer at the age of seven was not the achievement of a swift
horse, it at least indicated a rating in excess of good packhorse.

The slide in the family fortunes could be put down to external
and internal factors. The decisive external factor was undoubtedly the turbidity of the times. Not only did the court no longer

look after the families of conscientious officials, but the five or six conscientious families that had managed heretofore with great difficulty to maintain their existence found themselves no longer able to endure: they cast away the honourable title as they would an old shoe. The decisive internal factor was related to heredity. The Ma family steadfastly maintained the tradition of conscientious official, but meat and fish graced their table no more than twice a year, at New Year's and at Ch'usŏk Harvest Festival. A few pieces of jerky and a dried pollack was as much as they were accustomed to use for the annual rituals required by the five generations of the family. There were more than ten of these annual rituals. Thus it could be readily surmised that since great-grandfather's time the family had been afflicted by malnutrition. To expect bright children to be born of such parents was ridiculous. Indeed, in view of the fact that malnutrition had been a fact of life now for two or three generations, it was fortunate that a complete moron had not been born into the recent generations of the family. And while it could be maintained that the absence of a moron showed how the pride of the conscientious official tradition was able to offset psychologically the family's poor nutrition, at the same time the failure of Ma Chun's twenty years of study to produce any fruit could not be blamed entirely on the fact that passing the civil service examination had degenerated into an exercise in finagling. The presumption was that a hole had been bored in the Ma family brain. The tragedy of father and son was their complete failure to realize this. Normally the father is the unbending, preaching type, and the son is the one who rushes into the midst of affairs while scoffing at antiquated moral instruction. Ma, father and son, were quite the opposite.

Ma Chun, twenty-seven years old, was sitting the civil service examination for the third time.

'So how many applicants do you think there might be this time?' his father enquired. The father's tentative phrasing of the query was because he knew perfectly well that the number of applicants at the civil service examinations could not be targeted in units of hundreds.

'About twenty or thirty thousand.'

'And the usual ten or so to pass?'

'Yes, I suppose so.'

'How many names are on the short list?'

'Well, there's Kim Taeshin's son from Chandong, and a descendant of an academician from Ch'angdong... about ten altogether.'

The short list referred to names that were bandied about before the examination as likely to succeed, not because they were academically brilliant or of outstanding character, but because they were the sons of powerful families waiting their turn to pass the exam. These names went out to every corner of the land, and they almost always passed.

'That means five or six at most will pass on merit.'

'That's the way it always is, father.'

'If only there was a department for conscientious officials...' the father said with a deep sigh.

Without a special examination for the children of conscientious officials, passing the difficult higher civil service examination was like trying to pluck stars from the sky.

'It can't be helped, I suppose,' the father mumbled. 'You know the old saying *song-ji-shi-ja,* even saints follow the times?'

'Father, I understood the phrase means that the times make the saints.'

'The meaning is substantially the same. I can't go around the houses of the powerful asking them to put an official's skullcap on my grown-up son. You'll have to make the effort yourself. There's no other way.'

It wasn't the first time for the father to say this. The descendant of Ma So-and-so, conscientious official, might not be material for the short list when there was a long line waiting, but a little diligence ought to be enough to secure a county magistracy in the south. Ma Chun had a bad taste in his mouth every time the talk came round to diligence.

'How can the grandson of a conscientious official run around the *sarang*-reception rooms of the powerful?' he complained. To which his father replied, 'That's not the way of the world.

Why won't you do what everyone else is doing? If you don't get an official posting, our family is finished.'

'That's not right, father. You mustn't soil the name of a conscientious official. Not even if starvation is the price...' Ma Chun was too far removed from his father's point of view to finish the sentence.

'What a dreadful thing to say!' the father said angrily, but there was a solid note of ineffectuality in his voice as he continued, 'All those failures in the civil service exam have changed you.'

In the summer of Ma Chun's twenty-ninth year, his father had a stroke. The old man was paralysed on one side, and Ma Chun himself, or his wife, was left with the task of dealing with the patient's bodily functions. A young couple lived in what passed as servant's quarters at the front gate. In the grinding poverty in which the Ma family lived, they were lucky this young couple had not run away; they could not ask them to provide such a service. The Ma household was maintained for the most part by the stipends the seven slaves paid in lieu of work. They were called slaves and written up as such in the official documents, but they lived wherever they wished. Each of them presented the master's house with a bag of rice once a year. It was a secondary consideration that this was easier than paying family tax, poll tax and all the other taxes; the primary consideration was that slaves in *yangban* houses were exempt from military service. A conscientious official could not own farmland, but there was no common law prescription against him having slaves. You cannot have a law that says spin a spider's web in a living man's throat. However, when the old man passed the wretched family finances over to the son, the son began to have scruples about what the slaves were paying in lieu of work. This had not bothered him heretofore. Maybe he felt no pity for his wife, who, unknown to the neighbours, did piecework sewing. At any rate, he made up his mind that he would have to free all the documented slaves. There's no good cure for paralysis: this is true, but the old ways demanded that a son, however extreme his lack of filial piety, had to provide the odd packet of Chinese medicine for his father. But here was a case of an injudicious young man taking over the running of a family in circumstances so difficult that he could not provide meals much less medicine.

'What on earth are you saying? Your father's illness is one thing, but you have to think of the children's future too,' his wife pleaded, dark spots freckling the corners of her eyes.

'I know that. It's a huge responsibility, but a man of virtue cannot sit idly by in the face of injustice. Especially so in our case: we are a conscientious official family, supposedly a model to the world. It's not right for us to be living in such a degenerate way.'

Ma Chun noisily gulped down a large bowl of water and turned back to his desk as if he resented his wife's interference. It was too late to bemoan her fate in marrying a man like him. When a husband who has read a thousand books proposes some lofty purpose, what can the wife do but defer and follow him unquestioningly? Read the book of your choice, cover to cover; there won't be a single word telling you how to live in these circumstances, so what's the use of having read ten thousand books? There were times when he felt the urge to burn every book in the house, but days without a book to read were a dismal prospect. He had not discussed his idea of freeing the slaves with his father because he did not want to worry the latter needlessly, but his father must have gotten the information from the daughter-in-law. He called Ma Chun to his bedside.

'If you are really determined to do this, I won't stop you. When a child says he's going to do something that is right, a father can't very well stop him. But I have one condition.'

'What do you mean, father?'

'You must pay your respects to Lord Kim in North Village three times in the space of a month. We don't belong to the same political faction, but there are old family friendship ties between us. If you show your face there from time to time, he won't treat you coldly.'

Ma Chun was sick of hearing this.

'How do you expect me to mix with those office hunters?'

'I'm not telling you to do this so as to get a posting. Access to that kind of house will help you learn the ways of the world.'

'I can sit right here and know all I need to know about our world.'

'What do you know? You know nothing.'

'It's a world where nothing works and nothing is impossible. If you have money, you can get absolved of crime; if you haven't money, you can't do anything. It's that kind of world, isn't it?'

'You know that much, I see. So what's the point in acting different from everyone else?'

'I have to maintain the dignity of a conscientious official.'

Father and son reiterated their fixed positions day and night.

'Anyway, I won't go along with freeing the slaves unless you do what I say.'

The father enunciated clearly; there was no slurring of his words. He could have given a clear order to the son and that would have been the end of it. So this sort of conditional haggling showed the unusual relationship between father and son. In a way it could be said that the father's abiding concern was to open a path to the future by making reverse use of the son's narrow one-track approach.

'And why did you not do that yourself, father?'

The question seemed reasonable to Ma Chun. He could not understand how his father could make such demands of his son when he was not willing to get stained by the world himself.

'I didn't realize it at the time. You will find out yourself when you are a little older. I'm not telling you to start flattering Lord Kim. All you have to do is pay your respects; you can keep your dignity. If there are a lot of visitors and you can't get into the sarang-reception, you can leave a calling card and come home. That's all right, too.'

That much did not seem too dishonourable. The problem was that Lord Kim from North Village was typical of the kind of corrupt minister whose head the non-politically involved literati invariably called for when times were turbulent. Lord Kim indeed had the power of political preferment in his hand, but how could Ma Chun wear the mask of a literatus and frequent such a house? And how could he face the non-political literati who recognized the Ma family as repositories of the conscientious official tradition and who highly valued Ma Chun's personal integrity?

Ma Chun's circle of non-political literati acquaintances was extremely limited; he was known to an extent by the scholars who lived in the Confucian village outside East Gate and by those who lived in Namsan Valley. His reputation was not predicated on great virtue or personal distinction; rather it was based on his being content with the frugal life of that rare entity, the descendant of a conscientious official. And to Ma Chun, tired beyond words of not being able to demonstrate human greatness, the recognition of a group of upright literati was of great value, something, in fact, quite irreplaceable. These literati had failed the various levels of the civil service examination several times. The *Noron* faction had reached the end of its ten year cycle of power, but as long as the *Noron* government did not collapse, there was no way to rescue the people from the chaos into which their lives had fallen. So these literati demanded the punishment of a few corrupt ministers, who were to be examples of the reform of this god-awful end-of-the-century culture that was rotting every corner of society. Mostly *Soron*, they had experienced crushing defeat in the factional fighting under the previous king. There were even some who asserted they had no political colour, who claimed political transparency. Ma Chun also was *Soron*. Ten years ago a *Soron* could join the ranks of the minor officials fairly readily, but in recent times a *Soron* couldn't even get the post of assistant curator of graves. The two sides were thus clearly demarcated. You could sit sedately in the palace or in the reception room of a palatial house surveying a city population of less than 180,000, or you could be on the other side with a handful of foolish, hopeless literati, men filled with rancour and resentment, accustomed to oppose just for the sake of opposing. Of course, Chosŏn society had a tradition of revering literati, even if it was mostly show. Accustomed to listening to their literati, the people were reluctant to sweep them out indiscriminately for being a bit reckless in what they said. Against this broad national background, Ma Chun's feelings about his good reputation among the literati, his awful dedication to friendship, was both pitiable and foolish, a bit of self-indulgence springing from the inferiority of the defeated.

For better or for worse, Ma Chun had no understanding of the way things were. His problem remained the same: should he oppose his father, or should he continue to live on the basis of false slave documents? In other words, instead of rooting out his own corruption, should he risk the sneers of his friends, get a job and earn his living? It was one or the other.

After several sleepless nights of soul searching, Ma Chun went to the Confucian village outside East Gate to see his close friend Ch'oe Ch'iyŏl. Supposed to be a literati village, in reality it was a slum of thirty or forty thatched crab shell houses grouped under a steep hill. Inside the city gate, roads had been widened, sewage systems fixed, the appearances of the capital maintained, but one step outside the gates presented scenes unchanged since Shilla and Koryŏ. This was especially true of places like the Confucian village where the residents only had the one well since their grandfathers' time.

'Anyone at home?'

A loud cough was followed by a gentlemanly hail.

Ch'oe Ch'iyŏl ran out quickly.

'No need to shout,' he said.

'What's up?'

'Were you tailed?'

'No, I don't think so.'

'You have to be careful these days. They're watching everyone coming in and out of the house.'

'What for?'

'What for? I'm being watched since I sent that memorial to the king demanding the clean-up of corruption.'

'So what? What you said wasn't wrong, was it?'

'That's what kills me. I wouldn't mind only it's doubtful if the memorial ever got to the king.

'It's fine to lament the times, but be careful you don't go too far.'

Coming from Ma Chun, this was very incisive advice.

Ma Chun proceeded to bare his soul. Ch'oe Ch'iyŏl was not impressed.

'You can't be serious, not at this stage of your life. OK, if you suck up to the *Noron* establishment and set your heart on fame and honour, there's nothing you can't do. After all, you're the descendant of a splendid conscientious official; you have character, you have education. But wait a bit longer. You won't starve. If things are really bad, we'll all help. Don't lose courage now.'

This was Ch'oe Ch'iyŏl's counsel. Well not so much counsel as an effort to dissuade.

'My father didn't mean me to swindle the people with an official's scull-cap. He meant me to take a stipend, live honourably and work for the people: that's the way of the scholar too,' Ma Chun said. He felt his friend was right, but somehow he was a bit disappointed.

'That's easy to say,' Ch'oe Ch'iyŏl said. 'But you know what the official world is like. Can an upright man like you put up with it? Suppose you get a county magistracy without having to lay anything out. If you want to keep it, you'll have to pay off the governor and make seasonal payments to various officials. You're crazy if you think you can live honourably on your government stipend. That much should be obvious!' Ch'oe Ch'iyŏl kept striking the floor in his excitement.

'But with the conscientious official image, things could be a little different.'

'That's what you think. If what you say is right, why appoint someone like you? The only policy is to drive out corrupt ministers and reform the government.'

'Will things improve if the *Soron* get in?'

'Not necessarily so. But there are clean people among the *Noron* too. We need to open the way to clean government; we need upstanding officials who transcend factionalism. Don't destroy the image of conscientious official.'

On this they were perfectly agreed.

The host detained Ma Chun late into the evening. Another guest, who had not visited for a long time, was scheduled to arrive from Namsan Valley. They would have dinner together and then Ma Chun could go. Ma Chun knew the guest, Pak Chinsa, a leader of the young literati in Namsan Valley. Last year a large number of the Yŏngnam literati had come up to Seoul, and while they were waiting for a memorial to go through channels, they staged a sit-down demonstration outside Kwanghwamun for which they were duly arrested. Pak Chinsa circulated a declaration criticizing the court's management of affairs. This was the start of Pak Chinsa's reputation as a man to be reckoned with. He was dragged before the Correctional Tribunal and subjected to intense torture. Afterwards even his supporters referred to him as outrageous. At any rate, he was a special kind of existence, a man who went around spitting out insults that would have meant disaster for an ordinary well-behaved literatus – and getting away with it. Whispered criticism of the *Noron* administration was not his way; he could not care less who heard him, he cursed loudly and openly. That's how it was today too.

'They should be slaughtered in Chongno,' Pak Chinsa declared. 'Did you hear,' he continued, 'that there was an uprising of the people in Chinju? They're playing it down for fear it might spread to other areas, but it seems to have been very big. The heart of the people is the heart of heaven; it can't be repressed at will. Do they think power has no limits? It's utterly unjust, utterly!'

A bowl of bear soup – and that was several months ago – was all the meat Ma Chun had tasted in some time. Two or three cups of wine brought a relaxed glow to his limbs, and while enjoying a certain release from tension during Pak Chinsa's on-going outburst, one side of him reacted negatively.

'Nowadays there isn't a single recording secretary that hasn't been bought off. That's the world we live in.'

'I know, I know.'

For the most part Ma Chun just listened to Pak Chinsa and Ch'oe Ch'iyŏl. If his esteemed father had heard the conversation of these two gentlemen, he would have reprimanded his son severely for sitting down to dine with them. Every age has its gripers. They express no regret for the lack of ability or character that prevented them from gaining preferment; they do not even consider the possibility of personal responsibility. All they do is curse the world at large and boost their egos with complaints about the distortions of the recording secretaries. One thing is certain: the man who leaves his name in history never belongs to the griping multitude. Ma Chun figured his father's admonishment would have been in these terms. And he felt the admonishment would not have been without merit. Normally when he faced his father, his attitude was similar to the attitude of Pak Chinsa and Ch'oe Ch'iyŏl, but today his father seemed to make sense.

Ch'oe Ch'iyŏl's counsel was no better. It cost him nothing to go on and on about the literati preserving loyalty; it was as easy as eating cool porridge. Ma Chun's friends said they would help him if things got really bad, but since they could barely feed themselves, what could they possibly do for him? This was just irresponsible talk. If they got summoned right now to the palace, who could guarantee they wouldn't rush into court dress and run off in answer to the call. The result of these unhappy thoughts was that Ma Chun's trip outside East Gate did not help much in solving his problem.

In the event, it was his father's dying words two months later that were instrumental in Ma Chun coming to a decision. His father had not much body function left, but he could still manage a bowl of rice. It happened to be harvest time and one of the 'paper' servants living in Suwŏn had sent a bunch of brass coins. Ma Chun sent his wife off to the market and she set such a rich table it upset his father's stomach. In the middle of the night, his father got severe stomach cramp. He was just able to twist his tongue around the words, 'Ca... call the physician in Kwanggyo, Doctor An.'

Ma Chun couldn't wait for the dawn curfew; he took a servant and set out. He was stopped twice on the way to Kwanggyo. Both times he pleaded he was going to get a physician for an emergency at home. He gave the guards a few coins he had prepared for the purpose. Even Ma Chun had this much common sense.

It was a little out of character for his father to look for this particular physician who was regularly in and out of North Village. However, he was rumoured to be very good with the needles. Ma Chun knocked at the gate. A servant came out rubbing sleepy eyes.

'Tell the physician Ma So-and-so from such-a-place urgently requests his services.'

The servant went inside and reappeared after an interval.

'The physician says he knows no such person,' the servant snorted.

'That's impossible....Tell him it's an emergency; he has to come.'

'Look here, sir, there's no good in keeping at it. Even with a sedan-chair, you wouldn't have much chance! I mean, who goes out in the middle of the night? Bring the patient at first light.'

The servant rattled the gate closed and drew the bolt. Actually the son-of-a-bitch was right. Even with a formal request and a palanquin at the ready, who knows how a celebrated physician would react to someone – one hand as long as the other – seeking his services in the middle of the night? His father had been thoughtless and he himself had been stupid. Had the request come from Lord Kim in North Village, the physician would have been so happy he would have danced naked with the girl in his bed and thrown on his clothes. But for conscientious official Ma So-and-so? The presumption was that the physician had roared at the servant, 'Don't make me laugh!'

Ma Chun sought out a pharmacy, had an elixir pill made and hurried home. Already the colour of death was in his father's face. He put his lips to his father's ear and whispered, 'The physician is down the country, he's not at home. Here, eat this pill.'

He broke the pill in two and put half of it in his father's mouth. His father shook his head and spat it out. He took his son's hand.

'It's all over now,' he said. 'It's a bitter thing to go without seeing you wear official garb, but....' he mumbled and died. This was not so much a lament as the expression of a dying wish. At least Ma Chun believed so. Apart from three or four very minor officials who were acquainted with his father, a few old Confucian scholars, a few friends such as Ch'oe Ch'iyŏl and Pak Chinsa, and the immediate family, about ten people came to offer condolences. Had Ma Chun written a few hundred death notices and had he circulated them where power is exercised, perhaps there would not have been such a dearth of people to send condolence money to the household of the last surviving conscientious official in the land, but quite apart from the fact that such behaviour would have been totally unthinkable, Ma Chun could not provide the writing materials, and in any case he had no messenger to deliver them. Ma Chun buried his father beside his mother in the family grave in Kwangju.

Ma Chun did not leave the house for the next hundred days; he prostrated himself repeatedly in front of his ancestral tablets. Deep in his heart he was convinced that implementing his father's dying wishes would not only gain him forgiveness for his lack of filial piety during his father's lifetime but would also pave the way for him to reform his base attitude to life, namely, using false documentation to make a living.

Mourning dress was worn for a period of three years. It was customary not to go out to a government position until the permanent burial took place after two years. Today it is normal to change clothes for going out purposes, but this is only an expedient misused by officials to avoid having their posts taken away. Ma Chun wanted to hear himself being addressed as 'sir'. Accordingly, before the permanent burial took place, he began to feel the need to busy himself in carving out a position.

Looking back, the idea that taking public office inevitably meant doing evil things seemed like a form of premature cowardice. And the lame excuse of asking himself how the descendant of a conscientious official could possibly beg for a bureaucrat's skullcap reflected an attitude that was cowardly and narrow-minded. If he became an upright official, who could dare point a finger in criticism? Ma Chun's father would have been delighted by his son's new resolve. Ma Chun himself felt that at the age of thirty he was finally growing up.

The following year, a few days after the post-burial memorial service, Ma Chun washed his hair, fixed up his top-knot and addressed his wife:

'I am going to Lord Kim's in North Village. Tell Yŏngchil to make the necessary preparations.'

'Lord Kim's?'

'That's all right. There's no need for you to concern yourself.'

When a poor scholar without any office pays his respects to a powerful minister, he has to take at least one servant; otherwise he might not even get his calling card processed.

Lord Kim's house was a huge establishment; it was said to be about 150 *kan*, and the area outside the front gate was a sea of confusion. Bearers gambled in groups beneath the stone wall. There were four-man sedan chairs, and single-wheelers; and for the less well-heeled there were palanquins; and then there was an array of messengers and merchants on donkeys or on foot. A man who appeared to be a steward sat on a mat in the gateway. He processed each calling card individually, recorded it and sent a servant inside with it. A little later the name was called if the interview had been granted. Ma Chun waited five turns, all in vain. Not even beggars were driven from the door. This was ridiculous, but since it was presumably due to the huge number of visitors morning and evening, he decided not to take umbrage at his rejection. He failed again the next day. He was very annoyed but decided to give it one more try. He signed himself as Ma Chun, direct descendent of Ma So-and-so, conscientious official.

Sure enough Ma Chun was called immediately. There were twenty or thirty visitors already sitting around a very large room. Two officials of the third rank and one of the second rank sat grandiosely in the highest place. It was an honour for Ma Chun to be part of this company even if he was seated in the lowest place. Eventually, there was a muddled nasal call from the yard, 'Lord Kim has risen from bed.'

The visitors reacted as one, folding their hands and rising to greet Lord Kim.

'I have some official business this morning, I'm wearing official garb. Forgive me.' Lord Kim's resonant voice rang out.

'Not at all, Lord Kim!' the attendant multitude sang out in unison.

Lord Kim laughed out loud. Ma Chun had no idea why Lord Kim was laughing. Had not literati the right to mingle on an equal basis with the prime minister, Ma Chun thought, straightening up deliberately? Assisted by two maids, Lord Kim sat down on two silk cushions. A manservant quickly brought in the long smoking pipe and a brazier.

'It's so early for you, Lord Kim.'

'I came today to escort My Lord to the ministry.'

A conversation ensued between Lord Kim and an elderly third rank official. Obviously there was no such thing as equality of rank among ministers.

'My Lord, I'm taking up my appointment tomorrow, thanks to you,' said a man with low drooping shoulders seated in the middle of the group.

'Ah, Mokch'on, is it?'

'No, My Lord, Kwach'ŏn.'

'Is that where it was? Don't make any mistakes down there.'

No mistakes! Such a beautiful way of putting it. No mistakes in governing the people, and no mistakes in dutiful repayments either!

Lord Kim took a look around those seated in the room.

'Which of you is the grandson of the conscientious' official? he asked.

'It is I, My Lord. My sixth ancestor's name was such-and-such,' Ma Chun said and he gave the Chinese characters.

Lord Kim inclined his head in thought momentarily.

'I think I've heard that name. But is the conscientious official system still in operation?' he asked with a slight laugh. The group laughed with him.

'I think we are the only family left.'

'I thought all the families had already returned the title. It's very commendable in this modern world that recognizes only money.'

'You praise us too much, My Lord.'

'It is indeed a happy occasion for the representative of a conscientious official household to come calling on My Lord,' said one of the guests.

A man with such ability in witty flattery would be useful. Lord Kim looked at the interlocutor with undisguised pleasure.

'It is ten years to the day since I first came to My Lord's *sarang*-reception room.'

'Is that so?'

There was another resounding laugh.

'And what is your desire?'

'P'aju county magistracy.'

'From today consider yourself magistrate of P'aju.'

'Sir?'

'I will inform the Ministry of the Interior. You can be getting your belongings ready.'

'My Lord!'

Had no one else been present, the man would have burst into a flood of tears.

'Well, shall we go to the ministry?' Lord Kim belched heftily a couple of times and set out slowly. The visitors followed Lord Kim out and lined up outside the gate to send him off in his four-man sedan chair. Outside the gate there was a restless crowd of rejected suitors and onlookers stretching as far as the main road. As Lord Kim's entourage was about to leave the lane, a young scholar wearing a formal dress hat threw himself on the ground and blocked further progress with a clamourous wailing 'My Lord!'

'Get out of the way!'

The guards rushed in and began to beat the young man mercilessly with their clubs. The young scholar lay there like a frog turned upside down holding its belly. The onlookers laughed. A male slave allayed their curiosity by explaining, 'He's crazy. He's been coming like this every day for a month to see Lord Kim.'

Unlike this young Confucian scholar, Ma Chun had reaped the rewards of his ancestor. He signed himself as the grandson of a conscientious official: without this he would have no fat chance of getting into Lord Kim's *sarang*-reception, not in a year.

When Ma Chun got home he knelt down in front of his father's shrine, lit incense, and in a voice touched with emotion said, 'Father, I went at your bidding today to pay my respects at Lord Kim's household. The delirium of riches and honour was enough to make me dizzy. I saw one lucky man get himself a township on the strength of a not very exceptional piece of wit, but father, as you know, your undutiful son has no such eloquence. What am I to do? I don't know if I can entertain much hope, even if I pay my respects every day for a year.'

You did well, son. What you did is not without embarrassment for a literatus, and you cannot expect the affairs of the world to be as you would wish them. You must grin and bear it and continue to do your best. Once again I leave you these words: if you do not get an official posting, our family is finished. And you cannot go back to the country, not even if you want to: without land you can't be a country squire.

The voice of the memorial tablet was like the living voice of his father.

'But father, inside I'm hurting and confused. I'll do as you say: I'll keep going to Lord Kim's, but how am I to face the friends who hold me dear? How am I to put up with their criticism and ridicule?'

Nonense! Was all your reading over the last twenty years for their benefit? After cultivating the heart, isn't it only reasonable to care for your family and your country? You shouldn't associate with such a pack of scoundrels. What they say is the groaning of empty bellies. Son, yangban government will not be done away with easily.

His father's abrupt use of a low-class Wangshimri inflection hit Ma Chun with strange power.

The same goes for this damn Noron administration.

'Yes, you may be right.'

People say kind things when they are dying. And what they say after they die must be the truth. Ma Chun made up his mind, come rain or wind, not to miss paying his respects to Lord Kim next day and the day after. His purpose was to see how the world goes around. He was amazed to find that the world now appeared in quite an opposite light. There was no question of donning an official hat and court dress and going off to the palace to sit there all day. Indeed he had no commitment as to when such a day might dawn, but the words in which the sacred cows were couched, the just scholar, for example, and even the conscientious official title seemed faded, whereas the actions of the guards in putting the squeeze on the merchants in the market place did not seem quite as offensive as heretofore. The underlings, after all, were just feeding themselves; there was no need to regard them as a public nuisance. Thus he developed a more liberal disposition.

Ma Chun may not have been able to look after himself, but he developed the skill of looking at the world through eyes borrowed from those who *were* able to look after themselves. Naivety would be a nice name for it, but in plain language, you would have to call it stupidity. In the end, what he had secretly feared all along happened. Ch'oe Ch'iyŏl appeared on the scene. He bowed in front of Ma Chun's father's shrine, then sat down facing Ma Chun and got right to the heart of the matter.

'They say you've been going a lot to North Village. Is it true?'

Ma Chun did not answer.

'Have you got a post?'

There was a note of scorn in Ch'oe Ch'iyŏl's words.

'It was my father's dying wish. Do you think I like it? You have to understand my feelings?'

Ma Chun put on a tearful face and dragged out his lame excuses.

'To think that *you* could be got at!'

Ch'oe Ch'iyŏl heaved a sigh of lamentation. Suddenly he lowered his voice. 'I understand wanting an official posting for your father's sake. But you have to rethink the idea of being recommended by Lord Kim. Do you think this *Noron* world is going to last forever? I'm telling you this because I cannot keep it from you. On the first day of next month we are rising up.'

Blue steel flashed in Ch'oe Ch'iyŏl's eyes.

'Rising up? What do you mean?'

Sudden fright made Ma Chun pose the query.

'The scholars outside East Gate and the literati from Namsan Valley are rising up. And that's not all, the *chung'in* from Ch'ŏnggyech'ŏn are with us too. It will be settled this time, one way or the other!'

'Settled! What do you mean?'

'We'll go in force to Kwanghwamun and petition the king directly. In the past no matter how many memorials we presented, corrupt ministers either fabricated the contents or sat on the document while we bore the pain. It won't be like that this time.'

'So how will it be?'

Ch'oe Ch'iyŏl checked outside. He lowered his voice further.

'Every man will have an axe in his hand; we're going to show some spirit.'

'Isn't that rebellion?'

'What do you mean, rebellion? We are going to petition the king directly about the concerns of the people. Any official who blocks us is a traitor. We are determined to smash the gates of the palace with axes and appeal to the king.'

Ch'oe Ch'iyŏl, fists clenched, puffed and panted.

Ma Chun shivered as if icy water had been thrown on his back.

'Why are you telling me this?'

There was a note close to complaint in Ma Chun's voice. Ch'oe Ch'iyŏl gave a quiet laugh.

'I know you're not going to tell Lord Kim about us. I'm not going to ask you to come out with us. All you have to do is stay quiet, pretend you heard nothing. You decide where you stand yourself. As a friend that's all I have to say.'

This 'I've said my piece, pretend you heard nothing' stuff was a bit ridiculous and the informing Lord Kim thing seemed rather insulting: all in all Ma Chun was not very happy. Did Ch'oe mean he lacked courage? Or that he would not betray the trust of a friend? It was all so ambiguous Ma Chun decided to interpret positively: he chose the second meaning. Even if Ma Chun knew nothing about Ch'oe Ch'iyŏl's plot, he realized that the times were complex and volatile enough for some like minded son-of-a-bitch to hatch such an insidious scheme. But as his father said, the world was not going to be turned upside down by a few hundred yellow-faced small-fry barely able to swing an axe; and even if their petition was delivered directly to the king, how could they hope to cut down Lord Kim who was the king's most trusted minister. They would be taken as traitors; three generations of their families wiped out.

It was now about two months since Ma Chun had begun frequenting Lord Kim's house. He could toss a joke or two at the steward on the gate now, and he did not need a calling card to gain immediate entrance. At this stage he could easily play the part of confidante to Lord Kim. When word got out that someone had become a confidante of Lord Kim, racketeers came with bundles of money in return for favours, but so far nothing like this had happened to Ma Chun. He realized, albeit a little sadly, that this might be due to the foolish reputation of conscientious official. If indeed someone came with a large amount of money looking for a special favour, what to do would have been a cause of great anxiety, but so far he had survived by deflecting such talk with the observation that such things were far removed from the life of an honest frugal man.

Finally, it was the morning of the first day of the month. Ma Chun set out from home rather early. He took his servant Yŏngchil with him just as he had done yesterday. His feeling was that Ch'oe Ch'iyŏl's whispered plot was an exaggeration in order to frighten a colleague and also perhaps to prevent him from turning against him. Ma Chun's walk was a step more refined, though there had been no change in his nutritional deprivation.

'Yŏngchil,' he cried. 'How old are you this year?'

'Thirty-five, sir.'

'Three years older than myself....Life has indeed been unkind to you.'

'It is not necessary to say that, sir.'

'The others went off to live in luxury. They send a bag of rice a year, while you and your wife wear your bones to powder in the service of our poverty-stricken household.' Ma Chun's voice was drenched in sentiment, something very unusual for him.

'Not at all, sir.'

'However, the way of heaven is not without feeling. You have been delivered from hardship's path. When I become the head of a township, you'll be my secretary. One must never treat badly a first wife married in days of poverty. Similarly, a servant who has been loyal in the bad times must not be cast away like an old shoe.'

'Are you on the short-list, sir?'

'Not really....'

Further explanation would be reading scripture in a cow's ear. More importantly, a rumour Ma Chun had heard a few days ago from his wife suddenly began to trouble him again. His wife had picked up an interesting comment from some passers-by, who said, quote, 'Lord Kim is being showered with criticism, but he is associating closely with a conscientious official, an indication that his situation may be better than imagined.' She passed on the comment to her husband.

'Of course, it's better!' He passed over the comment at the time as having little significance, but recently he had begun to wonder if there was any connection between the comment and the fact that Lord Kim had become very friendly. But such doubts were only dog meat. Lord Kim's warmth came from their deepening friendship. Soon the long awaited 'What is your desire?' question would become a reality. From the moment he opened his eyes today, he had that lucky feeling. A row of familiar faces sat determinedly in the big *sarang*-reception. As soon as the 'My Lord has risen from bed' announcement was made, they quickly rearranged their robes. Lord Kim came in with a splendid flourish. He wore ordinary clothes today and seemed to be in very good humour.

'All's well under Heaven,' he said with a loud laugh.

'That goes without saying, My Lord,' all replied in unison.

'And the weather is fine...By the way, is the conscientious official Ma So-and-so here today?'

'Yes, My Lord, I'm here.'

'I see. Is it a place in the Academy you have set your heart on?'

'No, My Lord. I beg to inform you that I have been hoping for a position in the country.'

'A position in the country! What magistracy is vacant at the moment?' Lord Kim asked his secretary.

'There is no vacancy at the moment.'

'Ha, ha, the fool doesn't understand. Make a vacancy!' Lord Kim thundered.

The disconcerted secretary rummaged through his papers.

'Chŏng'ŭp is vacant at the moment.'

Ma Chun felt as if he were floating like a cloud in the sky.

Lord Kim gave a self-important cough and turned to Ma Chun. 'Chŏng'ŭp is a bit far away,' he said, 'but you don't mind.'

Ma Chun had waited breathlessly for this moment.

'My L-O-R-D!' An unexpected cry rang out.

'My Lord, there's been a riot!' an officer of the guard gasped. 'There's a sea of white gathered in Kwanghwamun, a riot.'

'Shut up,' Lord Kim growled. 'How dare you make such an unseemly fuss. Get out this minute!'

Things were not good. The commander of the guard swept in on his horse.

'My Lord, you can't stay here. The rioters insist on seeing the king; they have axes. Shall I deploy the gunners and wipe them out?'

'Commander?'

'Yes, My Lord?'

'That's a stupid thing to say. They are all our people! Wipe them out, you say! No, we won't do that. We'll go and take a look.'

Lord Kim was indeed an exceptional man. Whatever he was feeling inside, on the outside he did not blink an eye. Ma Chun was so impressed he found himself following the retinue. About a hundred guards escorted the party. The entourage entered the palace through Kŏnch'unmun. If only that misfortunate officer had arrived a moment later, Ma Chun would have been magistrate of Chŏng'ŭp. This was all the result of Ch'oe Ch'iyŏl's rash adventure. Ma Chun could not control the anger he felt for Ch'oe. He followed Lord Kim's party up onto the pavilion at Kwanghwamun. The crowd was as big as the one that gathered for the funeral of the last king. They spread bags and mats on the ground and the leaders in the front row prostrated themselves and shouted something. Whereupon everyone straightened up, joined their hands in front of their breasts and bowed twice. At intervals a cry rang out.

'Your Majesty, hear our plea, we beseech you. Drive out corrupt ministers; let justice rule in the land.'

Looking down on the scene, it was apparent that Ch'oe Ch'iyŏl and Pak Chinsa in the front row were brandishing axes, fanning the ardour of the crowd.

'The document will be presented to the king as written. Advise them to disperse and attend to their affairs.'

The officer got his instructions and went outside the gate to thunder them to the crowd, but the commotion only grew worse.

'There's no other way: we'll have to deploy the gunners,' the commander of the guard said, but just as Lord Kim was nodding in agreement, something unexpected happened. A figure rushed toward Kwanghwamun with his axe high in the air. It was Ch'oe Ch'iyŏl. Just when it looked like he was going to smash the gate, he bashed himself on the head. His unfocussed eyes were bloodshot and wild. The people rushed in with a cry and lifted Ch'oe Ch'iyŏl on to a sack. Pak Chinsa shouted a few words to the people. Sounds of wailing vibrated on the air.

'He was a loyal subject. Find out his name,' Lord Kim instructed, a tremble in his voice.

'They say his name is Ch'oe Ch'iyŏl and that he lives outside East Gate.'

When Lord Kim got this report he said,

'If Mr Ch'oe is not dead, tell him I'm appointing him magistrate of Chŏng'ŭp. He was indeed a loyal subject.'

Lord Kim turned to the commander of the guard.

'Commander,' he said. 'We have nothing to fear from those who bash their own heads with axes. In the evening fill them with wine and meat and send them home,' he announced with great liberality, laughing his characteristic resonant loud laugh. Beside him the bespectacled recorder's writing brush moved diligently.

I'm building a straw hut beneath a rock (shijo)

I'm building a straw hut beneath a rock
in a landscape of mountain and water.
Those that do not understand laugh at what they see,
but folly
and rustic simplicity somehow seem to become me.

Yun Sŏndo (1587–1671)

CONFUCIUS GOES MODERN

Emperor Kojong set up a telephone at the grave site of his father, Taewŏn'gun, so that he could pay his respects morning and evening. It is not clear who answered the phone.

The tree is diseased (shijo)

The tree is diseased;
no one rests in its pavilion.

When it stood tall and verdant, no one passed it by.
But the leaves have fallen,
the boughs are broken; not even birds perch there now.

Chŏng Ch'ŏl (1536–1593)

INCULTURATION AT THE END OF CHOSON

A foreign trader took out his false teeth to clean them. The local people, who had gathered shamelessly to witness the foreigner's weird culinary habits, gasped in dismay. 'He's taking himself apart,' they cried and took to their heels.

You couldn't be too careful with a foreign devil!

THE SWINGING TWENTIES

The early part of the Japanese occupation was an extraordinary time. Modernity and the old Confucian world were in conflict. Confucianism, however, still managed to maintain a precarious niche.

After annexation in 1910, an increasing number of young Korean intellectuals, intent on university education, went to Tokyo where they came in contact with current trends in Japanese literary circles. In poetry, this meant symbolism; in fiction, it meant naturalism. In an era when London poets were extremely hazy in their understanding of symbolist theory, it was only to be expected that Korean poets, with third hand information from Japan, would have even hazier ideas. The young Korean intellectuals presumably had excellent Japanese, some English and less French. Most of their translations seem to have been made from Japanese texts, with an eye perhaps on the English, and what theory there was seems to have come from Japanese translations of English sources. What emerged from a complex skein of influence was a poetry full of Pre-Raphaelite colours, characterized by a *fin-de-siècle* atmosphere of decadence, pessimism and world weariness. 1890s London was reincarnated in 1920s Seoul, to the extent that Kim Tongin (1900–1951) paraded up Chongno decked out in tall hat, tailcoat, striped pants, spats and carnation. Whether the carnation was a bow to Baudelaire or to Oscar Wilde no one really knew or cared; it was the gesture that was significant. Chŏng Chiyong's 'Cafe France,' published in 1926, does not seem much in translation, but it functioned in its time as a rallying point for those committed to modernity. After an introductory verse describing the café in exotic terms of lanterns and palm trees, the speaker describes the young men on their way there.

Café France

One wears a rubashka;
another a Bohemian cravat;
'Skin and Bones' leads the pack.

Slits of snake eyes night rain,
light snivelling on the pavement,
we're off to Café France.

One head a tilted apple;
one heart a wormy rose;
a third, a drowned sparrow, races ahead.

'Mr Parrot, sir, good evening!'
'Good evening.' (How does my friend do?)

Chŏng Chiyong (1903–?)

The very idea of a Café France in the Seoul of the time was exotic. Couple this with the Russian jacket, the French cravat, the snake eyes rain, the wormy rose, the overall sensuous for-eignness of the detail, and the use of foreign language. Suddenly you begin to realize the impact exerted by the poem on young writers groping for direction in a world that had few signposts. It was not Mr Prufrock, but it was *modern*.

This tapestry of an exotic avant-garde literary world has to be seen against the background of the horrors of the Japanese occupation. I knew several poets who grew up with Japanese as virtually their first language. At least, that's what they told me. Some of them were over thirty, they said, before they penned a line in *han'gŭl*. I had a friend who served as a lieutenant in the Japanese Imperial Army. The honour code of the Imperial army officer corps was his proudest boast. These men loved Korea and were proud of Korea's independence, but they talked about Japanese times with affection and rarely volunteered information on the oppression that must have been a major part of it. Some of them talk about falling in love with their Japanese primary school teachers, who were invariably not only dedicated teachers but also symbols of elegance and taste, quintessential *mŏtjjaengi*. Some of their memories may have been too painful to discuss. Whatever the reason, there is an ambivalence in the presentation of oppression and modernity in the colonial period. I find it difficult to reconcile the bitterness and rancour of the colonial experience with the exoticism that modernity enshrined. Art and politics seemed separate worlds.

Collaborator in Korea invariably means someone who collaborated with the Japanese. Collaboration with Americans, Russians, Germans, French, British or Chinese – and there were plenty who collaborated – doesn't count. It seems a reasonable conclusion that everyone who managed to do reasonably well economically under the Japanese collaborated or cooperated to a lesser or greater extent. Such sentiments, however, are heretical. I did a series of broadcasts a few years ago. I thought the idea was interesting, a foreigner talking about his favourite Korean poets and reading what he considered their best poems. For me, Sŏ Chŏngju, by a mile, is Korea's best modern poet. I am aware that Sŏ Chŏngju got himself in trouble on a number of occasions. A handful of poems were highlighted as evidence of a pro-Japanese stance. Sŏ Chŏngju himself admitted his indiscretion. He also accepted patronage and financial support from Chun Duhwan's unpopular regime. These were two not inconsiderable goofs, and when I proceeded to talk with great affection about Sŏ Chŏngju and my own friendship with him, the reaction was instantaneous. Messages of protest deluged the station boards. Many were very patronizing. They said things like, 'The foreigner cannot be expected to know these things, but the station authorities should know better than to have a collaborator praised on station airwaves.'

Collaboration is a very emotive topic. A lot of people were tarred and feathered for perceived betrayals in old Ireland. So I know that it behoves the foreigner in Korea to tread lightly in what is a minefield of passions. The great translator-missionary, James Scarth Gale, was accused of being pro-Japanese, as was the first Horace Underwood who founded Yonsei University. Neither were collaborators. Gale loved Korea and did more to introduce Korea and her culture to the West than anyone else in his time, but he made the mistake of seeing plusses in Japan's Korea policies – roads, railways, electricity, communications, the infrastructure of industrialization and so on. Many of the early missionaries shared his views. Underwood was a pioneering educator. He cooperated rather than see his beloved Yonsei University go down the Han River. Catholic priests, including my own Columban confreres, cooperated by bowing at Shinto shrines; they did it to keep the Japanese police off their backs and off the backs of their parishioners. It is the old moral principle of the act of two effects, which sometimes can have Machiavellian overtones. Prime Minister Chang Myun, a committed Catholic, was accused of collaboration because as a young professor he was in charge of a Catholic youth organization that participated in worship at Shinto shrines. Cardinal Kim, who served in the Japanese army was also accused of collaboration. He made the point that those who had not lived through the period should not make such accusations. It is not a very persuasive argument, but the cardinal was such a patently good man and such a clear symbol of opposition to Park Chunghee's *yushin* reform that charges of collaboration didn't stick. In addition he had been punished in his school days for refusing the pledge of loyalty to the Emperor of Heaven, a pledge which Park Chunghee apparently made. The first generation of great literary and political leaders, among them Ch'oe Namsŏn and Yi Kwangsu, were tarred with the collaborator's brush, as was Ch'oe Manshik, author of *Peace Under Heaven*, a superb satire on collaboration.

In the '60s collaboration was not an issue. The collective energy of the nation was caught up in the struggle against normalization of relations with Japan. Many of my teachers in Graduate School, however, were accused subsequently of pro-Japanese sentiments, including one who got up from his deathbed to put his seal on my PhD dissertation. Having to make this imposition on a dying man was singularly the worst moment of my forty-nine years in Korea, but the authorities assured me that if I wanted my degree I had better do it. I was too weak to say that no personal gain warrants this sort of invasion of a dying man's privacy. I regret it to this day.

In judging the collaboration issue, it is important to see the full spectrum of the clash between nationalism and modernity. Sŏ Kiwŏn's satire on the phenomenon of the collaborator teaches some home truths while demonstrating how Confucian rituals continued to operate within the colonial system.

THE MAROK BIOGRAPHIES: MA YŎNG'S TALE

Ma Yŏng was a political agent in the Government-General. More precisely, he was Superintendent Kinoshida's nark in Chongno Police Station. The background to his becoming that most hated of entities, a police informer, was not without extenuating circumstances. However, a prolix introduction of such trivialities at the beginning of this account is not to the purpose. Suffice it to say that the noble ambience emanating from Ma Yŏng's single character name indicated that he was the seed of a family line of some substance.

The difference between a Japanese police nark and a councillor in the Colonial Privy Council was of course one of gravel and white jade. Yet Ma Yŏng had succeeded in gaining admittance to Councillor Kim's *sarang*-reception. No mean achievement, and it was due entirely to Ma's family pedigree. As far as Councillor Kim was concerned, Ma Yŏng was welcome in his house because he was from a reasonably good family. Ma Yŏng's attitude toward Councillor Kim was one of total awe and respect. It must be borne in mind that Ma Yŏng's personal circumstances prevented him from finding this attitude repugnant. After all, the pedigree of the Ma household could not be measured with the same ruler as Councillor Kim's household. Until annexation the councillor's household had enjoyed the abundance of a Chosŏn dynasty minister of state.

Councillor Kim always remembered that Ma Yŏng's father, deceased now for several years, was one of the upright Confucian scholars who refused thank you money at the time of annexation. Thus Ma Yŏng's life was a slur on his father's name, though Ma Yŏng, both then and now, chose to take a broader, more variegated approach to his father's memory, and no one had the right to question this. Those three razor-thin ten *wŏn* notes that his father had returned to the *myŏn* office secretary often gleamed in front of his eyes, leaving him with a profound sense of loss.

Ma Yŏng had just come out of Hwadong Lane and was about to cross the bridge over the stream that connected with the main Samch'ŏngdong road. He wanted to get to the police station fairly early today.

Old Hwang came out of the real estate office with a load on his back.

'How's business, Ma Chusa?' Hwang said in greeting. He employed the honourific title *chusa*, which was used to address lower echelon civil servants. His question was not prompted by ignorance of who Ma Yŏng really was; neither was there any malice in his tone.

'Don't mention business,' Ma Yŏng replied. 'The gold mine boom has gone over the top now. How are things with you?'

'People looking to rent a room are as scarce as beans in a drought. But you're a man who can adapt to circumstances, Ma Chusa, you have no worries.'

Ma Yŏng straightened his hat – Japanese style, with ear flaps. 'That's a bit of a joke,' he said with an ambiguous laugh.

'Neighbouring cousins should look after each other,' Hwang said.

'You're right,' Ma Yŏng replied.

Hwang's conversation may sound like a chancer's stratagem to play on the weakness of a nice guy – not your typical police messenger – in an effort to wheedle a pack of cigarettes out of him, but in fact this was not so. Local naivety has its charm: the Ma family had always treated the locals well, and the locals – whether or not Ma Yŏng's real profession troubled them in their hearts – treated him in their turn as a man who made his living as a miner, thus indicating that there was not a complete dearth of people who thought of him as a man of character.

Ma Yŏng emerged from the hot-and-cold atmosphere of the locale. At sight of a rickshaw driving briskly by, he swept off his hat and bowed to the waist. Councillor Kim, dressed in morning coat, was sitting on the rickshaw, curtains thrown open to greet a fine spring day. He held his expansive tummy and laughed graciously.

'Good morning, Excellency,' Ma Yŏng said in greeting. 'I regret I have not been able to pay my respects for some time.'

'I'm glad we met,' Councillor Kim said. 'Call in for a minute this evening.'

'Certainly, sir. I will see you this evening.'

Councillor Kim gave the impression something had come up that he wished to discuss. Ch'adal, the driver, towel wrapped around his head, spat on his hands and started off at a lively pace. For a driver, the son-of-a-bitch lived in the lap of luxury. Ma Yŏng was impressed every time he set eyes on the councillor's rickshaw. This was no ordinary rickshaw. The spokes of the wheels were done to a silver sumptuousness; the seat covers had the sheen of silk. On bright sunny days the dazzle made the passer-by lower his head. Ma Yŏng felt a throb of pain in his heart as he wondered whether there would ever be a day when he would drive in such a vehicle.

Councillor in the Privy Council was the greatest honour and the highest office to which a denizen of Chosŏn could aspire. Councillor Kim's eldest son had graduated in spring from a technical college in Tokyo; he was supposed to go straight into the Government-General. The younger son, attending an acclaimed Tokyo university, was supposed to be studying for the senior civil service examination. There was not another man under Chosŏn skies quite so blessed as Councillor Kim.

Ma Yŏng, lost in a dream that he had attained the stature of Councillor Kim, trudged along under the wall of Kyŏngbok Palace. Establish a big reputation, gain the trust of the Japanese, get yourself referred to as a unique son-of-a-bitch or a brainy son-of-a-bitch – that could be the route to an appointment as chief clerk in the East-West Colonial Company. No. His academic background was inadequate for such a post. But there was no reason he couldn't make Chief Security Guard in the Government-General.

Ma Yŏng's dream was shattered the moment his jodhpur clad legs put him in front of Superintendent Kinoshida, who had charge of the dissident control section in Chongno police station.

'You're a bastard, a right bastard, a rice worm!' Kinoshida roared. 'You feed on your pay and produce nothing.'

This was a terrible bawling out, quite untypical of Kinoshida. Ma Yŏng swallowed hard in an effort to regain his composure.

'Did I do something wrong, sir?'

'What do you mean by that story yesterday about the student in Chungdong? Better bring in nothing at all than unsubstantiated rumours.'

'I'm sorry, sir. These things happen. Cases of people being abusive about Japan have become rare. Perhaps it's due to the widespread effect of the new cultural policy.'

In terms of Ma Yŏng's brain capacity, this piece of flattery represented a rare level of wit. Superintendent Kinoshida gave a snort, but his mood had improved.

'Are you making fun of me? You Chosŏn people are incorrigible. More effort is called for here. Understood?'

Ma Yŏng had been associated with Superintendent Kinoshida now for three years. He had been a big help to the superintendent during the major events of the period – the Kyŏngshin School general strike, and the mass arrest of the Justice Party. Ma Yŏng flattered himself that he had been a considerable help to Kinoshida in getting him those two decorations. So he figured the superintendent's language on this occasion was excessive. But he also firmly believed that to get angry or pull a face in circumstances such as these would only be a repetition of his deceased father's folly.

'I will make every effort, sir.'

A deflated Ma Yŏng, in restless mood, went snooping to Pagoda Park where he listened in on the old people's conversations and eavesdropped on the boozers in the back lane wineshops. With these tactics, it was impossible to get any usable information. He came home, a model husband and a model father.

'You're early today.'

Ma Yŏng grunted a noncommittal response.

In his time Ma Yŏng had had his share of women. However, when his eldest son went into normal school, he made the effort to restrain himself from throwing his hard-earned money at the wineshop prostitutes and began to make do with the shriveled breasts of his first wife from hard times. He had two other children who in due course would also go to normal school. These fine prospects carried great hope for a great regeneration of the Ma family. The flaw in the jade was that his eldest son recently had become suspicious of the nature of his father's employment.

'Why are you so late?' Ma Yŏng asked his son.

'School was late,' the boy answered sullenly and went into his room without looking at his father. Ma Yŏng, figuring his son was at that age when children give back answers to their parents, showed great wisdom in controlling his displeasure.

As soon as Ma Yŏng finished supper, he hastened to visit Councillor Kim's house. Sŏngch'il, who lived in the servant's quarters, opened the gate as always. With the pack of cigarettes

Ma Yŏng gave him clutched in his hand, he escorted his guest into the *sarang*-reception, as he would someone of distinction. The pack of cigarettes was not really a bribe to gain easy admittance to the house. The visitor has his pride; this was just a small token called for in a house as large as Councillor Kim's where the steely glint of power was evidenced in the German shepherd – or whatever breed the dog was – tied up in the front yard.

Ma Yŏng tossed a sugary smile at the dog, which was growling with bared fangs.

'Mr Ma from Hwadong has arrived.' Sŏngch'il imitated the formal tones of an usher. Ma Yŏng coughed gently and opened the door.

'Come in. Sit here. There's no need to be formal.' Councillor Kim was warmer than ever. To Ma Yŏng's surprise, a tray of wine and side-dishes was brought in. Councillor Kim dismissed the servant girl and poured the wine himself.

'Yes, indeed, we could all take your father for a model. Not everyone could do what he did,' Councillor Kim said.

He's at it again, Ma Yŏng thought, a sour taste already in his mouth. However, he bowed his head humbly.

'Of course,' Councillor Kim continued, 'there have been not a few in history who raised armies and tried to repay the favour of the king – foolish gestures by people who did not understand the times. Your father, however, knew his place and preserved his integrity. He is different to people like us. We live – reluctantly maybe – but we live off a stipend from the Government-General. He was different, really different.' What Councillor Kim meant, of course, was that he was drinking with a low-class son-of-a-bitch. The excessive praise lavished on Ma Yŏng's father, so far from engendering feelings of love and admiration, served only to make the son see his father in an ugly light; his feelings were strange and disturbed.

'You are too kind.'

'Actually I called you because I have an urgent request for you.' Councillor Kim deliberately lowered his voice. His second boy, T'aeyŏl, had come home last winter vacation and had not returned to school. The boy kept saying he had to research something for his graduation thesis.

'Maybe he's in love?'

'Don't be ridiculous. If that were all, why would I be worried?' Councillor Kim had respected T'aeyŏl's wishes about not getting married until after graduation. The subject of marriage had been strictly avoided. Were he to sow his wild oats with a bar girl, Councillor Kim would have put it down to the joys of youthful experience. This was quite different. His son's ideology had become suspect; he was associating with diabolical characters.

'Excellency, a son of yours would not behave like that.'

'You don't know what you're talking about. A father knows his children. Don't you know your children?'

'Well, yes, I think I do.'

Councillor Kim had been so worried he had confronted his son. He pressed hard, but the boy kept denying he was doing anything harmful to the family. A father's eyes, however, are not deceived. If the boy got embroiled in an anti-Japanese scheme, that would be bad trouble indeed.

'If this goes to the police, we're finished. A single subversive document would mean disaster. You'll have to watch T'aeyŏl's movements carefully.'

'I understand.'

'You have to handle trouble before it happens. And if in the course of the investigation you get the feeling that the police are going to be involved, you have to stop that too.'

'But I don't have any power?'

'Don't worry about money. Do you understand?'

'Yes, sir.'

It was almost as if Councillor Kim wanted to ask Ma Yŏng to guide his son along the broad bright road to success but figured this was too much to expect.

Councillor Kim held out a white envelope.

'We must keep this between ourselves.'

'Of course, Excellency, how could I refuse a request from you.'

Ma Yŏng accepted the envelope with both hands as if he were getting an award and put it in his inside pocket. When he got back to the privacy of his own house and opened it, he found coincidentally that it contained three ten *wŏn* notes.

If you live right, fortune sometimes rolls your way. This was a bonanza, a chance to eat the pheasant and the eggs. Next day Ma Yŏng enthusiastically began the task of sniffing out the situation. He whirled around busily, hoping that young Master T'aeyŏl would team up with some dissidents to hatch an awful plot. Fortunately he had never met T'aeyŏl, but he could not tail him in the hat and jodhpurs he invariably wore, so he got himself a cheap suit for the purpose.

T'aeyŏl came down Samch'ŏngdong Road between ten and eleven every morning. The first day he went into a tearoom in Ch'ungmuro, stayed there for two hours and then went off with three companions to a secluded lane in Naesudong. Ma Yŏng jotted down the house number and nameplate in his notebook. The second day T'aeyŏl had a boisterous outing with his Naesudong companions in Shiktowŏn Restaurant. For anyone with money, these were really fine times. As Councillor Kim said, he would prefer to have his son playing around with the girls, within the limits, of course, of not dissipating the family fortune, rather than becoming ideologically tainted, but judging from the young man's ability to make the *kisaengs* laugh and his prowess in performing pop songs, Councillor Kim was engaging in needless worry.

Background checks on T'aeyŏl's companions showed one going to Koryŏ University, one going to Yŏnsei, and one who was not a student at all and lived outside West Gate. This one seemed a bit suspicious, but Ma Yŏng could find no concrete grounds for suspicion.

A month went by in this way. T'aeyŏl came out of a stationer's in Chongno with a huge box in his arms. Ma Yŏng entered the store.

'What did that student just buy?'

'Why do you want to know?'

'It's my business to ask.'

'A mimeograph machine. It's not stolen. It's the same as the new one over there.'

'I see.' Ma Yŏng's heart popped like a hand mill. Subversive documents and handbills were commonly printed on mimeograph machines. In these cases, the detectives began by searching the stationer's. Any way you looked at it, it was crazy to buy a mimeograph machine in broad daylight in the middle of Chongno! Maybe the young man had no fear of the tiger, or maybe he felt protected by his own high wall? Ma Yŏng could not tell. At any rate, Ma Yŏng felt himself gently floating in the air. Accomplishment was staring him in the face; this was his opportunity to capitalize on fate.

After some earnest reflection, Ma Yŏng realized his obligation was not quite so simple. If the police were notified about subversive handbills sent in the mail or scattered in the streets, it would be difficult to keep T'aeyŏl from implication on the grounds that he was the son of a councillor in the Privy Council. T'aeyŏl would be taken into detention, investigated, charged, and judged. Only then might Councillor Kim solve the problem by making a personal request to the commissioner. Councillor Kim had trusted Ma Yŏng with his request precisely to block disaster before it happened. This was no time for being wishy-washy. Ma Yŏng made a report to Councillor Kim that very night.

'If your son had moved the mimeograph machine elsewhere, I might be able to do something, but if he prints subversive documents here in the house, how can I find that out? Excellency, you will have to find that out yourself.'

'That's a problem all right.'

Councillor Kim, arms folded, had his eyes closed.

'I can't very well go into the servant's quarters,' Ma Yŏng said. 'Yes, that's true.'

'It's not nice to have to say it, but you will have to keep your son under strict surveillance.'

'I understand. If I need you for anything I'll let you know.'

Need me for anything? Ah yes. The father would not be eating his heart out like this if he thought that confronting the son over the mimeograph machine would bring the boy to give in easily and promise not to do anything dangerous again. Obviously the son would make a scene; saliva filled Ma Yŏng's mouth.

Councillor Kim came out with Ma Yŏng to the middle gate; this was an unusual gesture. It was such a palatial residence, you could only guess the size of the main building from outside the high surrounding wall. And yet even while living in the midst of honour and riches, one son gone wrong could line a man's face with anxiety. There was indeed justice in this world, Ma Yŏng felt.

The envelope Councillor Kim handed over seemed so light that Ma Yŏng checked it quickly in the moonlight as soon as he got out the gate. The sum was much smaller than he had expected. I'm not Councillor Kim's personal private eye, he thought. Digging up as much as I did called for some generosity in the final payment. If the minister had the effrontery to think he could buy silence with this, Ma Yŏng had no choice but to turn the information over to Superintendent Kinoshida. Why was Councillor Kim being so stingy? Well, stingy or not, it didn't matter now. When you can't get the pheasant, take the chicken. Ma Yŏng smacked his lips in testimony to his tangled feelings and went home only to find his son rolling around in his room drunk as a lord.

'What's going on here? Why's he like that?'

The boy wasn't old enough to be smoking or drinking. Ma Yŏng was at a complete loss.

'He's becoming a delinquent. That's what.'

'That's a terrible thing to say! Tell him to come over to the sitting room.'

'Leave him there. You can find out all about it in the morning.'

What his wife said made sense. He put a brake on his displeasure. Actually he was a little afraid of the eldest boy and his wife knew it. At the same time no parent could ignore a child still wet behind the ears getting into alcohol. Ma Yŏng did not want his father's honour trampled by this kind of unpleasantness.

As soon as the son washed in the morning, his father called him to the sitting room.

'Sit down there,' he said. 'What do you mean by this kind of behaviour? Who taught you to drink'

'I wasn't taught. I just tried it.'

'Show some respect! Tell me what happened.'

'I'm going to quit school.'

'What? Do you realize what a sacrifice it was to send you to school? You've got a hiding coming, young man.' Ma Yŏng had gone white. His hand shook as he slapped the whip off the floor. The son got up immediately and rolled up his trouser legs.

'The kids tease me and shun me. They call me the Jap stool-pigeon!'

Ma Yŏng choked at his son's tearful pouting cry. If they called him the stoolpigeon's son, he could understand it, but the child himself was no stoolpigeon. The sudden thought made Ma Yŏng pity his unfortunate son.

'Sit down. It's difficult to explain this so that you can understand, but when they say such things, tell them this. Tell them, my father may be friendly with the Japanese, and he may go to the police station from time to time, but he never does anything harmful to the people of Chosŏn. If they persist, say this. You sons-of-bitches, do you know any man of Chosŏn who doesn't butter up the Japanese. From the Government-General down – police, teachers, *myŏn* clerks, tram conductors even – is there anyone who doesn't have to beg for his food under the Japanese? You sons-of-bitches, your fathers are wealthy landlords, aren't they? Well, it's just the same with land-lords. The police protect them and come down on the dissidents. That's how the landlords live their fine rich lives. Well, am I wrong?' Ma Yŏng brandished his fist and foamed at the mouth as if he were addressing not his son but all those who were pointing the finger at him.

'Who's sneering at whom?' he added, still breathing heavily in his excitement. 'Do you understand?'

'Yes, father.' The son hastened to reply because of his father's menacing demeanor.

Children everywhere are a continuous headache, but letting off steam like this brought a great sense of relief to Ma Yŏng. He gave his son a large sum of money and told him to buy whatever he needed for school.

Subsequent to this shock affair, there was a complete blackout of news from Councillor Kim's for about ten days. Councillor Kim had said he would let Ma Yŏng know if he needed him. To go in advance of the call would be an indication that he wanted something. He controlled his inclination to visit.

Ma Yŏng had been so involved in Councillor Kim's household affairs that he had been careless with his police informant duties. With promotion upcoming, Superintendent Kinishoda was impatient and cantankerous, and Ma Yŏng found it difficult to put up with his abusive hectoring. Thought he'd make a bundle, but it hadn't worked out. And now for a pittance, his head was on the block. Painful indeed.

Ma Yŏng took advantage of a time when he knew Councillor Kim would be out of the house to set a lure for Sŏngch'il. He bought him some makkŏlli to soften him up. In return he got some astounding information.

'It's terrible. He put the son in a storeroom and locked him in.'

The eldest son and Ch'adal, the son-of-a-bitch, had joined with Councillor Kim in incarcerating T'aeyŏl, leading Sŏngch'il to lament the staggering lack of humanity in a rich man's house.

'He was driven into a corner.'

'What do you mean?'

'Nothing, nothing at all.'

Ma Yŏng recalled the story of how Yŏngjo starved Prince Sado to death in a rice bin. Was a councillor post in the Privy Council so important? Could a high-ranking civil servant in the Government-General be so crazy? Shit! Ma Yŏng felt like spitting in his face. Just a moment! Ma Yŏng's none too brilliant mind rolled this way and that – perhaps there's something in this for me, he thought.

'Are they feeding him regularly?'

'They bring him sumptuous meals, enough to break the legs of the table. At first he kicked the food away without lifting a spoon, but now he's eating well. The mistress pleads in tears, but it's reading scripture in a cow's ear.'

'That's a rather learned reference. Who does she plead with?

'She pleads with his lordship and she pleads with her son.'

'That's terrible. Can you believe it? A child should be filial to his father, and a father should rear his child with love. Is power so important? Can you call yourself a man and behave like that?'

'I agree totally.'

In the end Ma Yŏng came to a decision. He would be faithful to his position as a police nark, and at the same time he would bring Councillor Kim back to a realization of parental responsibility. To do this, he determined to leave aside the question of money and to do what he had to do.

Ma Yŏng, nostrils flaring, reported the entire affair to Superintendent Kinoshida. I say the entire affair, but in the event, he chose, of course, what seemed good, and that was what he reported. Superintendent Kinishoda was never one to leap into the unknown, not even when the news was of enormous significance.

'Find out the details. We're dealing here with a councillor in the Privy Council. One false move and we're dead.' Kinoshida slid a finger across his throat to demonstrate the point.

'You are joking.'

'I'll give you three days to get proof. If you're right, we'll round them up.'

'Councillor Kim too?'

'Out, fool!'

Ma Yŏng withdrew to this thunderous shout.

As Ma Yŏng passed along the dimly lit corridor outside the interrogation room, there was a boom and a bang as if the earth were caving in, followed by repeated screams like a pig getting its throat cut. Clearly someone was getting the bamboo baptism. Ma Yŏng could tell immediately the type of torture by the acoustical effects and the screams. If Councillor Kim's son were brought in, he would get a rub of the leg screw. On the one hand, Ma Yŏng felt pity; on the other, he had a sense of elation. Yet inside he was troubled.

Reporting the Councillor Kim affair to Superintendent Kinoshida was his job. So why had he a bad taste in his mouth, why was he hot in the face like someone caught doing something wrong? He would have to go and see for himself, if only to satisfy his curiosity about the father's reaction to locking his son up in a storeroom.

It was an early summer night; the moon was at the full. Ma Yŏng bought a box of cakes and knocked at Councillor Kim's gate. Sŏngch'il's pattern of behaviour was different this time: he went inside first and did not come back to let the visitor in for quite some time. Clearly guest admissions were being strictly controlled. The storeroom where T'aeyŏl appeared to be incarcerated was attached to the lower part of the servant's quarters. For days now, there had not even been the sound of breathing, much less any crazy ranting from the storeroom. Exhaustion may have been the explanation. In the moonlight, the shadowed fringes of the area seemed as spooky as a tomb.

Ma Yŏng, without giving the usual warning cough, turned towards the house.

'Excellency, I have neglected to call this last while.'

'Ah, was something the matter?'

Councillor Kim looked ten years older. With his deep sunken eyes, and his sharp pointed chin that looked as if it had been smoothed with a plane, he had changed into a completely different person. It did not require a reader of faces to divine this dark cloud as an evil omen.

'Excellency, you are a bad colour.'

'The frozen heart that haunts the dummy!'

Councillor Kim suddenly took Ma Yŏng's hand. His tone of voice was close to pleading.

'Morning and evening I go into the storeroom. In tears I try to persuade him, but it's like the east wind in a horse's ear.

He says he won't give up his ideology and he won't betray his friends, not if he has to die for it. I wish I knew what that bloody goblin ideology is....'

'Drive the Japanese out of the peninsula, isn't it?'

'My good man, the Chosŏn dynasty lasted five hundred years. You think they'll cough up a peninsula they've just swallowed.'

'Yes, you have a point there.'

Moving from the central facts to silly talk about historical points of view showed that both Councillor Kim and Ma Yŏng were pitiable specimens with at least one nut loose in their brains.

'It would be wonderful if I could let him out. But those bloody friends of his! What happens if they get together and bomb the Government-General? I'm caught no matter what I do. Do you understand what it's like to be caught like this, not to be able to breathe?'

'Excellency, you have granted me your favour in the past. I cannot keep a secret from you. The truth is, the Chongno police have already begun their investigation. To my knowledge, they began to dig into a reading circle in Yŏnsei and your excellency's son's name came out. They may come down on this house within a few days.'

Councillor Kim held the pack of cigarettes in his trembling hand and looked for a match.

'I knew it would come to this. Is there nothing that can be done?'

Ma Yŏng lit the minister's cigarette.

'When a child grows up, you can no longer force it to do what you want. I'm afraid you are going to lose a son.'

'Suppose I appeal to the chief superintendent in Chongno?'

'It would be futile in a question of ideology. No use at all. But try this. Hold your son's funeral,' Ma Yŏng muttered grimfaced.

'What did you just say?'

'Nothing works when it's a question of ideology and independence struggles. But if you remove the three characters – kim t'ae yol – from the family register, the police might as well be looking for a goblin.'

Councillor Kim was about to strike his knee in approval when he thought, 'But you can't change names whenever you feel like it.'

'Saving his life is the first concern.'

Two streams of tears lined Councillor Kim's emaciated cheeks.

'If I do it, he won't listen. I know it's a lot of trouble, but you have come this far, you'll have to save him.'

Councillor Kim opened the safe, big as a kimch'i pot, big enough for a good-sized bank, and took out a bundle of money. He was asking Ma Yŏng to give the money to T'aeyŏl and to tell him to get far away to Manchuria or China. Councillor Kim closed the safe, sank down where he was sitting and threw down the storeroom keys with a clatter. Ma Yŏng took charge of the money and went to the storeroom.

'Master Kim, do you know me? I am in your father's debt. I live close by. My name is Ma Yŏng.'

'What brings a Japanese police nark here?'

Judging from the reply, T'aeyŏl was perfectly fine, in contrast to what Ma Yŏng had been led to believe. The lamplight revealed that the so-called storeroom was bigger and more comfortable than Ma Yŏng's living room. The golden embroidered chrysanthemums on the bed linen formed a fine contrast with Taeyŏl's face. T'aeyŏl was hunkered in the corner, dangerous as a wild animal about to pounce.

'I have not come to arrest you. Your father says to give you this. Do you understand? Do you understand your father's real meaning?' Ma Yŏng reached across half the money just as he had predetermined.

'I'm trapped.'

'Believe me. I'm a Chosŏn man too. Change your name – Pak, Ma, whatever. And before you go, say goodbye to your father.'

'I have no father.'

The young man's muttered complaint was reminiscent of Ma Yŏng's son's childish complaint. And since His Excellency Councillor Kim was sending his son T'aeyŏl to the other world, the 'I have no father' cry made sense.

Back in the *sarang*-reception, Ma Yŏng was able to render a complete account of his achievements to Councillor Kim. A coffin was rushed to the house in the middle of the night and the family doctor was summoned. This was to get certification of sudden death. As the young man was unmarried, no mourning guests were allowed, and the funeral took place hurriedly on the third day. Broken by their bereavement, the parents were unable to accompany the bier. It was a small, lovely, flower-decorated bier easily carried by four men.

A woebegone Sŏngch'il, repeatedly blowing his nose, walked in front, while Ma Yŏng, dressed in a black suit with a black armband, and the eldest son, dressed in mourning garb, followed side by side behind the bier. They were bringing the body to the family grave in Koyang. It was a desolate procession, like a funeral in a house whose fortunes had collapsed. The procession wound down along Ch'onggyech'ŏn, and when it got to the entrance to Hwadong, Old Hwang from the real estate office, Ma Yŏng's wife, and the local people all clacked their tongues in sympathy for Councillor Kim's younger son, gone in the flower of youth.

Impromptu Song *(hanshi)*

The tiny pond is like a tub, the water shallow and clear.
Lines of grass and cattails spring up anew; the reeds sport new
   shoots.
I call the boy; he takes the bucket to fetch water.
I'm cultivating plantain so I can listen to rain on the leaves.

Sŏ Kŏjŏng (1420–1488)

THE HONOURABLE FORSYTHIA

In Japanese times, it was customary to have a secluded, unnumbered seat in the back of a public auditorium for the exclusive use of the attendant policeman, whose job was to ensure that any disturbance, particularly of a political nature, was dealt with forthwith. More than half of the constables on the force were

Japanese nationals who had failed to get positions in the police force in Japan but had succeeded in the colony.

A prominent Korean public speaker at the time was wont to gesture towards the back of the auditorium at the beginning of his speech and say, 'I see the honourable forsythia has bloomed', an announcement that was invariably greeted with gales of laughter from the Korean audience, while the poor Japanese constable looked around in total confusion. The Korean for forsythia is *kae-nari*, dog lord or honourable dog!

CONFUCIANISM TODAY

What about Confucianism today? Confucianism is so embedded in the marrow of the Korean bone that it will never totally disappear. The shell is intact even if the intuitive heart is largely gone. I say largely, because intuitive insights into human living never totally disappear. Korea's best poets kept intuition alive. Sŏ Chŏngju's work is a repository of Zen insights. Ku Sang, too, was a great exemplar of the simple heart of the cultivated man.

Playing Alone

'Harabŏji, are you as famous as people say?'
the little girl next door asked one day –
this was before she began primary school.
'What do you think fame is?' I asked her.
'I don't know,' she said.
'It isn't anything good,' I told her.

This year she's in second year middle
and her class is studying a poem of mine.
She said she knew the poet well.
'So what did you tell them?' I asked.
I said you were an ordinary *harabŏji*
and that you often looked like a boy
playing on his own.

I was delighted by her reply.
'You did well,' I said. 'Thank you.'
I felt lighthearted all day.

Ku Sang (1919–2000)

Koreans don't seem to know what Confucianism is anymore except to say that it is all-pervasive in society, whatever that means. Self-cultivation and inner freedom, which are the enlightening elements in Confucianism, have disappeared from the discussion, tragically so because what remains is a stifling formalism (*hyŏngshikchuŭi*), already apparent in Chŏng Kŭgin's *kasa* and verified by Ma Chun's Tale. A *malssŭm* (words) culture reigns supreme: endless meetings, endless talk. Committees are formed, staffed often by people with noble academic qualifications but little competence in the particular field. Papers are delivered, replies are composed, reports are written. Congratulations all around, followed by a lengthy lunch or dinner. The contented and the discontented go home; nothing changes.

The Zen master says: Words are fingers pointing at the moon. If you watch the fingers, you won't see the moon. Contemporary Korea is absorbed in the fingers. A culture that encourages social divisions discourages creativity; a culture that discourages diversity discourages creativity. I'm not sure that the *yangban/* inferior axis is all that relevant anymore, but the reluctance to be different is hugely important in terms of creativity.

Many aspects of the bureaucracy that we commonly label Confucian aren't Confucian at all. Western bureaucracies are much worse. Try exchanging your Korean driving licence for an Irish licence. Of course, it can be done, but in the process you'll learn ugly things about the bureaucracy in Ireland that you never dreamed about. Or try presenting any document in the US if your name is spelled differently than in your passport – Kim Chŏl, Cheol, Jol, Jeol. Remonstrating won't do you any good. American officialdom will beat anything you have ever seen in Korea.

I have already suggested reading Yi Munyŏl's novella *Our Twisted Hero*. It's the best introduction I know to the negative elements of the Confucian legacy, the perfect exemplar in action of the sunflower syndrome, the flower that always looks upwards with a smile. In the Confucian bureaucracy, you always take care of the level immediately above you.

And read the *hanshi* (poems in Chinese) of Chosŏn dynasty bureaucrats. They are the best introduction to the positive legacy of Confucianism.

It Faired and Rained Again *(hanshi)*

It faired briefly and rained again; rained and faired.
If that's the way of heaven, what can we expect among men!
Honoured one minute, reviled the next;
disinterested in fame, then courting it.
Flowers bloom, flowers fade: how can spring be in control?
Clouds come, clouds go: the mountains don't fight.
To the men of the world I say:
find joy where you can; that's what life's about.

Kim Shisŭp (1435–1493)

A lot of the fun of living in Korea comes from bumping into the shell of Confucianism. The early missionaries talked and wrote about it gleefully, but no one talks or writes about it very much anymore.

THE THREE PINES

The three pines represent three friends of the same age, all growing old together. Although the three trees are the same age, they are never the same size or shape. Confucian society did not teach equality or democracy. Order was based on hierarchy; one should know one's place and stay in it. Each tree spreads its branches in different directions so as not to encroach on the space of the others. Still they stand close together to protect each other and to use their combined strength to stand up to the fury of the storms. One may be damaged by age, disease or the severity of the gales of fortune, but the other two trees support it and protect it, so that even though battered, it can survive and enjoy life within the friendship of the group. In this way friends should remain friends forever. (Frank Mullany, *Symbolism in Korean Ink Brush Painting*, Global Oriental, UK, p.69.)

It was just after the Korean War in a small town in Kangwŏn Province. The county chief, the *hanyak* doctor (oriental medicine) and the parish priest were bosom pals. They were also boozing pals. Scotch was the drink of choice and most of the time there was plenty of it, supplied partly by friends in nearby Camp Long, an American base, and partly by a flourishing black market. If there was no scotch, *soju* was an adequate substitute.

The county chief had a problem. The county office had been bombed during the war and civil administration was a shambles for the lack of a decent workspace.

'Leave it to me,' the parish priest said.

As a foreigner and a priest he had ready access to the American base. The soldiers liked his easy way and sense of humour. Besides, General MacArthur had been a great supporter of the missionaries.

The parish priest headed off to Camp Long to see the general.

'General,' he said. 'It's up to the American army to help rebuild this country. We really need a county office in my town. Can't you help?'

Note the phrasing. He didn't ask 'Can you help?' That's western. He asked the negative question, 'Can't you help?' That's the Korean way. It adds a little bit of pressure.

'What do you need?' asked the general.

The parish priest had his homework done. He was well informed on the construction business, having built several churches himself in recent years. He quickly listed the requirements: timber, blocks, cement, fittings, whatever was required to put up a working county office. The trucks began to arrive the following Monday. Local workers were mustered. The parish priest sold some American relief grain to pay them – totally in breach of the relevant regulations governing relief grain but common practice at the time – and the work began.

Six weeks later, office complete, the county chief and his staff were ready to move in. But first there would have to be a dedication ceremony, with a presentation of plaques of appreciation to the key people in the project. The county chief planned a nice ceremony followed by a reception. On the morning of the ceremony, the parish priest said the early mass and got himself ready in his best suit. He decided to take a quick look at the site and check the place settings for the dignitaries at the reception table. There was a name card for the Home Minister and for several of his ranking staff, one for the Governor of Kangwŏn Province and several of his ranking staff; there were also name cards for Kangwŏn members of parliament and other provincial dignitaries; there was even a name card for the American general and the bird colonels on his staff. But there was no name card for the parish priest. The parish priest couldn't believe his eyes.

'*Kaesaekki* son-of-a-bitch,' he muttered and turned away in total disgust.

As soon as the parish priest got home, he made a beeline for the drinks cabinet. He took out a bottle of Johnny Walker Black – he only drank the best – and poured himself a generous double. The ceremony went off without a hitch. Words of gratitude rang out on all sides; the home minister spoke, the governor spoke, the county chief spoke and the general spoke. Plaques of appreciation were presented. There was scotch at the head table and barrels of soju at the minor tables. The dignitaries drank to their heart's content until about four in the afternoon and then left in ones and twos. The only blot on the day, a minor hitch, had been the lack of a translator for the American general's speech. When the last guest had gone, the county chief turned to the doctor. 'The *shinbu saekki* never showed up,' he said. 'We had no translator. Strange. *Ap'unga* – is he sick?'

'I have no idea,' the doctor said. 'We better go and see.'

So the chief and the doc piled into a jeep and drove to the priest's house. They noted with some satisfaction that the priest's jeep was in the yard. Obviously he was at home. Regular visitors, they just walked in. They found the parish priest slumped in his chair with a bottle of whiskey beside him.

'Shinbunim, shinbunim!' they greeted the priest in unison.

The parish priest didn't get up to greet his friends. He looked sourly at the county chief and then turned his gaze to the painting of 'The Three Pines' that hung on the facing wall. The doc had given it to him as a New Year present a few years ago. The priest sighed and addressed his greeting to the doctor.

'What sort of *kaesaekki*,' he said 'would walk into a man's house with his hat on?'

The chief and the doctor were a bit taken aback by the priest's greeting or lack of greeting but decided to pass no remarks. The chief was accustomed to wearing his hat wherever he went. In old Korea a man's hat was a badge of prestige. They sat down. The priest poured them a shot of scotch, then repeated his question, 'What sort of *kaesekki* would walk into a man's house with his hat on?' The question froze the county chief for the second time. Then the parish priest turned in a most friendly way to the doctor and began to regale him with sweet talk. After about ten minutes he turned again to the county chief.

'Tell me,' he said, 'What sort of *kaesaekki* would come into a man's house with his hat on?'

This was too much. The county chief left in a huff.

The parish priest and the doctor drank on for about two hours. They talked about affairs in general. Not a word about the opening ceremony. Suddenly the parish priest turned to the doctor.

'Where's the chief,' he said. The doctor, deadpan, said, 'I've no idea. I think he must have gone home.'

'*Ap'unga*? Is he sick?' asked the priest. 'Let's go and see him.'

The doctor and priest climbed into the parish jeep and drove down to the chief's house where they were met by his wife. 'Come in, come in,' she said. 'He's inside. He'll be delighted to see you.'

The parish priest strode into the living room. 'How are you?' he asked. 'This *kaesaekki* of a doctor never told me you were sick.'

The chief's wife brought in some *anju* dainties and a bottle of whisky and the three men started to drink again. The parish priest punctuated the conversation with constant references to the *kaesaekki* doctor who hadn't told him his friend was sick. He did it once too often. The doctor got up and left in a huff.

The county chief and the priest drank for several hours. They talked about the affairs of the town and the province. Not a word about the opening ceremony. Suddenly, the priest said to the chief, 'Where's the doc?'

'I have no idea,' the chief said, 'he must have gone home.'

'*Ap'unga*,' asked the priest? 'We better go and see.' Once again they piled into the jeep and headed for the doctor's house. It was now about two in the morning. They knocked on the door; the doctor opened it.

'Great to see you,' he said. 'Come on in. We'll have a drink.'

'*Yŏbo*,' he shouted at his wife. 'Get up. We need some whisky and eats.'

The three men sat down and drank amicably until it was light, discussing the affairs of county, province, and nation. Not a word about the opening ceremony.

Several days later the parish priest belatedly got his plaque. He discovered that the name cards were for outside visitors only; there were none for local dignitaries. And of course, a place had been reserved for him at the top table.

The parish priest took a bottle of Johnny Walker Black out of the cabinet and walked down to the new county office. The doc was with the chief. The priest walked in unannounced. In a loud voice he cried,

'*Ya! Kaesaekkidŭra!* We'll have a drink.'

Crane Painting *(hanshi)*

A lone crane, eyes trained on the distant sky,
stands on one leg in the cold of the night.
The west wind worries the bamboo grove;
I'm drenched in autumn dew.

Yi Tal (1539–1612)

THE WIDOW KIM

The Widow Kim accrued her widow title surreptitiously. A *kisaeng* all her life, she never married and she had no children. When she retired from the entertainment trade, she decided to return to her home town in Kangwŏn Province. Everyone in town knew her lurid past; the details, in fact, grew in the telling. By the time local tongues tired of wagging, the widow had bedded a range of notables from prime ministers to scholars, from sons of the finest noble houses to sons of the most prominent business families in the land. Juciest of all were the accounts of her relationship with her *kidung sŏbang* (pillar man), a lovely Korean term that meant lover, bodyguard and protector. To minds trained in Confucian ethics, it was bad enough to have been a *kisaeng*, but to remain unmarried and not have children offended filial piety on the treble. Although the Widow Kim couldn't care less about Confucian ethics, she did care about making a successful reentry into her home turf. She felt that a gesture towards respectability was necessary to facilitate her desire to be part of the local community. Hence the adoption of the widow title. This kind of fabrication was not unusual. Generations of local gentry had fabricated the details of their family registers in order to promote themselves to *yangban* status. The creation of personal myths was so deeply imbedded in the local culture that no one was likely to demur unless there were other more offensive considerations. The widow was careful not to try to forge close ties with the Confucian elite, not because she despised them, which she did, but because she knew that no matter what she did, they would never accept her. Confucian society was both class conscious and hypocritical as evidenced by the penchant of many *yangban* to despise *kisaeng* but delight in *kisaeng* dalliance. The church on the other hand was egalitarian in its theology even if stuffy in its administration. All are equal in the sight of God. The widow began to attend church, noting with real pleasure that the Confucian elite would not be pleased. She liked the idea of belonging to a social group that was anathema to many Confucians. She spent the usual six months as a cat-echumen, passed several rigorous doctrine examinations and was baptized. In her new faith life, she became a key member of the parish, active in the Legion of Mary and various other commit-tees, a woman who knew how to get things done and who was generous with her time and money. Of course, the *kisaeng's* habits of a lifetime didn't disappear easily. When she sat, she didn't keep her knees together; she smoked like a chimney in front of her betters; and she delighted in dirty stories. The conservative men of the area, both Christian and Confucian, found her ingrained habits offensive. Her generous contributions to the parish, how-ever, kept the Christians quiet, and the Confucian elite showed a certain tolerance because most of them at one time or another had enjoyed the thrills of *kisaeng* dalliance and were afraid that the widow might know some of the details. That tolerance wilted, however, when her existence impinged on their well-being.

The trouble began when the parish decided to buy the moun-tain behind the church. The mountain had been the local grave-yard for generations, used by Catholics and non-Catholics alike. It was not consecrated ground, however. Catholic graves had to be blessed as needed, and to a people culturally infatuated with a theology of eternal reward and the rituals that accompanied it, this was not a satisfactory situation. The underlying principles of exclusion endemic in Korean culture demanded CATHO-LICS ONLY in a Catholic graveyard! Keeping the riff-raff out included the so-called Confucian elite. The Confucian elite may have considered themselves several steps above everyone else, but the Catholics regarded them as *waein*, outsiders.

The paper work for the purchase of the mountain was duly completed and the bishop, unaware of the machinations of exclu-sion that were being contemplated by the local Catholics, regis-tered the property in the Diocesan Corporation. Part 1 of the project was complete: the parish now owned the mountain. The fact that the land was registered in the diocesan corporation was an irrelevancy. The parish owned the mountain and the parishio-ners presumed that they could use it as they saw fit. The next step was the formal exclusion of non-Catholics. The parish council proposed to build a wall around one section of the mountain and make that section an exclusively Catholic graveyard. This was much too serious a question to be decided unilaterally, so the parish priest, against the best advice of the parish council, referred the matter to the bishop. Building the wall involved a petition to the Ministry of Education and Social Affairs. The bishop was not interested in any project that had to be referred to a government ministry. Life was stressful enough without getting embroiled in the inner workings of government bureaucracy.

The Confucian gentry were exceedingly alarmed when they got wind of the proposal. Such a wall would interfere with the good joss of the mountain. Burial here had always been according to the strictest principles of *p'ungsu* science, the traditional wind/water discipline that governed these matters. Ensuring the eternal rest of one's ancestors impinged heavily on the peace and prosperity of descendants. The bishop's lack of interest in the project had nothing to do with indifference to *p'ungsu* or insensitivity to Korean culture although a casual observer might have accused him of both. He knew from experience that property negotiations with any government ministry would be protracted and complex and he had neither the time nor the inclination to get involved. The lack of interest of the parish council in the Confucian elite's joss problems was not a denial of the importance of *p'ungsu* in matters of burial. The niceties of *p'ungsu* were always rigorously implemented in Catholic burials. Great care was taken to ensure that the coffin was lying at the proper angle *vis-à-vis* the four directions and the *yin* and *yang* properties of mountain and water as determined by *p'ungsu* science. No Catholic wanted to rile his ancestors either. This was a matter of priorities. The gain from excluding *waein* from the Catholic graveyard had to be weighed against any possible offence given in terms of *p'ungsu*. The act of two effects had come to impinge on East-Asian lives. Needless to say, the local Catholics had never heard of the act of two effects. The bottom line was that sensitive negotiation and cultural accommodation would only be required in the event that the parish leaders failed to get their way.

The Confucian gentry were well aware of the bishop's disinclination to get involved, and they in their turn were reluctant to anger the foreign devil unnecessarily. They knew that the bishop's seal was essential for the local Catholics to have their way. Time was on their side. Prudence told them to sit and wait.

The Widow Kim's case, however, precipitated affairs. While the Confucian elite were considering all the options, the widow decided that her campaign for respectability demanded a proper grave site to accommodate her body when the baleful day of reckoning came. All matters related to Catholic deaths and funerals were administered by a parish organization called the *yŏngnyŏng* committee. The committee handled everything – the purchase of the grave site from the parish, the preparation of the body for burial (which also included coffin, death shroud, incense, flowers, *makkolli, soju* and all ancillary services), the writing of funeral banners, the provision of mourners for the wake and the funeral procession, and of course pall bearers. The parish priest took no part in funeral negotiations. There were still a lot of superstitious practices associated with funerals, sufficient to ensure that a prudent parish priest took a back seat. It was better for intrinsic theological reasons and also for community relations if he stayed in control but not in charge. Thus the *yŏngnyŏng* committee was given wide latitude, which in turn resulted in the committee arrogating significant powers to itself.

The widow went to see the chairman of the *yŏngnyŏng* committee. Death is such a morbid subject that she did not approach the chairman empty-handed. She brought a goodly supply of *soju* and dainties. There was no undue haste in broaching the subject of her visit. Seasonal greetings were exchanged and three bowls of soju were drunk – three not four, in deference to the death-four character in Sino-Korean – before the widow deemed it fit to introduce the reason for her visit. There was a succession of *kurungas* (is that a fact?), followed by several *kurundaes* (but or by the way), and a sprinkling of *olchis* (you're right) before the terms of purchase were agreed. The fee was handed over and the documents were sealed. The widow was now a fully-fledged denizen of the village endowed with inalienable rights, among which was the right to burial in her own grave.

The Confucian elite quickly heard of the widow's gambit. For them the purchase of the grave was an outrage. To bury a *kisaeng* in their midst, a woman without family or descendants, was Confucian sacrilege, an affront to their illustrious ancestors who had been buried on this mountain through the generations. The good joss of the living and the undisturbed rest of the dead would be ruined forever. Unhappy ancestors made for unhappy descendants.

The Widow Kim moved quickly and decisively to cement her advantage. She sent more *soju* to the *yŏngnyŏng* committee members to appease any incipient opposition and she secured the services of a few local lads to dig her grave. The grave was duly dug, an empty coffin was placed therein and the grave was filled again. The young men built the grassy mound on top, the omphalos, symbol of the womb of mother earth to which the widow would eventually return – though not for quite some time, she figured. Game, set and match or whatever the Korean equivalent is. The empty coffin was extra insurance on her right to burial in her own grave. The widow made sure that word of what she had done spread like wildfire through the town. The Confucian elite – to their consternation – found themselves virtually stymied.

It was only at this stage that the matter came to the notice of the parish priest, an Irishman who was erudite in things Korean, familiar not only with the principles of *p'ungsu* but also with the cultural lives of the Confucian elite and the minor superstitions of his flock. He was almost the perfect neutral arbitrator. Almost, because there was one part of the equation in which he lacked real expertise – kisaengry. Of that he knew nothing beyond the dictionary and the confessional. And he was wise enough to know that both in Ireland and in Korea, the general principle governing confessions is to tell the priest your sins but not your business.

The village headman whose daughter was married to the catechist was prodded by the Confucian elite to broach the matter with the foreigner. For the headman to have to meet the priest in even minimally hostile circumstances was an occasion of great embarrassment. He made many bows and offered profuse apologies; the parish priest reciprocated in kind. There were long comments on wind and weather, the state of the nation and the plight of the local farmers in these difficult times. Finally the village headman broached the subject of the graveyard in general and the widow's grave site in particular, separate problems but intimately related. He reminded the parish priest of the importance of *p'ungsu* in the cultural life of the community. Any wall constructed on the mountain would jeopardize the alignment of mountain and water, with the gravest consequences in terms of *yin* and *yang*. The grave of a Confucian was chosen – at great expense – by a professional geomancer. The principles governing the four directions and the alignment of mountain and water were integral to the calculations that allowed the geomancer to come up with a *myongdang* (propitious) grave site. Any wall built on the mountain would destroy the *yin* and *yang* of his calculations. The occupants of the graves would be exceedingly angry, and the baleful consequences of their anger would be felt in perpetuity by the succeeding generations of the families. Such a thing could not be. Confucian mores were very strict. Finally, almost by way of afternote to his expansive introduction, he introduced the subject of the widow, ranging through the unfortunate circumstances of her life and emphasizing the confusion that an unconnected woman, without husband or progeny, would introduce into the halls of *pun'gmansan* (the Korean Hades) were she to occupy the grave site which purportedly she had recently purchased. When the geomancers were consulted on the problem, the headman said, they suggested that the evil effects of a wall across the mountain could only be negated by building another wall at the bottom of the mountain. By sheer coincidence, the village head continued, the proposed second wall – most regrettably – would run across the entrance to the church, and the local Catholic community – even more regrettably – would not be able to get to mass any more. The parish priest nodded gravely throughout. He showed the utmost consideration for his visitor but no hint of anything approaching panic or consternation at the implied threat to his church community. When it was his turn to speak, he began by recalling the story of Sai Weng, a fortune teller from a part of northern China where the horse was the principle means of transportation. The parish priest was a great believer in the rhetoric of indirection.

'Sai Weng's horse ran away to Hudi in the north,' the parish priest began. The headman was perplexed by this *tong-mun-sŏ-tap* (east-question-west-answer) development, but he held his peace. The parish priest continued. 'Sai Weng's neighbours came to him and said, 'We are sorry to hear that you lost your horse.'

'Who knows,' Sai Weng said, 'This may be good fortune.'

Even as Sai Weng spoke, the parish priest continued, his horse returned, bringing a fine stallion with her. So the people of the village congratulated Sai Weng.

'Who knows,' Sai Weng said, 'This may be bad luck.'

As he had predicted, his son fell off the horse and broke his leg. Next day, the people visited Sai Weng to offer their condolences. But he said, 'We should never come to hasty conclusions. This may turn out to be good fortune yet.'

A year later, the northern barbarians invaded and many young villagers went to the battlefield. Sai Weng's son, however, stayed at home because of his leg. As a result, he was saved from being killed in the war.

'The story of *Sai Weng's horse* reminds us,' the parish priest concluded, 'that good fortune and bad fortune come and go in our lives. Ultimately it is very difficult to say if any one event is good or bad joss, and we should be very reluctant to take decisive action in matters that deal with community well-being.'

The village headman was enormously impressed by the parish priest's East Asian approach to human affairs. The parish priest smiled as much as to say that as far as he was concerned an amicable agreement had been reached and the matter was resolved. The village headman came away from the encounter more than a little bewildered. His bewilderment changed to consternation when he heard next day about the widow putting an empty coffin in her grave. Women in the Confucian world were not supposed to be quite so pro-active. Immediate action was called for. The village head went to see his colleague – a lapsed Catholic – who lived at the other end of the administrative district, and he outlined the sudden thickening of the plot. Together they visited the Confucian man of substance who owned the lane into the church and who had disputed right-of-way with the bishop from the moment some years earlier when the bishop began to build the church. In a typical display of Western insensitivity the bishop went ahead with the building without bothering to acquire access rights through an easement or an agreement on right-of-way. The Confucian man of substance was more than a little pleased to find himself poised now over the bishop's neck like the sword of Damocles, *muyong kŏm* in Korean, the sword that casts no shadow, He had blocked the alley on several occasions in the past much to the chagrin not only of the Catholics and the parish priest but also of other residents in the area. In the past public opinion had always forced him to relent. After all he had to live here too. Now public opinion – with the exception of the Catholics – would be on his side. And truth to tell, even some of the Catholics were nervous about building the wall on the mountain and riling the Confucian ancestors.

The Confucian elite were aware that the widow had struck a decisive blow by burying the coffin. Any counter measure would have to be covert. A number of hardy local youths were engaged for a moonlight sortie. It was rumoured that several of the young men, apparently willing to do anything for the promise of a good booze-up, had already participated in the widow's gambit, but that cannot be verified. The project was to dig up the widow's coffin. The young men fell to the task with a will, salivating already over the *soju*, dainties and further possible delights that awaited them. The coffin was dug out.

The parish priest called a meeting of all the parties involved and offered himself as arbiter in the negotiations although he had no intention of saying anything. The parish council, the head of the *yŏngnyŏng* committee, the two headmen, the owner of the lane and some half dozen of the local Confucian gentry, and the ex-*kisaeng*, the Widow Kim, were invited. The widow was at her flagrant best, sitting in her usual provocative posture and puffing smoke in the direction of the Confucian elite. The Confucian elite made no effort to hide their displeasure. The parish priest had an acute attack of the giggles, but being naturally a grave man, if the outrageous pun can be excused, managed to control himself. The widow had the names of six young men who had participated in the dig. She spat out the name of each of the offenders through a fine smoke ring directed at the Confucian elite. She was outraged, she said, in her finer sensibilities. Not since the attempted violation of the regent Taewŏn'gun's ancestral grave in the previous century, she proclaimed, had anything like this happened in Korea. She did not know − or care − that the earlier grave robbing expedition was led by a French priest intent on reparations being paid for the lives of three French priests martyred by the regent.

This affair, the parish priest knew, would bring no good to anyone. He regretted not having saved the story of Sai Weng for this quite perfect occasion. The good fortune of one and all was at stake.

The meeting ended with a series of threats and counter threats. The threats all involved litigation, bluffing for the most part, because both sides knew that in any litigation the lawyers rob both sides.

Fate took a hand. A cousin of one of the young men involved in digging up the widow's coffin was hit by a car when he was coming out of a winery in Hongch'ŏn. Another of the young men came down with a severe dose of gonorrhea contracted in the celebration after the widow's coffin was dug up. The mother of a third young man took mysteriously ill and died.

The word went out quickly that the widow had hired a shaman to put the Korean comether on all involved. When the lapsed Catholic headman took to his bed with unexplained symptoms, the Confucian elite threw their collective hands in the air. The avenging angel was coming much too close. Another shaman was called to clear the air. For a considerable fee – reputedly paid by the Widow Kim – the shaman performed a cleansing ritual. Confucianism and Catholicism were able to accommodate local cultural realities by looking in the opposite direction. The young men who had dug up the widow's coffin put the coffin back in its place. The parish council dropped the plan to build the wall on the mountain; the property owner decided against blocking the alley. Peace reigned in the valley.

Plum *(hanshi)*

Plum like snow; snow like plum.
Snow hits my forehead; plum blooms forthwith.
Now I know that Heaven and earth are one pure force.
I'll trample the snow; I'll come to see the plum.

Sŏ Kŏjŏng (1420–1488)

Ch'usa, Kim Chŏnghŭi

Scholar, calligrapher and poet, Kim Ch'usa left an indelible mark on the spiritual legacy of Chosŏn.

When a new moon rose above the eaves,
Ch'usa dreamed of great orchid painters
from the past, one painter a night,
as he drank his wine in double draughts.
First he poured a double in ritual aspersion,
and then like the moon drinking water,
he consumed the wine in brimming doubles.

(Sŏ Chŏngju 1915–2000)

8

THE CHOSŎN BUREAUCRACY

THE STATE COUNCIL (Ŭijŏngbu), which was the supreme policy making and administrative organ in the government, was composed of three ministers of prime minister rank: chief councillor, minister of the left, minister of the right and four high officials: chief secretary of the left, chief secretary of the right, assistant chief secretary of the left, and assistant chief secretary of the right.

Six Ministries (*Yukcho*)
Ministry of Appointments (*Ijo*)
Ministry of Taxation (*Hojo*)
Ministry of Rites (*Yejo*)
Ministry of Justice (*Hyŏngjo*)
Ministry of Public Works (*Kongjo*)
Military Ministry (*Pyŏngjo*)

The Six Ministries were originally under the State Council, but eventually the king controlled them directly. Each ministry was directed by a minister (*p'ansŏ*), deputy (*ch'agwan*), vice-minister (*ch'amp'an*), and beneath these there was a councillor *(ch'amŭi),* a fifth rank secretary, and a sixth rank secretary.

The Royal Secretariat (*Sŭngjŏngwŏn*) operated as a liaison office between king and government; it had six royal secretaries (*sŭngji*), one for each ministry.

Two organs served a watchdog role over king and government. *Saganwŏn*, Office of the Censor General, was the watchdog over the royal family; *Sahŏnbu*, Office of the Inspector General, was the watchdog over the government.

Hongmun'gwan, Royal Archives, was a think tank of special advisers who carried out research, gave advice, and formulated policy.

Officials in the *Sahŏnbu, Saganwŏn* and *Hongmun'gwan* did not rank highly in the bureaucracy, but they wielded extraordinary power. Posts in these departments were coveted by aspiring officials as they were the certain road to advancement.

Royal Guards
The Royal Guards evolved into an agency directly under the king, which dealt with rebellions and threats to the dynasty. It overlapped with the Ministry of Justice. There was a third judicial organ responsible for the defence of Seoul.

Office charged with publication of Confucian texts.
Office to draft messages and statements from the king.
Office to draft diplomatic messages and notes.

Korea had eight provinces: Hamgil, P'yŏng'an, Hwanghae, Kangwŏn, Kyŏnggi, Ch'ungch'ŏng, Kyŏngsang, and Chŏlla. Each province had a governor who was administrator, judge, and military commander. The governor was served by district magistrates, each of whom had an administrator with multiple functions, a police chief, a judge, and a tax collector.

Governorships were for one year; district magistrates also had limited tenure. A governor never served in his home province.

The district magistrate supervised local petty officials who were organized in six groups corresponding to the Six Ministries. The district magistrate had a district council composed of local *yangban*, which acted only in an advisory capacity.

9

THE BUDDHIST INGREDIENT

In Chamshil (hanshi)

A vagabond for ten years; I've travelled east and west.
I'm like mugwort on a hill.
My way and the world's way offer bumpy alternatives.
Sniff a flower; say nothing: that's the ultimate choice.

Kim Shisŭp (1435–1493)

Jubilee Temple (hanshi)

This temple from the past is covered with autumn grass;
a scholar's inscription endures on one of the stones:
'A thousand years flow by like water;
clouds return to see the setting sun.'

Paek Kwanghun (1532–1582)

Most things beautiful in Korea are Buddhist inspired. The monks were smart enough to pick the most beautiful valleys in the country as temple sites.

Tiny Room in Flower Sage Temple (hanshi)

Nine turns in a hundred paces, I climb the high mountain.
The house hangs in the air – it only has a few rooms.
The sacred spring is clear; cool water flows.
Old dark walls are spotted as if with green moss.

A stone-head pine ages under a sliver moon.
Clouds drape a thousand mountain peaks at the rim of the sky.
The dust of human affairs cannot reach this far.
Leisure is the hermit's joy through the ages.

Chŏng Chisang (?–1135)

Cho Byunghwa (1921–2003) says that the most beautiful things are saddest. They are saddest because things change. Living this mutability taught him primeval loneliness and primeval emptiness. 'I am within them,' he says, 'my poetry is within them, my consolation is within them.' He learned a freedom of the spirit that affirmed and denied everything, and with this freedom he depicted a lonely self. It's a Buddhist point of view learned from his mother. Life and death are a continuum; death is a continuation not an end.

The road is an important symbol in Cho Byunghwa's poems and paintings. 'Dialogue,' a late poem dramatizes the theme. For the old man bereft of dreams, the road is short, but for the boy weighed down by dreams the road is long. Were this a more percipient world, more open to the things of the spirit, 'Dialogue' would be on many lips. As it is, the poem is buried in obscurity:

Dialogue

An old man and a boy
walked side by side.

'How far are you going?'
the old man asked the boy.

'A long way,' the boy replied.
'How far are you going, sir?'

'Over the next hill,' the old man said.
'What have you in your satchel, boy?'

'Dreams,' the boy replied.
'What have you in yours?'

'Nothing now,' the old man said.
'Are dreams heavy?' the old man asked.

'Yes,' the boy murmured,
'very heavy.'

Korean Buddhism is mostly Zen in spirit; the largess that
eschews the conventional response is central. Zen insight into
the nature of reality infuses buildings, paintings, pottery and
poetry with the kinds of feelings we associate with Wordsworth
in *The Prelude*. If you take the Zen ingredient out, as the Neo-
Confucian ideologists tried to do at the beginning of Chosŏn,
passion and poetry die.

Wŏlmyŏng, the Monk

Whenever Wŏlmyŏng, the Shilla monk, had something special
to ask one of the gods of heaven, he did not do it personally; he
took the heart of a flower and sent it with the message instead
– surely the stuff of poetry.

But when the moon rode the sky, and he wished to entice
the girl within, to call her down near his lips, he used no inter-
mediary; he put his pipe to his lips and piped her down.

What do you think ... shouldn't we allow the monk this
much privacy?

Sŏ Chŏngju (1915–2000)

'Why Complain, Why Sigh?' is a traditional song that features
the ageless line, 'Life is a spring dream' (*Insaeng-il-chang-ch'un-
mong*), which always brings a smile to a Korean face. People take
their dreams seriously here. You'll get a phone call from a friend
you haven't heard from for a long time. Eventually you discover
that you appeared abruptly in a dream and the friend wondered
if you were all right. The older you get the more likely this is

to happen. A widow told me her husband appeared to her in a dream. She complained bitterly about being left alone to care for the children. He said he couldn't help it; life and death were beyond his control. 'Wait a moment,' he said. When he returned he had a lovely porcelain vase with a hydrangea in it, which he handed to her. She gazed at the hydrangea in wonder, and when she looked up, her husband was gone. It's a beautiful dream. Don't ask me what it means.

Song of Three Dreams (hanshi)

The master tells the guest his dream;
the guest tells the master his dream.
Two friends tell two dreams;
they themselves, meanwhile, are the stuff of dreams.

Sŏsan Taesa (1520–1604)

THE DIPLOMATIC CORPS GOES BUDDHIST

The artist arrived out of the blue. The ambassador – poet, art connoisseur and diplomat – had arranged the visit. The artist was tall, with granite features, eyes like deep pools, hands that a stone mason might have owned, and a lovely accent, rounded vowels straight off the lathe. Friendly, easy to talk to, his eyes were the only indicator that he was a painter of note. A feature of his art was to apprentice himself for six months or more to new methods in a strange culture. It might be the aborigines in Australia, or a pygmy tribe in Africa. This time he had come to Korea to apprentice himself to a noted painter, poet, dancer monk who resided in one of the hermitages of Tongdo-sa, a famous temple between Kyŏngju and Pusan. The idea was to learn the powerful brushwork of Buddhist painting, where the painter holds the brush like a chisel.

The ambassador gave a welcoming reception in the residence. As the artist's official training master, Hyean sŭnim was obviously invited. The ambassador also asked another famous monk, Chunggwang, known popularly as the Mad Monk, thinking the two monks would be a support for each other in what was largely a foreign gathering. I was the official interpreter. The Mad Monk got his name from his flamboyant art style and his propensity to do daft things. He had a considerable reputation at home and abroad. In New York he made *Time* magazine and his paintings sold for tens of thousands of dollars. On occasion he was known to spill a bucket of paint on a canvas, strip off, roll across the canvas, then spring to his feet and announce the completion of another masterpiece, which duly, by all accounts, sold for a considerable sum.

Hyean *sŭnim* made a grand entrance accompanied by a coterie of ladies resplendent in Korean traditional dress. The ambassador asked him would he have something to drink. 'Have you any water?' the good monk asked. The ambassador, a tad surprised, looked to me for help, which, I'm afraid, was not forthcoming. Then he turned and asked a waiter to bring water. Without waiting for the glass of water, Hyean *sŭnim*, to the ambassador's astonishment, strode into the dining room and helped himself to a brimming glass of white wine from the dinner table.

In the meantime Chunggwang had arrived, accompanied by another coterie of lovely ladies, also arrayed in traditional Korean dress. He lined his team up around him in the opposite corner to Hyean *sŭnim*'s team. No nod of recognition passed between the two notable monks. My interpretation skills, to my immense relief, were not called on at any time in the course of a hilarious evening. Chunggwang had a show of his paintings due to open next day in Insadong. It was a major art event, and a splendid full-colour brochure, which presumably cost an arm and a leg, had been prepared to commemorate the occasion. A hundred copies of the brochure were duly delivered to the front door of the embassy residence and passed out to the guests to a chorus of oohs and ahs. One-nil, Chunggwang, I figured.

Hyean *sŭnim* was a new name to me, but I knew about Chunggwang from his personal notoriety and also from the fact that he wrote some poetry. His 'hit' poem, if I might be pardoned the pop expression, was titled 'I Am Shit,' but you need to tag *irosoida* to the end of the shit word to get the feel of the line in Korean – I Am Shit-i-ro-so-i-da. You will agree it has a bit of a ring to it. I crossed the room and gave him a polite but friendly greeting. He looked me up and down and said,

'I'm enlightened, you're not.'

'I know,' I said, 'priests are rarely enlightened, but I'm working on it.'

'Ah, you're a priest?' he said. 'You're right, priests are never enlightened. They could do so much good in this world if they'd only spread a little love around. They're not married, they have no commitments and the world is full of the lame and the halt. What's their problem?'

I had no answer to this thrust. I veered the conversation away.

'Kim Chiha says there's no such thing as belief until you pass it through the bowel,' I said by way of diversion, knowing he liked the fundamental nature of the excrement idea. Kim Chiha, the noted civil rights activist, had made this comment about his Christian faith.

Chunggwang looked me up and down.

'I wrote a poem about that,' he said.

'I know,' I answered. 'I've read it. I Am Shit-i-ro-so-i-da.'

There was a pause in the conversation. Finally he said, 'You're all right.'

The conversation was closed. I turned away.

Dinner with much wine and many speeches followed. After dinner we went back into the outer reception room. Again the teams divided. Hyean's team took up the fireplace alcove on the right; Chunggwang's team was arrayed on the settees to the left.

About twenty minutes went by while we sipped coffee and after-dinner drinks. Suddenly Hyean sprang to his feet, whipped off his *turumaegi* cloak and said, 'I think I'll sing!'

Chunggwang rose to his feet, assembled his cohort and said, 'There'll now be a slideshow of tomorrow's exhibition. Follow me.'

Two-nil by my reckoning.

While Hyean danced and sang, Chunggwang led his team out of the living room, went upstairs, commandeered the first big room he saw, ushered his troops in, set up the slide projector and proceeded to give a commentary on the paintings due to be exhibited next day.

The ambassador ran the finest soirée in town. Anyone of note in the art world who came to Seoul invariably dined at his table. But the Hyean-Chunggwang night was easily the finest night in the embassy's history – though perhaps not for the ambassador. When two monks take over your house, lock, stock and barrel, what are you going to do?

Lodging in the Head Monk's Quarters

Priest on priest's floor,
bridging two traditions,
inexplicably comfortable,
uncomfortable with both.
I stirred in the night
to the rhythm of the drum,
to the droning of the monks,
to the reverberations of the great bell.
The straight backs of monks at prayer;
the magic of their incantational chant;
the spell of the maroon against the grey;
the kaleidoscope
magnetized me into the night yard again.
Under a sequined sky
I was free; I was bound.
The monk idea is invariably the same:
tides of empty and fill.
It's when the idea is subsumed
by order, by the collective
that the bucket is kicked and Tao spills.
'Find happiness wherever you can,'
the wandering monk cried!
The great systems answer,

regrettably,
with an indignant growl.

HAE-U-SO

The loo in Kim Sakkat's museum in Yŏngwŏl bears the plaque
ch'ŏngbang, meaning washroom, I presume. They told me in
Yŏngwŏl it's the normal word for toilet in Korea, but I haven't
met anyone since who ever heard of it. Korean like English
has many names for lavatories. The normal term *hwajangshil* is
literally make-up room, derived presumably from toilette. The
sign hanging in many temples, *Hae-u-so,* the place for loosening
(disentangling) your worries, is a real stroke of linguistic genius.

Shilla Future Expertise

The people of Shilla had the extraordinary habit of picking particularly fine things in the future – a hundred, a thousand, a million years on – and advancing their existence so that they could
be enjoyed here and now.

The Mireuk Buddha – the Goddess of Mercy – is not a
Buddha of the past or the present: prophesy places it in the
distant future. The people of Shilla took this Buddha, advanced
its existence and lived with it face to face. When Chinji was
king, the monk Chinja walked from Kyŏngju to Kongju in
Ch'ungch'ŏng Province. The walk took ten days; a bow at
every step and the prayer, 'Mireuk Buddha, deign to appear!'
And the story goes that the bright-eyed monk met the Goddess of Mercy at the gateway of Suwŏn-sa Temple in Kongju.
King Chinji said: 'Lovely, really lovely: refined, congenial, and
with elegant flowing-wind *p'ungnyu* taste; I kept Mireuk by my
side as a *hwarang* for seven years. The *p'ungnyu* referred to here
is not, of course, an imported foreign philosophy; it came down
to us from Tan'gun times. And it was so good that the people
pu – shed
– –
it right out to the future, and that was wonderful. The trees that

lined the roads recognized this being from the future, and that was wonderful too! It would appear that green leaves are more forward oriented than past reflective.

Sŏ Chŏngju (1915–2000)

Pak Mog'wŏl, a poet with a distinctly Christian sensibility, had an instinctive feel for Buddhist roots in the culture. He was a man who oozed spiritual oomph.

Blue Deer

The old tiled halls of Blue Cloud Temple
stand on the distant mountain.
The mountain is called Rose Mist.
When spring snows melt,
the inner folds of elm leaves burgeon
in a twelve twist unfurling,
and white clouds circle in the
crystal eyes of the blue deer.

Pak Mog'wŏl (1916–1978)

A lovely melancholy infuses the temples when the landscape is bathed in autumn colours. You feel it in the colours, in the empty *sarang* and in the spiralling incense thread.

Written on the Monk's Scroll in Pong'ŭn-sa Temple *(hanshi)*

Autumn breezes blow across the old hermitage;
fallen leaves cry in mountain rain.
The empty *sarang* extension is hushed; no monk inside;
an incense thread spirals from the stone terrace.

Ch'oe Kyŏngch'ang (1539–1583)

Contact with Buddhism invariably brings out the theme of the worldling, a constant thorn in the side of the man who aspires to wisdom.

Kamno-sa Temple (Sweet Dew Temple) (hanshi)

This is no place for a worldling guest;
thought grows lucid when you get to the top.
The mountain is in autumn mode; all the better;
the colour of the river is even clearer at night.
A white heron disappears in solitary flight;
a solitary sailboat glides lightly on the water.
Shame on me: for half a lifetime I've sought
fame and honour in a constricted world.

Kim Pushik (1075–1151)

Visit to the Hermitage of Master Ka (hanshi)

Desolate the monk's room beside the ancient tree;
one lamp, one incense burner in the shrine.
No need to ask the old monk how he spends his days.
A chat when a guest comes; when he goes, a nap.

Yi Kyubo (1168–1241)

A shadow is reflected in the water (shijo)

A shadow is reflected in the water;
a monk is crossing the bridge.
'Monk, stay a moment, let me ask you where you're going!'
Stick pointed
at white clouds, he passes without a backward glance.

Chŏng Chŏl (1536–1593)

Mention Cho Chihun's 'Old Temple' to any Korean friend.
You will be surprised by the reaction. The sentiments in the
poem are part of Korea's cultural furniture, familiar to everyone,
an embodiment of the serenity that we all strive to attain. The
'Buddha smiles' line transports me to Sokkuram Grotto and
the smiling Buddha image there, and I begin to understand the
peace and tranquillity this poem purveys.

Old Temple

The novice –
fine of feature –
falls asleep,
overcome by the drowsy
beat of wooden clappers.
Buddha smiles:
no comment.
Ten thousand *li*
to West Posthouse.
Peonies fall
in the dusk dazzle.

Cho Chihun (1920–1968)

A FATEFUL BLOW

There are things that a man must not do to save a nation

– John O'Leary

Every Korean is familiar with the tragic story of crown prince Sado who was imprisoned in a rice bin by his father King Yŏngjo and starved to death. Sado's son, subsequently King Chŏngjo, eleven at the time, clung tearfully to his grandfather's coat-tails pleading for the life of his father. The boy's pleas fell on deaf ears. Yŏngjo was adamant; the crown prince died.

Chŏngjo treated the memory of his father with great reverence. He kept his father's memorial tablet in Yongju-sa Temple in Suwŏn and cared for the grave with such dedication that even the caterpillars feasting on pine leaves around the grave site risked the royal anger.

Yongju-sa Temple became a bastion of Buddhist power. The monks, however, were not always well-behaved. Some of them were known to get drunk and rampage through the streets of Suwŏn. No woman was safe from their lustful attacks; no man stood against them for fear of reprisal.

A new magistrate was appointed to Suwŏn, a gallant man who immediately arrested the leader of the rampaging monks.

'How dare you take me into custody!' the errant monk cried in a fit of pique. 'The monks here are held in high esteem by the king himself,' he shouted, and he showered the new magistrate with invective. The magistrate wrote a memorial to the throne in which he outlined the outrageous conduct of the monks. Chŏngjo wrote back:

> This evil has happened because of an excess of benevolence towards the monks of this temple where my father's memorial tablet is enshrined. Out of respect for my father's memory, it is my wish that you deal leniently with the offenders. Let the monk you have in custody be given a single blow of the club in punishment.

The magistrate could not believe the king's judgment. Such leniency was gravely at odds with the magnitude of the offence. For days the magistrate could think of nothing else. He racked his brains for a solution to his dilemma. Eventually he came up with one. He called together his assistants and instructed them to seek out the strongest men in the country. These strong men were to vie with one another in a test of strength until the strongest man among them was determined.

All was done to the magistrate's satisfaction. The strongest man was chosen. For ten days he practised his technique on a variety of animals including deer, wild boar and a huge ox. The idea was to kill the animal with a single blow.

Finally the fateful day arrived. People gathered like clouds on the plain of Suwŏn and a scaffold was built while they watched. The chief of the rampaging monks spread his buttocks on the scaffold. He wore a perverse smile. The drums rolled. The strongest man in the world, a red bandanna wrapped around his temples, raised the stout oak club in his hand, took aim, and with a roar like thunder brought the club crashing down on the monk's buttocks. The oak club split in two; the monk's back bone was smashed in pieces. He died on the spot.

The magistrate sent an official report to the king in which he stated with regret that the monk had expired after a single blow. Chŏngjo wrote back praising the efforts of the magistrate to carry out his duties to the letter.

There were no more monk rampages in Yongju-sa Temple.

The Nun's Dance

Fine, white cowl –
folded butterfly wings;

blue shaved head –
gossamer screened.

Sad-beautiful
the light on her cheeks.

Mute candles melt on the empty night terrace;
the moon sets with every falling paulownia leaf.

Sleeves reach across the width of sky;
pŏsŏn white socks point-fly in answering rhythm.

Black eyes lift gently
to focus on a star in the distant sky.

Two tears glisten on lovely peach cheeks;
the anguish of the daily grind turns to starlight.

Hands angle, furl, stretch to the limit:
imaging a sacred joining deep in the heart.

Third watch: crickets sleepless through the night;
fine, white cowl – folded butterfly wings.

Cho Chihun (1920–1968)

The Making of the Great Buddha Image in Hwangnyong-sa (Yellow Dragon) Temple

Buddha, bodhisattva, poem, whatever – if you're making a work of art, one that you want to keep forever, and your workmanship is inferior, go find someone who can do it right and entrust the commission to him. Don't play the fool and persist with something that's not right. Never, never!

Take the artistic material, iron or gold, load it on a stout boat, hoist sail and send it across time and space. And when the boat has floated around every conceivable country in the world – it may take hundreds or even thousands of years – eventually – somewhere – the perfect creative artist will be found who will give the material its perfect mystic shape.

The material for sculpting the great Buddha image in Hwangnyong-sa Temple came originally from India. Loaded on a boat, it journeyed across distant seas with the message 'Send me elsewhere if the making does not work out!' It circled all the countries of the world in search of an artist, and after a thousand years and some three hundred more, it arrived in Shilla where it met its master and came to created being.

Sŏ Chŏngju (1915–2000)

The principle of getting the best man for the job is clearly stated, but often modern Korea does not use a lot of energy getting the best man. Who you are and who you know are often more important than how well you do something. This is especially surprising in a culture that takes art, face and transcendence very seriously.

The Way (hanshi)

It's never been possible to fabricate nature.
Why do I look for enlightenment outside?
All I know for truth is that there's no action in the heart.
Thirsty, I brew tea; tired, I take a nap.

Hyegŭn (1320–1376)

PAEKP'A AND CH'USA

On his way into exile, the famous painter-calligrapher Ch'usa Kim Chŏnghŭi composed a pen name, Sŏkchin, which he sent to his best friend Paekp'a the monk, telling him to use it himself or give it to a disciple. Paekp'a did not use the name, nor did he give it to anyone. He put it in the drawer of his desk and left it there.

When it was Paekp'a's turn to die, he summoned his disciples and gave them the Sŏkchin name, instructing them to find the right owner among those who inherit the Buddha spirit from them.

Ch'usa, still in exile, was told about Paekp'a's dying wish. He composed a memorial, *A Big Man Knows How to Write a Big Hand,* the only memorial he ever penned. It stands to this day in Paekp'a's hermitage in Sŏn'un-sa Temple.

Koreans have an intimacy with Buddhist practices that allows them to relate easily with temple and monk. This easiness is not quite so evident in the way they relate with priests, ministers and the Christian churches. Buddhism in Korea is in the bone. It expresses itself in a lovely fun ambience unknown in the Korean Christian tradition. How beautifully *shijo* after *shijo* pokes fun at prized institutions!

Epiphany *(shijo)*

Ah, I saw him;
I saw my monk supreme.
Such beauty wrapped in an old ragged robe!
A camellia
Flowered in midwinter's cold and crept into an old pine tree.

Anonymous (18th century)

Rip your black robe asunder; fashion a pair of breeches *(shijo)*

Rip your black robe asunder; fashion a pair of breeches.
Take off your rosary; use it for the donkey's crupper.

These ten years studying Buddha's Pure Land, invoking
the Goddess of Mercy and Amitabha's saving hand,
let them go where they will.
Night on a nun's breast
is no time for reciting sutras.

Anonymous (18th century)

Death is a fundamental reality in the Buddhist way of life.
No need for anything more than acceptance.

Destination

It is my turn next;
lower me into that tiny solitude.

Cho Byunghwa (1921–2003)

In 'Ritual Service for a Dead Sister' Wŏlmyŏng's grief is
palpable. He makes an offering to the spirit of his dead sister,
and as he sings his song a mad wind blows away the paper
money used in the ritual.

Ritual Service for a Dead Sister (hyangga)

You left
on the life-death road
with no word
of farewell:
we are two leaves, torn
by early autumn winds
from a single tree,
scattered who knows where.
Let me abide in the Way, I pray,
until we meet in paradise.

Ch'ungji sings his 'Death Song' with memorable poignancy.
Acceptance, transcendence, life and death....

Death Song *(hanshi)*

Sixty-seven years have passed;
all is consummated this morning.
The road home is smooth;
I won't lose my way.
My staff may be all I carry,
but thankfully my legs won't tire on the way.

Ch'ungji (1226–1292)

'Like the Wind Leaving the Lotus' dramatizes the oneness of life and death. For me, it is Korea's finest modern poem. Who else but Sŏ Chŏngju would have penned it?

Like the Wind Leaving the Lotus

Sorry,
not utterly sorry,
just sorry enough

for parting,
not utter parting,
but parting with the promise
of meeting again,
in the next life perhaps;

not like the wind
coming to the lotus,
but like the wind leaving therefrom;

not like the wind leaving
a couple of days ago,
but like the wind leaving
a couple of seasons back.

10

EXCLUSIVITY MYTHS

FOREIGNERS WHO VISITED KOREA at the end of the nineteenth century – Elizabeth Bishop and the French anthropologist Bourdaret, for example – note that the Koreans are bigger and better-looking than their East Asian counterparts. They see the Koreans as multiracial in their origins, with Caucasian and Mongol characteristics. The Italian, Rossetti, said they were a mix of East Asian and South East Asian stock. The British painter, Landor, said it was as if all the different racial types of Asia had settled in the tiny peninsula. Yi Kwangsu, a prominent nationalist and educator, who was eventually tarred with the pro-Japanese brush, wrote in his *Chosŏn minjok non* (1933) that there was no record that Koreans were traditionally regarded as a homogenous people. Shin Ch'aeho, the noted historian of the first half of the twentieth century, had no problem with Koreans having multiracial origins. Yet every handbook on Korea notes on the first page that Koreans are a homogeneous people. It's that formidable excluding principle again – in Korea all the people are Korean – which keeps coming back to haunt foreigners who have ambitions to make a mark in Korean society. Homogeneity is obviously seen as something rare and precious, an identifying mark that singles Koreans out from the peoples of the world. What this means for mongrel people like the Irish with their mix of native Irish, Celt, Viking, Norman, Scots, English and God only knows what other blood is not quite clear. Identity is a crucial concern for Koreans, perhaps inevitably so against the backdrop of Japanese oppression. While Japan struggled to annihilate any notion of a Korean identity separate from that of imperial Japan, Korea struggled to preserve a clear national identity. That's why the provisional government in Shanghai adopted Taehanmin'guk in 1919 as the official name of the country, rejecting the name of Chosŏn which the Japanese favoured and the North Koreans still use. This clear vision of a distinct national identity led to a preoccupation with Koreanness, and a tendency to mythologize in order to achieve that goal, as evidenced by the claim to racial homogeneity, which takes no account of Arab, Indian, Mongolian, Chinese, and Japanese intrusions into Korean bloodlines, not to speak of the gene input of Hamel's red-haired crew.

The drive to discover or create the uniquely Korean is a central theme in contemporary academic writing. Take, for example, the penchant to present *han*, *hŭng* and *mŏt* as defining elements of Korean identity. If you are not Korean, we are told, you cannot understand *han*, *mŏt* and *hŭng*. Non-Koreans, however, relate to all three concepts within their own experience. Many believe these concepts are in fact universal with subtle regional differences. *Han* and *hŭng* are Chinese terms: discussion of these concepts goes back to antiquity. *Mŏt*, on the other hand, is a vernacular term and has only been a subject of discussion in Korean academic circles since the publication of Shin Sŏkcho's 'Mŏtsŏl' in the March 1941 number of *Munjang*. Since then there has been a stream of articles by learned members of the literary establishment.

English does not have corresponding words for *han*, *hŭng*, and *mŏt*, a regrettable oversight by the founding fathers of the language, which by some acrobatic feat of logic is taken in Korea as proof positive of the Koreanness of the concepts. It is not a very good argument. All it really proves is that Korean is more sensitive in some matters than English. There are plenty of equivalent examples across the languages of the world. I remember a series of seminars in Graduate School about the superiority of the Hopi language to English in a variety of contexts, all of which I have long since forgotten. The bottom line was that Hopi had many words of gorgeous accuracy for which English had no equivalents.

UNIVERSALITY OF *HAN*

No one in the English-speaking world has much difficulty in identifying with the ideas and feelings that *han, hŭng* and *mŏt* elicit. *Han* is the quintessential sense of bitter wrong that has dogged the Korean people throughout their history. There is just as much *han* per square inch in Ireland as there ever was in Korea: the *han* of a divided nation, the *han* of years of political and cultural exploitation; the *han* of the widow; the *han* of the childless woman; the *han* of the woman who sacrifices her own life to look after her ageing parents; the *han* of the abused daughter-in-law. Ireland even has a category of *han* unknown in Korea: the *han* of the old bachelor who never got married, either because of a domineering mother or because of the poverty of his circumstances. The Irish experience of *han* is repeated across Europe and into Russia, not to speak of Africa, the Middle East, and East Asia. In fact, wherever you have communities that have suffered oppression over an extended period, you will find some version of *han*. It may differ a little from region to region, but basically *han* is *han*. Ireland's short story writer, Frank O'Connor, has an interesting theory that the short story thrives under circumstances of *han*. He illustrates his case with examples from Russia, England, Ireland and India, noting how England with the largess of temper that comes from empire has tended to excel in the novel rather than the short story, whereas Russia, which has known both empire and grinding misery, is distinguished in both the short story and the novel. Ireland and India, archetypal *han* countries, have produced their best work in the short story. Joyce, Beckett and the current crop of first-rate Irish novelists, John Banville and Colm Toibin, for example, would be a little offended, but it is an interesting theory developed with cogency in O'Connor's acclaimed study of the short story, *The Lonely Voice* (Macmillan: 1965) The Korean experience lends even more weight to O'Connor's argument. The short story is by far Korea's strongest literary genre in the twentieth century.

TANJONG'S *HAN*

One of the great embodiments of *han* in Korean history is the boy king Tanjong (1441–1457), who was deposed by his uncle Sejo and subsequently killed at Sejo's command. Tanjong wrote a lovely *shijo* filled with intimations of approaching death:

The cuckoo calls; the moon is low on the mountains *(shijo)*

The cuckoo calls; the moon is low on the mountain;
I lean against the balustrade thinking of distant friends.
The anguish in your voice suffuses my heart. Were you silent I
   would not be sad.
To friends from whom I have parted, I say:
do not come here in spring when the cuckoo calls and the
   moon is bright on the pavilion.

The bird in the poem has traditionally been called the cuckoo. The cuckoo, however, doesn't call at night. Scops-owl would probably be a more accurate translation. Sometimes tradition wins.

CHO KWANGJO'S *HAN*

Cho Kwangjo (1482–1519), a brilliant if rather divisive intellectual who was put to death in the Ki'myo Purge of 1519, is another fine example of pristine *han*. As a young man, Cho Kwangjo lodged in the home of a newly married woman and quickly became the object of her desire. As Sŏ Chŏngju tells the story: 'She looked at him with the eyes of love, flapped her wings and attached herself fast.' Kwangjo refused the woman's favours. The woman took the pin from her hair and gave it to him, the ultimate sign of her love. He accepted it at first but came back later, stuck it in a crack in the wall and took to his heels. Sŏ Chŏngju notes:

Had Kwangjo been capable of accepting the woman's favours, of indulging in a giggly interlude, would he not have been able to forestall the death by poisoning at the order of the king that greeted his thirty-eighth year? Had he laughed and giggled through such times, he might have lived and thus have saved his father, mother, wife and children from tears.

Intransigence is seen as the bedrock of *han*. Sŏ Chŏngju's view reflects Korea's age old double standard. What would have been a giggly interlude for Cho Kwangjo would have been adultery for the woman – Sŏ Chŏngju would not have thrown stones.

Hŭng

It's in the swing of the hips of a
countrywoman going to market.
It's in a young ajumoni's shrug, dunting
the baby a bit higher on her back.
It's in the toss of an ajosshi's head
to the rhythm of a farmer's band.

Hŭng is the excitement generated by the apprehension of beauty. It is triggered by almost anything – sunrise, sunset, wine, music, dance, poetry, a painting, a companion, a beauty, an insight into life, a fish biting and so on. We have already seen how a disapproving Yi T'oegye of Chosŏn tells us that *hŭng* is the feeling produced by vernacular songs. He had in mind sentiments like those expressed in the Koryŏ *kayo* in which the woman pleads with her trader husband to avoid the sirens of the marketplace and come back home.

HŬNG IN POETRY

Shijo is full of *hŭng*, the *hŭng* of spring, love, friendship, wine, music, fishing:

I nodded off; I lost my fishing pole

I nodded off; I lost my fishing pole.
I danced a set; I lost my raincape.

White gull, laugh not at an old man's folly.
Ten li of peach blossoms
are in bloom; I am filled with the joy of spring

Ko Un, one of Korea's most feted contemporary poets writes in 'Big Spring:'

Big Spring

Look!
Fish surface
from deep holes,
ice on their backs.
How could sky be unaffected?
The wild goose
takes his family
to the Songhwa River.
Something big is going on
in this country now.
A big spring.

Ko Un (1933–)

The big spring is *hŭng*. It is also Zen or Tao.

KIM INHU'S PERVERTED *HŬNG*

Hasŏ Kim Inhu (1510–1560) was an official during the turbulent reign of Myŏngjong. After the Ŭlsa Purge in 1545, he returned to his family home on the pretext of sickness and devoted himself to scholarly pursuits. Stories abound about his love of wine and the prodigious amounts he consumed. When Myŏngjong appointed him to an official post and ordered him to come to Seoul, Kim Inhu loaded his old donkey with kegs of wine and set out to take up the appointment. On the way he visited a winehouse which had a fine bamboo grove and garden. He spent ten days there, drinking till the wine was gone. 'Ah, hell, I'm going home,' Sŏ Chŏngju has him say, 'It's a disease, a disease, so fine a disease I'd hate to give it to anyone.' He aborted the trip and went back home.

UNIVERSALITY OF *HŬNG*

Hŭng is not an exclusively Korean feeling. Anyone who ever took a fishing rod in hand and felt the nibble of a fish knows it. Anyone who likes music knows it; Bach at first light, for example. It's what Wordsworth felt in *The Prelude* when he saw the waterfall; what Hardy felt driving up the hill on the way to Castle Boterel; what William Carlos Williams felt when he looked at his famous red wheelbarrow; what Seamus Heaney felt when he watched the thatcher or water diviner at work. In rhythmic terms, its most characteristic movement in Korea begins in the shoulder; in Ireland it begins in the feet. Anyone who has seen a farmer's band perform will know the shoulder movement and the buzz of excitement that goes with it; anyone familiar with Irish music will know the characteristic tap of the foot and the excitement that goes with jigs and reels. The rhythm and movement of a farmer's band is quintessentially Korean, the tap of the jig and reel are quintessentially Gaelic, but what is felt in the heart in both cases is *hŭng*.

MŎT

Professor Kim Chonggil tells us in *The Darling Buds of May* (1991) that *mŏt* is a phonetically corrupted form of *mat* (taste), and that the word first occurred as late as the second half of the nineteenth century. He tells how Professor Kim Hŭnggyu found the phrase, *matto morŭgo*, in a *p'ansori* version of the classical Korean romance *Hŭngbu chŏn* (*Hŭngbu's* Tale), written presumably in the latter half of the nineteenth century. The phrase literally means 'without knowing taste', but in the context it is used in the sense of 'unwittingly' or 'carelessly', the present day version of which is *mŏt to morŭgo*. The word *mŏtchige*, the adverbial form of *mŏt*, occurs in an An Minyŏng *shijo* in his collection, *Kŭmok ch'ongbu*, edited in the 1870s. Professor Kim believes that the word *mŏt* began to be used in the second half of the nineteenth century, together with words like *mŏtjaengi* or *mŏtjida*. Those of you who know a little Korean will be familiar with these words. One obvious problem with *mŏt* as a defining concept of Korean sensibility is explaining how you can hang an entire aesthetic on a Korean word that has only been current since the latter half of the nineteenth century, when the whole world knows that the vernacular was not held in very high esteem until the surge of nationalism at the end of the enlightenment period. In fact, the word *han'gul* itself was not coined until the twentieth century. *Ŏnmun* (vulgar writing), an obviously deleterious expression, was the term in common use.

Mŏt is a popular rather than a scholarly term. Very difficult to define, it reflects the perception of beauty, refinement, taste, and elegance in people and things. A man of *mŏt* is a gentleman in the fullest sense of the word, the complete, rounded human specimen. He is refined, urbane, charming, attractive looking, maybe even sexy, with overtones of dandy and swinger. *Mŏt* is both inward and outward; inward *mŏt*, however, reflects the real essence of *mŏt*. The man of *mŏt* is inwardly untrammelled; he has broken from the constraints of the conventional – shades of Lady Suro and the old man who dared pick the azaleas for her; the man of *mŏt* has reserves of emotional largess; he holds himself open to aesthetical experience; he tastes life to the full. *Mŏt* is more in the heart than in the mind; more outward looking in love for others than inward looking in preoccupation with the self; more platonic than sexual; it is found more consistently among our forefathers than among our contemporaries.

All this is universal. Wherever people have concerned themselves with beauty, whether in nature, art or in the spirit, there has always been *mŏt*. What is different is the attitude that individuals, cultural groups, and nations take to beauty.

MŎT AND THE BEAUTIFUL

The discussion of *mŏt*, then, rightfully begins with a discussion of attitudes towards the beautiful because while *mŏt* and the beautiful are by no means synonymous, they are so closely related that overlap is inevitable. Chŏng Pyŏng'uk, a prominent scholar of the last generation, notes that when Koreans look at a rose, they do not see an array of individual petals, each subtly distinct from each other, each totally distinct from every petal of every rose that ever existed. They are not interested in the physical make-up of the individual flower. They see a rose that is the essence of every rose; they see a symbol of the universal. Beauty as it appears to the eye takes a back seat to beauty as it appears to the heart. This explains why one does not readily find the kind of poem in Korean that Gerard Manley Hopkins wrote in English. When Hopkins saw a blade of grass, he felt compelled to define its essence, to see how it differed from every other blade of grass, to marvel at its uniqueness, and to refer the mystery of its existence back to the glory of God. A Korean poet is interested in the moral aspect of things. He sees his rose as symbolic of a spiritual reality embodied in nature. The beauty of the rose is a healing beauty; contemplating the rose relieves man of the accumulated burdens of life. Hopkins put his blade of grass under microscopic scrutiny. The Korean poet universalizes his blade of grass.

Yi Ŏryŏng's idea of point of view in traditional Korean art reinforces the conceptual quality of the Korean approach to nature. He gave a paper many years ago at a PEN Conference in Walker Hill in which he noted that perspective is a Western technique. Korean poets, he said, and he used Sowŏl's 'Mountain Flowers' to illustrate his theme, see all points of view at once. It's as if, he said, the poet were riding a helicopter, untrammelled by the physical restrictions of the Western point of view. The idea may not stand up to critical scrutiny but it is a very unusual conception and shows the continuing Korean preoccupation with the conceptual aspects of things.

MŎT AND P'UNGRYU

The commentators try to give some historical depth to the concept of *mŏt* by linking it with the Chinese term *p'ungnyu*, but the link is tenuous. Shilla *p'ungnyu* is a version of Chinese fengliu which, according to Professor Kim Chonggil, originally meant 'social morale' but came to mean a 'carefree, detached style of life,' associated with lute, poetry, wine and female entertainer. Fengliu reached its full development during the T'ang dynasty and subsequently found its way into Korea as *p'ungnyu* and into Japan as *miyabi*.

Sŏ Chŏngju explains the *p'ungnyu* concept in '*P'ungnyu* Discrimination':

> The Shilla poet, Ch'oe Ch'iwŏn, said that *p'ungnyu* as first understood in this country was a fine amalgam of Buddhism, Taoism and Confucianism. Ch'oe Namsŏn ... claimed that the old Korean term *pu-ru*, meaning the light of heaven, was matched to the Chinese characters *p'ung* and *ryu* (wind and flow).

P'ungnyu then is a concept with strong religious overtones: it is the light of heaven in a man's inner being. However, in the practice of *p'ungnyu*, that is, in the life of the *p'ungnyugaek* (aesthete) there are always strong overtones of music, poetry, wine, and *kisaeng*. It is notable in the Sŏ Chŏngju poem that whereas the elucidation of the principle is religious–spiritual, the practical illustration is from the *kisaeng* world. The poem continues:

> In considering these two explications, imagine, if you will, old *p'ungnyu* melodies in secluded rooms in the back lanes of the night twanging perforce from the strings of *kayagŭms* strummed by aged *kisaeng* whose hearts are filled with all regret: something comes to you, as if from home, across the shimmering haze of the centuries. Especially if you think these thoughts while gently stroking a fine old Chosŏn white or a Koryŏ green.

Notice how Sŏ Chŏngju mixes the notion of *kisaeng han* with the notion of artistic fineness. In *The Darling Buds of May* Professor Kim says that Alan Heyman, a specialist in Korean music and dance, is wrong to think that *mŏt* occurs from the interaction of *hŭng* and *han*. *Mŏt*, Professor Kim claims, is rather the Janus face of *hŭng*. He says Alan Heyman was probably reflecting something learned through his long association with Korean music and dance. Many of the great exemplars of *mŏt* in history have also been great exemplars of *han*. Non'gye, for example, the *kisaeng* who threw herself off the cliff in the arms of the Japanese general, and Hwang Chini, the celebrated sixteenth century *kisaeng*, are symbols of *han* as well as *mŏt*. The fact that Sŏ Chŏngju uses *kisaeng han* to illustrate his idea of *mŏt* shows how much myth making there is in these identity defining exclusive concepts.

The progression from T'ang fengliu to Shilla *p'ungnyu* seems relatively clear, although it is not quite clear where the Shilla religious connotations of *p'ungnyu* come from. The problem occurs in getting from Shilla *p'ungnyu* to modern *mŏt*. There is no linguistic link. The argument is developed by means of historical examples on the presumption that *p'ungnyu* and *mŏt* emanate from the same national heart. But since *p'ungnyu* in its original form is Chinese, it is difficult to see it as an exclusive definer of Korean sensibility.

AZALEAS AND *MŎT*

The archetypal Korean man of *p'ungnyu-mŏt* is the old Shilla man who scaled the cliff to cut the azaleas for Lady Suro. The old man is transcendent: he breaks through the mould of convention; he knocks down the walls of inhibition; he shows himself to be a man of emotional largess. He scorns the social norms that govern age, subservient wives and boorish husbands; he is oblivious of everything except an ideal beauty. The situation has a special emotional complexity in that Lady Suro, whom the old man recognizes as a 'flower,' is herself a lady of *p'ungnyu*, not just physically beautiful, but aesthetically beautiful. What is at stake here is a spiritual quality, an opening of the heart to emotional response, which enables a man to be above life while experiencing life's full intensity. This is not an exclusively Korean emotion. People everywhere identify with it.

EXPONENTS OF *P'UNGNYU-MŎT*

There are dozens of figures in history and literature that illustrate the Korean idea of *p'ungnyu-mŏt*. Some that come directly to mind are Chŏng Mongju, drunk as a lord, back to front on his horse, as he goes to face the assassin's club; Wŏlmyŏng the Monk piping down the lady in the Moon; Yi Sunshin strapped in death to the mast of his ship leading his men even after he expired; Prime Minister Yu Kwan cupping the rain in his umbrella hands; Hwang Chini cracking the flea before she sings at the Governor of Naju's feast; Non'gye jumping to her death with the Japanese general in her arms; Kim Tongin marching down Ulchiro in morning coat, striped trousers, silk hat and carnation; and Sŏ Chŏngju himself, perhaps the last of the old generation of *mŏtjaengi*, whose *mŏt* transcended the pettiness of the establishment.

UNIVERSALITY OF *MŎT*

Mŏt is universal. What distinguishes Korean *mŏt* from *mŏt* throughout the world is the Korean attitude to beauty. The Korean artist, as we have noted, looks to moral rather than to physical beauty; his concern is with the universal rather than the particular. The approach is conceptual, the emphasis is moral. The Korean approach is neither better nor worse than any other approach. There is plenty of precedent for it in the West, particularly in the tradition of poetry practised in Eastern Europe in the twentieth century – Czeslaw Milosz, for example, and the influence of his work on contemporary poetic practice has been enormous.

The implications of the conceptual approach to beauty are very wide-ranging. First of all, it focuses on ideals rather than on realities. Koreans look at the facade and dream great dreams. When things go wrong there is a great outpouring of moral outrage; blame is apportioned; myths of responsibility are created. Witness the collapse of the Wau Apartments; the explosion of the train in Iri; the collapse of Sŏngsu Bridge and the subsequent revelation that the bridges over the Han were all floating; the problems with the Samil Elevated Highway until it was removed to beautify Ch'ŏnggyech'ŏn; pollution in the Paldang Dam, Seoul's main source of drinking water; the money problems in the various governments of the last thirty years; the list is endless. The outcry every time is of tidal proportions, as if this were the first time such moral turpitude had raised its ugly head among us. The myth-maker resigns, the angry waters subside and everyone holds their collective breath until the process begins again. Who would have thought that the roots of a national attitude would be buried so deeply in the perception of beauty?

That's your basic introduction to life in Korea. You have encountered some dominant thought patterns, the class system, classical literature, modern literature, the art of making money, the Tan'gun story, the monolith of Confucianism, the heart of Buddhism, and the exclusivity myths – *han, hŭng and mŏt*. Scholars will tell you that it's a fundamental error to confuse Taoism and Buddhist Zen practice, but Taoism is so much a part of the fabric of all things Korean – Confucian, Buddhist, and Christian – that I find it inseparable.

All that remains before trying your luck in the mainstream is to take a closer look at the Korean heart. For this you must go to Sŏ Chŏngju's home village of Chilmajae in Chŏlla, where you will find the simple values that inspired an older Korea. How the human heart operated in that older Korea is the key to understanding how it operates today.

11

CHILMAJAE SONGS

Tidal Wave

ONCE, IN MY GRANNY'S, the flooding tide rode the stream, slipped through the hemp hedge, passed through the corn-field and gathered to a brimming fullness in the yard. I splashed around delightedly in my bare feet, looking for goby and shrimp; my joy went right into my teeth like the chirps of a baby lark. Normally the mere sight of me was enough to set granny talking about the old days: she would talk end-lessly, like the silkworm makes its thread, but today she stood there without a word and looked out to sea, her face already very old, reddening like the gentle rays of the evening sun. At the time I had no idea why she was doing this. Indeed it wasn't until she was dead that I found out. My granddad was a boatman, a fisher of distant seas. One winter before I was born, he was caught in a bitter wind and swept into the sea; he never came back. Presumably it was the sight of her husband's sea driving into her yard that rooted granny there, wordless, red-faced.

The Singer

When the song of Chilmajae's finest singer lost its edge, his antidote was to twirl the twelve-string streamer on his head; when his song got boring, he liked to stand a cowled monk on his shoulder. For the funeral bier he had a brass handbell that shone like the sun, which he hung on the front. The singer's song reached from this world to the next.

One morning when our village singer was not engaged in song, I saw him removing the contents of the honey bucket in the outhouse. What can I say! Our honey bucket was noted for the way it reflected moon and stars. He stood there, exposed to wind and rain, busily using our wonderful, roofless honey bucket as a mirror to dye beneath his topknot headband. He pushed his hair back up under the headband – nicely, nicely – and dyed it with appropriate decorum.

Perhaps this mirror, so special, so fertile, was also the source of his song, which was so luxuriantly effective in bridging this world and the next.

Exceptional Pressure in the Urinary Pump of the Esteemed Wife of Squire Yi

Squire Yi's wife's radish patch reputedly had the richest soil and the thickest stalks in the village of Chilmajae, and there was universal agreement that this was because of the potent urinary jet of the esteemed woman of the house.

King Chidoro of old Shilla, whose appendage was so big he couldn't find a match, finally got a girl to share his life – she had left a dung patty as big as an hourglass drum under a gnarled old winter tree. Whether there was enough ardour in Mrs Yi's pee to function as an hourglass-drum stimulant for her radishes remains an imponderable, but when the village kids were caught taking a short-cut through the radish patch, they discovered to their cost the potency of the good lady's jet.

'I'm telling you, you little skitters. I'll stick you between my legs and spray hot piss on your polls,' she would cry, whereupon the kids scampered off like young pheasants. They clearly knew the heat of that redoubtable pump!

Horse Blood

There are all sorts of ways of separating a man and a woman who have fallen in love; it depends on place on earth and time in heaven.

In our village, Chilmajae, the custom was to take hot, acrid horse blood, a dark, rancid brew, and spray it between the pair: that finished love forever.

The widow from Flax Field Valley – the house with the persimmon tree – was so beautiful even at forty that her eyebrows seemed to exude a fragrant, ritual incense. For several years she had maintained an infrequent relationship with a man nicknamed Togap (which translates as Bogeyman), and rumour was rife that she was buying rice-paddies and dry fields. One evening her wicker gate was roped off and the area was doused with hot, acrid, rancid, dark horse blood.

Needless to say, when the offending rogue came in the night with his lamp alight, he was stricken out of his love. 'Don't think that sharing a bed means sharing love,' he shrieked so that all the villagers could hear. Whereupon he took off for good.

Would you believe it? This horse blood rite came down through the Yi dynasty and into Japanese times, with precisely the same effect it had when Kim Yushin cut his horse's throat as he rode past Ch'ŏn'gwannyŏ, thus severing their ties of love. Would you not agree that it is far superior to, and much more poignant than, the silly methods of parting current in our time?

Kite Contest

The joy of a fight is in the winning, the saying goes; no one says there's joy in losing. But on the first full moon of lunar January, the skies of this village make losing into an art. It is our supreme example for the entire year.

A kite contest is all about toughness.

Go to the cruellest deepest sea and take the air bladder from the stomach of a croaker and boil it to paste.

Sharp, steely edges are crucial: collect crockery fragments sharper than any blade, and grind them down till you have innumerable tiny ice-shard blades.

It is essential to reflect the sun beautifully. Take the lovely gentle yellow mustard – the loveliest of all the colours – boil it to a paste in a stoneware pot, and rub it repeatedly on the kite string.

The kites, tied to the contestants' reels by all that length of string, fly above the highest mountain peak in the village in a display of all their talents, vying with one another in the contest. And should one kite cut the string of another, the defeated never cries in lamentation, 'I've lost, I've lost.' Instead, he sets out on the ultimate never-ending voyage of untrammelled freedom. The kite dances over the peak, as if mounted on the end of that cut string, till with a quiver it disappears in the distant sky. The kite carries with it a heart that wants to voyage forever, a heart filled since Shilla times with the lure of distant things.

And when such a man fails in village life and sets out on the illimitable wayfarer's road, he shakes the dust thoroughly from his bundle, gets up, and takes the road as lightly as the loosed kite. This is the greeting that sends him on his way: 'Fortune, fortune, you lucky son-of-a-bitch, yours is the finest fortune of all.'

The Bride

The bride was sitting with the groom on their wedding night, wearing her grass green blouse and bright red skirt, her side tresses barely loosened. Suddenly, the groom, spurred by an urgent need to relieve himself, rose hurriedly to his feet and rushed to get out, in the process catching his coat in the hinge of the door. The groom thought his bride, consumed with desire and unable to endure the delay, was pulling him from behind. Thinking this, he swept out of the room without a backward glance. When he had finished urinating, he took to his heels, still wearing the torn coat; his bride's demean had disturbed him deeply.

After a lapse of some forty or fifty years, business unexpectedly took him past the bride's home. Driven by a need to know, he opened the door of the bride's room. The bride was sitting there in her grass green blouse and bright red skirt, her side tresses barely loosened, just as she had been on their wedding night. Moved to pity, he went across and patted her shoulder. She turned to acrid ash, ash grass green and bright red, and sank in a heap to the ground.

Adultery and the Well

Incidents of adultery were as rare in the village of Chilmajae as eating rice-cakes in your sleep, but when an incident burst on the scene with all the explosive impact of sores erupting all over the body, Heaven, as if stung innumerable times by swarming bees, was first to feel the pain.

'So-and-so's wife and so-and-so's husband COUPLED!' As soon as the rumour broke, every trumpet in the village was out, blowing for all it was worth. And the gongs and the drums couldn't stay still: out they sprang and joined in the riot. With men and women, young and old, even chickens and puppies flushed out and part of the fray, what with the shouting and the running, Heaven could not but feel its pain.

Then the villagers escorted a pained Heaven to the cow-sheds: they took the cattle feed, scattered it in the village wells, filled them to the brim. For a whole year the villagers could neither draw nor drink water from any of the village wells. They sought out watering holes in the fields and in the mountain valleys where they quenched their thirst and drew their supply of drinking water.

Chaegon the Immortal

Chaegon, meaning in Chinese 'entitled to live in this world,' was the name of a legless cripple. With his two sound hands, he could weave straw mats or baskets, but this was not enough for him to feed himself, so the people of Chilmajae granted him the special right to whirl on his bum around the village and beg for his food. 'If Chaegon fails to live his allotted span, our village is bankrupt of all humanity, and we will not escape the punishment of Heaven.' The people were agreed on this, and so they looked after him, providing him with three square meals, and clothes and firewood to protect him from the cold.

One morning, in the Kapsul Year – or was it Ŭlhae? – when the rose-of-sharon was newly in bloom, Chaegon vanished. From breakfast time on, not a trace of him could be found on the face of heaven or earth. All that remained of him was the living memory, in the hearts of the villagers, of the cripple when he lived among them, crawling around like a turtle, awkward, ungainly. And the people worried about the punishment Heaven would mete out to them. But the years repeated themselves and still the punishment of Heaven did not descend on the village. Farming was as productive here as elsewhere. Cho Sŏndal, an old white-beard, said to know something of the Way of the Immortals, explained: 'Chaegon looked like a turtle, didn't he? Turtles and cranes have a life span of 1,000 years. The thought of such a long life here was unendurable, so he sprouted wings and flew off to heaven to live the life of an Immortal.' Cho Sŏndal further opined: 'Perhaps Chaegon felt so indebted to us, he tied a millstone tightly around his neck, submerged himself deep in the sea and won't come out.' To all this the villagers responded: 'Chaegon's never shown himself dead to us: what Cho Sŏndal is saying feels right.' Thus they were compelled to take Chaegon's turtle body, the live version as it existed in their minds, and attach wings to his oxters on both sides.

Gourd Flower Time

Hŭngbu is a character in a Chosŏn dynasty romance who is synonymous with simplicity and poverty. (Hŭngbu and his avaricious brother, Nolbu, are household words in Korea, symbols of an old world morality that Korean parents insist on instilling in their children.) A swallow uncovered to him the key to riches.

Long, long ago in old China, in an age more gentle than ours, the menfolk had a unit of time they called stroke-your-beard-time. Similarly, the women in the village of Chilmajae developed a unit of time called gourd-flower-time, which is still popularly observed today.

'The gourd flowers are open, it's dinner time, we'll go for water,' the womenfolk would say, showing that in the eyes and livers of these women, who carried the jars of spring water from distant wells, there was no power in heaven or on earth – pro-vided the barley bins in the houses of the poor were not quite empty – capable of smashing the pristine purity of the gourd flower hour when that hour came and the gourd flowers, puck-ered tight all day long, began to open in the fading summer light.

However, in a house as poor as Hŭngbu's, with the last of the barley gone, an empty corner came in the gourd flower hour, and a swallow from the south fluttered into the emptiness and appended this advice to its fluttering dance: 'Don't worry, Hŭngbu. Cannot the five cereals, the hundred fruits, coin of the land, gold, silver and jewels all be put into the gourd – fruit of the gourd flower?' Thus the household was brought to under-standing.

And so, to this day, the gourd flower hour cannot be smashed, twisted, subtracted from, or added to; it is retained and passed on in the purity of its original gold.

Honey Bucket

No matter how despised a man may be, or how poor his house-hold, he needs to have three honey jars where he can sit in soli-tary dignity and do his double business. The high and mighty of this world straddle celadon plum pots on oil papered pal-ace floors to do their thing, but is such fuss really necessary? What you need are three big, strong earthenware jars buried in a secluded place on the premises, a spot where sun, moon and stars shine brightest and here a man can exercise his ultimate prerogative of free and satisfactory expression. Best to have neither roof nor paper.

And whether several thousand bolts of sunstroke inhere in the broiling summer sun, or several tens of thousands of lightning bolts inhere in torrential summer showers, sit there with bared bum, a bamboo hat on your head to protect against the rain, and reach for a gourd leaf to wipe your backside. This is the last vestige of Korean honey bucket technique. Special, isn't it?

Moon and stars shine in the honey bucket too.

When Karam Yi Pyŏnggi was in his cups, he often sang the praises of a toilet lit by moon and stars. And when you come to do your business for the last time, isn't it a fine thing to do it with a certain poise and in a splendid setting? And doesn't the finality of it all make it even better?

Mrs Greatwater: The Sighs of a Childless Woman

Mrs Greatwater, a childless woman, took it upon herself to get her husband a concubine: she lived alone on the hill opposite the pine grove. Her name was derived from the name of her home village which was noted for the abundance of its waters. She herself was a fine, firm-fleshed, all-round jewel of a woman. Eyes, eyebrows, teeth, hair parting – she shone out among the women of Chilmajae: for sheer vitality she had no peer. Thus, on windy days, when she threaded the paths between the ramie fields, carrying a heaped basket of corn on her head, and when the ramie leaves flip-fluttered their underbellies in the breeze, the village people smilingly ascribed this also to 'Mrs Greatwater's vitality'.

And when that quiet childlike smile spread across her face like a flower blooming within jade, those who witnessed it, young and old, male and female, whether from the smile's sheer impossibility, or its sheer facility, were quite unable to prevent an involuntary miniscule arching of their lips. No one could look at her smile for an extended length of time because of her smile's extraordinary power to bare the viewer's teeth, resist though the viewer might. Perhaps the experience was too acute, for the viewer soon turned stealthily away and engaged in a little distraction. And not just people, the rumour goes, but also dogs and cats. 'Laugh and live like Mrs Greatwater,' everyone agreed.

At the age of forty-something Mrs Greatwater and her smile left this world, victims of a terrible fever, and another rumour was born in the village, a rumour which has been passed down to the present day. Someone, it would seem, heard Mrs Greatwater sigh. It was not heard in the usual black of night, nor on a dark dirty day, nor in the twilight hour: it was heard in the early morning, when the sun was high in the sky and the day was already clear and bright. The sound overlapped with the pine breeze rising on the hill behind her house in a marvel of harmonious whisper.

To this day when the villagers hear the soughing of the pines on bright mornings, they are wont to say. 'Did you hear? Mrs Greatwater is up and about early, with her monopoly on the sigh. She'll spend today too with a smile.'

The Women Under the Zelkova

Reputedly the women who live under the zelkova on the mountain in Chilmajae, whether as girls, young women, or ripe wives, never indulge in affairs of the heart, but when they reach the age of fifty and are on the brink of growing old, they are said to take to love with a vengeance. As girls they did as their parents bid; married, they did as their mothers-in-law bid – secondarily as their husbands bid. Did the burden of washing and cleaning leave them no leisure? One thing is certain: they have more ass-power than their husbands, most of whom, between the ages of forty and fifty, take off with broken heads to the other world. And now with leisure to stretch their knees, the women, reputedly, take to love. Mrs Pak and Mrs Kim are cases in point. With a room all to themselves, they now wield adult power: they can oil themselves and powder themselves to their hearts' content. Mrs Kim is fifty-one this year, but for the first time in her life she's a beauty. They say the man slipping from her room at first light wears a flow of red blood from his nose. The verdant zelkova on the mountain behind is seven hundred years old this year: all this must be an extension of its vigour.

12

KOREA'S GREATEST ASSET

MOST FOREIGNERS WILL AGREE that Korea's women are her finest product.

Woman

She comes each morning
with the sea on her head.

'Fresh oysters for sale, fresh oysters!'
she cries like the sunlight,

wrinkles rippling
though there isn't a puff of wind,

hands filled with thunderous storm clouds.

When will it rain,
when will it rain?

Her firm buttocks
are rolling breakers.

Faster than the dark,
lighter than a bird,

lovely, so lovely,
she strides beside the sun.

Kang Ŭn'gyo (1945–)

Korean women are beautiful, fearless, and intensely loyal; without them it's doubtful if Korea would have made it through the twentieth century. But forget that docile, subservient stuff; it's pure façade. Anyone who has been in Korea for a week will know the busy *ajumŏni* type pushing her way shamelessly to the head of the queue in the bank, the post office, the railway station or any government office. She is a figure of fun to Koreans and foreigners alike, but make no mistake, she can be very exasperating.

GOING TO THE BANK

Gugin Way, a longtime resident, had business in the local branch of his bank. He set out with his usual sense of anticipation, armed with bankbooks, *tojangs* (seals), plastic cards, three photographs, passport, birth certificate, residence permit, driver's licence, medical insurance, anything he thought might be useful. Experience had taught him it pays to be prepared. As usual, the inside of the bank was like Seoul Station at Ch'usŏk, lines at the money machines, lines at the counters, every seat full.

Some foreigners get impatient in these circumstances. Not goodly Gugin Way. He just took his place in the queue. Over the years he had cultivated a rare transcendence in the face of what he called the bureaucratic wait. It did not bother him at all, that is, until that archetypal character, the busy *ajumŏni*, arrived on the scene. She touched a nerve that quickly moved him from relaxed waiting mode to steeled for battle mode, not for battle-battle, with angry words, raised voices and so on, but for what he liked to call fun-battle, the kind of sortie that put the other customers giggling and sent him home with a chuckle.

The busy *ajumŏni* operated with consummate skill. She waited for a slight hesitation at the top of the queue, then nipped to the front of the line, brandishing a sheaf of documents, forcing the teller to accept her or be rude.

Gugin Way had seen this happen so often before that he was only momentarily disconcerted. He tapped the *ajumŏni* gently on the shoulder, aware of the impoliteness of touching in Korean culture, but feigning foreign ignorance.

'Excuse me, *ajumŏni*,' he said, deliberately giving her a grade of honorific less than he thought was merited. 'Are you in a hurry?'

She turned in surprise. '*Nye-e?*' she countered.

For his second sally Gugin Way raised the honorific form and moved from question mode to statement.

'Madam, you seem to be very busy,' he said, smiling, high form, very polite, with all the subtlety of a Panzer attack.

'No, I'm not busy at all. Were you waiting, sir?' she rejoined sweetly, giving him back a little of the high form treatment.

'No, no,' he said, 'I'm not waiting, I'm just here to pass the time.'

He paused to see what impact, if any, his sarcasm had, saw that it had very little and continued, 'But if you are really busy, you can go first.'

'No, no, *sŏnsaengnim*,' she said. 'You go first, you go first. I'm not busy at all.'

'No, no, madam,' the foreign devil said. 'You go first.'

By this stage gentleman and lady were bent double in gradually deepening bows, each deferring to the other.

'But *sŏnsaengnim*,' she said, 'You've been waiting for a long time.'

The foreigner had made the customary three deferrals.

'Well ... that's true, I suppose,' he said. 'Perhaps I had better go first after all. Thank you, it's very kind of you, madam, I'm sure.'

'Not at all, *sŏnsaengnim*,' she said, 'The pleasure is mine.'

Gugin Way chuckled all the way home, bolstered by the smiles on the faces of the other customers in the bank which translated said, 'You did good.' His only regret was that he had not used the alternative ending on his internal computer program for dealing with these situations, which has him say,

'Well if you're not busy and I'm not busy, there's a whole line of people waiting here who are busy. Why don't we let them go first, and you and I go to the back of the queue?'

Somehow he'd never had the courage to do this. It might turn simple fun into a lesser thing.

Woman

Erupting volcano
sealed universe
continuously flowing stream

unforgiving heaven
treacherous marsh
sky thrown open

term of all longing
sign of all craving
palace of secrets

erupting eternity
fertile desire
mystery that never dries

Cho Byunghwa (1921–2003)

INTERACTING

Korean women you know personally are invariably charming and kind, but women you don't know can be tough as nails. If you have to rent a house, avoid the woman owner. With the warmest of smiles she'll squeeze the last penny out of you. Unfortunately, Korean men know this very well, so invariably they send their wives to do the deal. Women police, women MPs, and women officials of all descriptions are sticklers for the letter of the law. Of course, there is nothing specifically Korean about this. Women officials in the West insist just as much on the letter of the law, but somehow Korean female charm leaves you unprepared for Korean female implacability. In the workplace women seem constrained to be more Confucian than their male counterparts, without understanding that Confucianism is supposed to free the spirit not strangle it. When you speak to them in Korean, they invariably answer in broken English. While a lot of men do this too, the numbers are not quite so damning

In the '70s and '80s, occasionally you met the regal *manim* type who swept into a room, calculatedly late, escorted by a large and noisy entourage. Her identity was unmistakable. I haven't seen this old style *manim* type for a very long time. She has a cousin I call the lesser *manim* type – you meet her frequently – who insists, with the greatest deference, on all the details of a schedule being done her way. You'll meet many lovely ladies in Korea. If you follow their directives, it's all wine and roses, but if you resist being bullied into doing things you don't want to do, you'll find yourself in trouble. I'm always in trouble because I try to follow the Yun Sŏndo model, which means not doing things I don't want to do.

Confucianism seeks to express itself in an inner freedom that enables people to transcend the conventional response. Freedom from your own ideas is the heart of enlightenment. But let's be fair; freedom from your own ideas is practically unknown among men or women, East or West. I, for one, have never managed to break free from mine.

Woman in Crisis

– Studies of women in history (6)

There were days
when I set the *paduk* board like a woman
but moved the counters like a man;
days when I scattered the seed like a woman
but reaped the harvest like a man;
days when I put down roots like a woman
but flowered like a man.
Like a man, then like a woman
I drew the bolt on the great main gate,
cut the ivy creeping over the wall.
Such perfect peace,

such perfect happiness!
There came a time
when my days of womanly love-dreaming
but manly living
splashed a black fearful augur
on the genial table of middle-age.
Wild-haired spectres feasted
within that augur of dark doom
and the fruits of love lay as a grave
in which a bloodstained moon was coffined.
Twilight shadows flickered in the distance –
the world's yardstick quivering in the stillness....
Why live, why live? The cry echoed on the riverbank.
A boat bobbed in the water
watched by a solitary woman.

Ko Chŏnghŭi (1948–1991)

NON-PERSON SADDLES HIS HORSE AND RIDES OFF IN ALL DIRECTIONS

There was a knock at the door of my apartment. I answered it myself. An officious looking lady, splendidly garbed in *hanbok* and armed to the teeth with documents, looked through me.

'No one at home!' she said.

'I'm home,' I said.

'Ah no,' she said, 'I mean someone I can communicate with.'

'What are we doing now?' I asked.

'You don't understand. Just sign here,' she said, reaching an important looking document under my nose.

'How can I sign if I'm not at home and don't understand?' I asked in my sweetest way.

She looked at me. I felt the thrill of success, the beginnings of *hŭng,* that quintessential buzz of excitement felt when the fish nibbles the bait. She was seeing me for the first time; puzzled, exasperated, but seeing. This was my cue to get annoyed.

'Mrs Kang,' I called into the kitchen. 'Could you come out here a minute? There's a lady here with something to be signed. She says I'm not at home, that I'm beyond communication. Would you deal with it? And when you're at it,' I added, 'tell her I'm glad I'm out, because were I at home, I'd feel obliged to give her a bit of my mind.'

Of course, my *ajumŏni* has no idea what I'm talking about. My sarcastic Irish barb is solely for my personal delectation.

Grass

Grass, summer grass,
dew drenched grass of Yoyogi fields,
gently, as if kissing a lover's lips,
I tread you with my bare feet.
Are you not truly the lips of the earth?

Should this, however, distress you,
I suggest that when I die
I turn to earth and go beneath your roots
to make you spring up high.
Should this still distress you,
I suggest that you and I,
animate as we are, each
walking the perimeters of immortality

shall meet again
on that eternal road.
Then you can become me and I you
and you can tread gently on me
as I now tread on you.

                              Namgung Pyŏk (1895–1922)

INTREPIDITY GETS IT WRONG

Women do not like being stereotyped and you can't blame them. The novelist, O Yŏngsu, stirred up a hornet's nest when he wrote about character traits of women on the basis of province of origin.

The traditional generalizations are, of course, outrageous; they reflect a male dominated world that no longer exists. Women find them very annoying, redolent of the worst kind of male chauvinism. Be warned: this is not ideal conversation at a dinner party. P'yŏng'an women are money conscious; their greed has brought ruin to many a family. Seoul women are *kkakjaengi*; they covet everything and think only of themselves. Pusan women lack guile and style. Kyŏngsang women are brusque and stubborn; they never contemplate compromise. Ch'ungch'ŏng women are slow but ladylike. Kangwŏn women are docile but dull of sensibility. Chŏlla women lack integrity but make great wives because they listen to their men and look after them. Of course, the men don't always respond in kind. Cho Yŏngnam's song 'Chŏlsang Province and Kyŏngna Province' is always greeted with howls of laughter. All that has been passed on is the accent.

LOVE AND MARRIAGE

You can't talk about Korean women very long without bringing up the topic of love. If you want to understand the politics of love, read the opening section of Hŏ Kyun's *Hong Kiltong*, Korea's Robin Hood romance from the Chosŏn dynasty. Minister Hong is in a welter of excitement after a dragon dream.

> My dragon dream portends the birth of a fine son, he thought. And though it was daytime, he rushed into the women's quarters. His wife rose to greet him. In his joy he took her hands and would feign have made love to her. The minister's wife frowned. 'Sir, you forget yourself. Such frivolous, base behaviour! I cannot comply,' she cried, and she removed her hands from his. The minister was most annoyed. Quite unable to contain his anger, he withdrew to the outer hall, deploring his wife's unwillingness.

Now it happened that the slave girl, Ch'unsŏm, was just about to serve tea. The minister looked at her, saw that her face was comely, took her by the hand into the next room and made love to her forthwith.

The passage records the begetting of Korea's very own Robin Hood.

Old Flame

The flame was stolen for a moment,
but while I basked in its heat,
I forgot the cares and fears of the world;
I was warm.

Thank you,
for everything you gave me;
also for the things you didn't.

Ch'oe Yŏngmi (1961–)

Marriage in Korea was traditionally a contractual business that ensured economic security and continuity of bloodlines. Love was not necessarily central. When it happened, wonderful, but love could always be found elsewhere. The old Korean adage was 'We marry our wives, but we love our concubines.' The sexes were separated at seven; strict segregation was practised. Kim Tonghwan paints a delightful picture of the politics of segregation in P'yŏngyang in the 1930s.

The Sin of a Smile

He asked for a short cut;
I told him the way.

He asked for a mouthful of water;
I drew him spring water from the well.

He thanked me:
I smiled.

Should the sun fail to rise over P'yŏngyang Fortress
surely the fault is not mine;
my only sin was a smile.

Kim Tonghwan (1901–?),

The last fifty years have seen a revolution in the way the sexes relate. In the 1960s and 1970s no girl would hold a boy's hand in public. Today subways and college campuses are filled with boys and girls kissing from first light. College girls today (and increasingly high school and middle school girls) are uneasy unless hanging on the arm of a boy. Korean women are asserting themselves not only in the love stakes but also in business, politics, art and sports. Power is gradually shifting from the old male elite to a new female elite. If women were subservient in Chosŏn, it is apparent that men will be (or perhaps already are) subservient in twenty-first century Korea. Turn on the TV. You will be amazed how often Korean women raise their voices in anger. In the old days they weren't supposed to do that. The substitution of one tyranny for another, of course, will hardly promote either an egalitarian society or unqualified happiness for the inhabitants.

Kashiri

'*Kashiri*' (Must you Go?) is one of Korea's great love songs. The word *kashiri* itself is such a lovely romantic word that limbs go limp and hearts beat fast when it is mentioned. Of course, no one treats it as a love song, much less a power song. It's more a second national anthem, except that no one knows the words or the tune. The magic is in the *kashiri* word.

Must you go, must you go,
must you leave me so?
Ah, *chŭng-jul-ga* the times are good now.

How can you leave
with a trite 'Fare thee well'?
Ah, *chŭng-jul-ga* the times are good now.

I should stop you, I know,
but you'd resent it so, you'd never return.
Ah, *chŭng-jul-ga* the times are good now.

So go, my brooding love,
go, but come right back.
Ah, *chŭng-jul-ga* the times are good now.

The girl begins by complaining about her lover leaving: 'Must you?' and 'How could you?' She believes she could stop him but concludes that stopping him would lead to so much resentment he might never return. In her wisdom, she sends him off with a tearful smile and urges him to come back as soon as he can. This, of course, is a Western interpretation. No Korean ever gave a single thought to what '*Kashiri*' is all about. For me, the song provides a stereotype of the woman who knows her own mind and tries to manipulate her husband/lover into doing things her way. There was an article in one of the English dailies a few years ago in which a woman talks about buying a nice present for her husband to mark Valentine's Day. She says she wants a nice present but not too nice because she doesn't want him to forget that she has not been too pleased with him recently. Eventually she decides the present will be to concoct a letter from a fictive girl friend, who professes her undying unrequited love. The letter, of course, sends the husband into a free-fall tizzy. It's an extraordinary gift, and an extraordinary exercise in psychological torture, which ends up with the woman innocently asking, 'Did I go too far?'

It Goes Without Saying

The beloved is not just the one you love; the beloved is the *all* you long for.

If all living things are the Buddha's beloved, then philosophy is Kant's beloved. If spring rain is the rose's beloved, Mazzini's beloved is Italy. Not only do I love the beloved, but the beloved loves me.

If love is freedom, the beloved is freedom. Is there not a fine restrictiveness in this lovely word freedom? Do you have a beloved? If you say yes, then you have not a beloved, you have the shadow of self.

I am a lost lamb, full of longing, wandering back from the darkling plain. In this spirit I write these poems.

Han Yong'un (1879–1944)

THE LIGHT OF HEAVEN

There's a lot of talk about love these days, but divorce rates in Korea are among the highest in the world. Women have been known to divorce husbands who failed in business. We are told it's about property rights and indebtedness, but you wonder. Marriage in Korea has a strong mathematical base. Romance is fine in theory but very often practicality is what counts. Young women prefer younger men, whom they imagine they can more easily control. One child is the norm in a household. Young men are becoming more feminine in their actions and looks, because – some say – they have been reared like princesses. The preference for male children is disappearing. Some young couples are choosing not to have children because of the economic burden that children generate, an attitude that was utterly unthinkable in traditional society. Men are much more openly loving to their children; I see them playing with their kids every day in my apartment yard. This is such a welcome, loving change from forty years ago! Men share chores in the kitchen, and parents are beginning to value living independently from their children. Again unthinkable in the recent past.

All this is the province of sociologists. My primary preoccupation is with the light of heaven, specifically with how culture reflects that light. You may recall that when Lee Myung-bak, then mayor of Seoul, tore down the 3.1 elevated highway, the idea was to let the light back into Ch'ŏnggyech'ŏn. An admirable conception indeed, but in executing the idea, he permanently stranded the citizens of Tongdaemun. The 3.1

was our main route downtown. I remember Ch'ŏnggyech'ŏn in the sixties. In the summer the stink was vile; whatever flowed there wasn't water. For years after the stream was covered over, there were little explosions. We used to joke about what's cooking in Ch'ŏnggyech'ŏn! I wonder did the mayor know of Se'o, the Shilla woman, who took the sun with her to Japan. And did he make a suitable offering before restoring the light to Ch'ŏnggyech'ŏn?

The Sun

In Shilla times, golden Shilla times
when Adala was king,
the sun clave to the loom of Se'o, wife of Yŏn'o,
for she was first to hang her heddles in the sky.
Wherever Se'o and her silk went,
the sun followed.
And because the people of Shilla knew this,
they followed Se'o when she rode the rock to Japan,
and they brought home a bolt of her silk.

Sŏ Chŏngju (1915–2000)

The bolt of silk was an offering to placate Heaven and have the sunlight restored.

Without the light of Heaven, we are told, nothing can begin in Korea. Women spend a lot of their lives in temples praying for light for themselves, their parents, their husbands, their sons, and their daughters. I hope the women of Ch'ŏnggyech'ŏn enjoy their restored light, but I will continue to moan about the gridlock the venture caused to those of us who live in Tongdaemun.

KOREAN WOMEN IN HISTORY

The first woman to catch the eye in Korean history is the Chinese wife of King Yuri, Koguryŏ's second monarch. The king went hunting one day and his queens fought in his absence.

Queen Zhiji, who was from Han China, was beside herself with rage – apparently Yuri's Korean queen had called her a foreign bitch. Zhiji promptly packed her bags and left for home. Yuri, back from the hunt, galloped after her but failed to persuade her to return. While resting in the shade of a tree, he saw orioles flying back and forth and composed his famous song.

Song of the Orioles

Fluttering orioles
cavort in pairs.
Who will go home
with this lonely man?

Yuri's bitter feelings, *han* to those acquainted with emotional bitterness in Korea, are mitigated somewhat for today's readers by the knowledge that the palace concubines would have been on red alert throughout that baleful night.

Paekche P'iri Pipe

No musical instrument evokes the spirit of Korea quite so beautifully as the p'iri pipe? In Sŏ Chŏngju's account, the p'iri is not an instrument for baring the soul; its music defines relationship.

Of all the variety of musical instruments –
bell, drum, and horn –
why on earth did King Ko'i choose the p'iri
for the proposed ritual offering to Heaven?
The p'iri is an instrument
with which a lover calls his beloved,
an instrument of single-minded,
plaintive ardour, played
when a fence separates lover and beloved,
not at all designed to bare the heart
to a universe that discounts the personal
in all its affairs.
The root of Paekch'e's failure to unite

the Three Kingdoms, it would seem,
was in that p'iri tune.

Sŏ Chŏngju (1915–2000)

LOVE IN SHILLA

Lady Suro is the most intriguing of Korea's ancient ladies. Her radiance was said to blow the mind of everything male in sight. She had a magnetic effect that pulled not only the Immortals from their chores in heaven but also the Dragon King from whatever he did in his lair under the East Sea. Lady Suro represents emotional and intellectual flexibility.

This is the same Suro who later achieved fame as the lady of the azaleas, the first great romantic in Korean poetry. Married to a bit of a boor, Lord Sunjong of Shilla, she knew she was flouting convention when she allowed the old man to tether his cow, climb the cliff, cut the azaleas and present them to her. A married woman accepting flowers from a man other than her husband was scandalous in the extreme! The old man, also contemptuous of the conventional response, reacts with the heart, demonstrating the essence of the Zen man. For Sŏ Chŏngju, at least, Lady Suro and the old man are models of the ideal modern Korean:

... the heart of a flower
that laughs when it sees a flower,
the heart of the unencumbered.

There was another Suro, Kim Suro, the founding king of Kaya, who was also famous for his ability to eschew the predictable response. Sŏ Chŏngju gives the story a modern twist:

Girl Getting Married

Hŏ Hwang'ok, on her way to be married to Kim Suro, the founding king of Kaya, took off her silk underwear and bowed to the mountain spirit. Obviously, the mountain spirit had been her lover. Kim Suro proffered not a word of blame, indicative that the Mountain Spirit had been a platonic lover like the wind among the pines or the breeze among the oaks. Or else Suro was one of those loving types of men who say, 'I'm not going to ask about a premarital affair with the mountain spirit!'

Sŏ Chŏngju (1915–2000)

Hwang'ok's deportment has not troubled the women of Korea. I imagine very few of them ever heard of her, and for the knowledgeable remnant, the myth that her lover was the Mountain Spirit takes care of any incipient guilt. Nor has another man bedding Ch'ŏyong's wife been a cause of national feminine disquiet either. Korea traditionally deals with Ch'ŏyong's problem by turning the adulterer into the spirit of the plague and making Ch'ŏyong a hero of forbearance.

Ch'ŏyong's Song (hyangga)

I revelled all night
in the moonlit capital,
came home and discovered
four legs in my bed!
Two are mine;
whose are the other two?
Legs once mine, now purloined,
what am I to do?

I never knew a Korean student who thought Ch'ŏyong's reaction was appropriate. The allegorical method has diminished Korean interpretations of literary crises ever since. In this case it sidesteps the notion that Korean women could be anything other than steadfast and pure. Shades of Ireland and the Playboy of the Western World!

I tinkered with the translation for years, until I found the word 'purloin.' Imagine, I thought, even Shilla has English words! With Norman roots!

The women of Shilla entertained deliciously romantic ideas. They seem to have been much more forward, carefree and creative than the women of Chosŏn, or even the women of today.

Getting Pregnant and Having Babies

There were some among
the women of early Shilla
who liked to swallow starlight
on the dark night road,
go home, share their bed
and get pregnant.
Ecstatic!

And when the baby came along,
the starlight scent, consumed ten months ago,
popped holes in the paper windows
like a thousand skylarks soaring in the sky.
What a prospect!

Sŏ Chŏngju (1915–2000)

Shilla women's sense of fair play and honour is quite remarkable. 'At the Rising of the Ch'usŏk Moon' is an extraordinary poem. Curiously, I've never known a Korean expert comment on it, favourably or otherwise. The difference in attitude must be in the lens through which we see the world

At the Rising of the Ch'usŏk Moon

At the rising of the Ch'usŏk moon
to the victors I say:
get not drunk on the victory feeling;
know, too, how to sorrow in the sorrow
of those you have vanquished.

And to the vanquished I say:
squat not with puckered foreheads;
rise up, dance, and sing.

But to those who in their sadness
know not to be sad, I say:
yours by right is the Ch'usŏk moon's light.

In old Shilla
at the rising of the Ch'usŏk moon
when the women wagered about
who could weave the most cloth,
it was the vanquished who rose first,
undulant in song and dance,
face to face in the moon's embrace,
escorted by the victors to the first place.

Sŏ Chŏngju (1915–2000)

LOVE IN KORYŎ

The sexiest lines in all Korean poetry are in the Koryŏ *kayo,*
'Spring Pervades the Pavilion:'

Spring Pervades the Pavilion *(Koryŏ kayo)*

The bed I make is bamboo leaves:
I spread them on the ice.
Though my love and I should freeze unto death,
slowly, slowly, pass this night
in love's enduring gentleness.

In 'Chŏngŭp sa,' the wife waits nervously for her merchant husband
to return. East Asian poetry is full of women climbing high rocks
to watch for their men. This woman – like most Korean women –
is very realistic: she worries, not without reason, that with money
in his pocket her man may fall into the fleshpots of the market
place. So she pleads with the moon to light his way home:

Chŏngŭp sa *(Koryŏ kayo)*

Moon,
rise high, rise high in the sky;
shine, shine, far and wide.

Is my man in the market place?
I fear he's mired in a sticky space.
Unburden yourself of all your gear.
Naught but night awaits me here.

'Song of P'yŏngyang,' one of the 'vulgar' Koryŏ songs that caught the censor's eye in the Chosŏn court is a terrific poem:

Song of P'yŏngyang *(Koryŏ kayo)*

P'yŏngyang,
P'yŏngyang, our first town.

Peaceful,
peaceful, the rebuilt fort.

I choose,
I choose, to leave the loom;

Love me,
love me, I'll follow in tears.

The pearls,
the pearls, they drop on the rock.

The string,
the string, will the pearl-string snap?

Alone,
alone, for a thousand years,

My faith,
my faith, will it disintegrate?

How broad
how broad, the Taedong River!

Boatman,
boatman, why do you sail?

Your wife,
your wife, don't you know what she craves?

You don't,
you don't, so you take my man.

Across,
across, sweet flowers bloom.

If he goes,
if he goes, he'll pluck those buds.

The P'yŏngyang girl's starting position is standard: she says she likes her life in the capital. What startles is her avowal that she is willing to forsake traditional securities for the love of a man. This is daring in the extreme. There's a lovely opposition between the claims of a settled life in the city and the excitement of the storms of love. The poem is filled with movement: the girl's willingness to leave P'yŏngyang, the flowing river, the boatman picking up passengers, the beloved about to embark. Movement reflects not just life's journey, but also the constant fluctuations of the heart: love and hate, joy and sorrow, serenity and anxiety. The certainty of the girl's love stands in sharp contrast to the uncertainty of the man's pledge. This is an archetypical theme. She says her love is so strong that she will not break faith, even if she is left alone for a thousand years. All, however, is not well. The love bond is tentative throughout. She never claims that the man she loves reciprocates her love. In fact, at this juncture, the beloved is not even listening. Already he is on the boat bound for the other side of the Taedong. In desperation, she turns her attention to the boatman. Does he not know, she asks, the sexual needs of his own wife? How can he take her man away? And then, almost by accident, she gets to her ultimate fear, rival flowers growing in profusion on the other side of the river: if her man goes, he will pluck those flowers! Husband or sweetheart, who knows?

This is not a song that persuades with cold logic. The feelings are universal, elemental: their tug is at the heart not the head; their vehicle is a rueful smile.

Most Korean women would be amazed to know that their ancestors were so forthcoming. You won't see a forty-year-old woman kissing her man in public. Public displays of affection are confined to TV advertisements or to young people on subway cars or school campuses or waiting at traffic lights and seem to be more an aping of Western ways than a demonstration of love and affection. Recently though I've been wondering have I got this wrong too? The way girls look deep into their boyfriends' eyes before belting them that ubiquitous Korean love thump – with or without the handbag – has me asking 'Could this be a relic from Koryŏ?' Never underestimate the foreigner's capacity to get the interpretation wrong!

LOVE IN CHOSŎN

Passion was the hallmark of Shilla and Koryŏ women. In Chosŏn, however, the pace of love appears to slow down and women and love find themselves on the back burner. This was inevitable in the wake of the blanket ban on passion imposed by Neo-Confucian ideology. The nature of Confucian class culture ensured that most women didn't make the records. With a few notable exceptions, those that are remembered were *kisaeng* or concubines.

HWANG CHINI

A special mystique surrounds Hwang Chini (1502–1540), the celebrated *kisaeng*-singer-poet of the sixteenth century. Her popular profile depicts her as a member of a despised class, a registered *kisaeng*. She associated freely with aristocrats, scholars, and artists and gained a reputation for defying social convention. She stands today as a symbol of art and the free spirit, a much admired woman who battled the odds to express her individuality.

I'll cut a piece from the waist (shijo)

I'll cut a piece from the waist
of this interminable eleventh moon night
and wind it in coils beneath these bedcovers, warm and
    fragrant as the spring breeze,
coil by coil
to unwind it the night my lover returns.

Hwang Chini (1502–1540)

The Hwang Chini myth sees her as a noble-minded, gracious, artistic lady, glamorizing what was a very inglorious profession. The myth is part of the drive to discover uniqueness in all things Korean. However, most Korean mothers would not want a daughter to be a *kisaeng*, and no scholar ever recorded a *kisaeng's* poems in his *munjip*. The status of the *kisaeng* was bottom of the ladder, and the *kisaeng* institution itself was constantly under fire both in Koryŏ and Chosŏn. It was tolerated because in providing sex for lusty bureaucrats it protected the daughters of the powerful. Kathleen McCarthy's excellent Harvard dissertation (1991) debunks much of the popular *kisaeng* myth. She points out that many records of *kisaeng* dalliance survive and that much of the activity was not related to music, dance or poetry. Here is Sŏ Chŏngju's version of the Hwang Chini myth.

Hwang Chini

Said Hwang Chini to her teacher Hwadam Sŏ Kyŏngdŏk,
you, sir, and I
are Kaesong's finest boast.
These many years by your side,
although I've been indecorous from time to time,
you never pinned me to your desire.
And if one other
can claim equality within our ranks,
surely it must be Pag'yŏn Falls
with its cool, constant, cascading splash.

Was Hwang Chini's pronouncement made wholly in jest?
I think not: I think she meant what she said.

Hwang Chini flitted through the land
like a fairy who had lost her cloth wings –
to Kŭmgangsan, to T'aebaeksan, to Chirisan;
and when in Chŏlla Province she sat among
the guests at the Governor of Naju's feast,
such her outrageous composure
that before she recited a poem,
or twanged the *kŏmung'o*, or sang a note,
she cracked the fleas in her clothes,
indicative of a poetic self-assurance
that affirmed indubitably
she meant what she said to Hwadam.

Sŏ Chŏngju (1915–2000)

SHINSAIMDANG (1512–1559)

Shinsaimdang, mother of Yi Yulgok, the great Confucian
scholar, was a poet, an artist and an all round cultivated woman.
The few poems that are credited to her are not wildly exciting, but her butterfly and insect paintings are highly praised.
For most Koreans she is a symbol of the best in Korean wom-
anhood, but she has her detractors, too, who say she comes
up short by Confucian standards because she lived at home
for twenty years after marriage without looking after her husband's household, which contravened prevailing mores. Other
commentators, however, quickly point out that it was the norm
for a woman to stay with her parents after marriage until her
children were reared and only then go to her husband's house.
Detractors go on to say Yulgok was her only child to achieve
distinction and that she didn't promote her husband's career
either. What exactly she could have done to promote her husband's career is not clear, but evidently she was not your typical
Confucian helpful wife type. She concentrated on developing

her own abilities at a time when a woman was expected to obey her father, then her husband, and in old age her son. Society did not look kindly on this kind of precocious individuality even though today it is valued highly. Some women's organizations opposed her face adorning the fifty thousand wŏn note on the grounds that she was being honoured as a wife and mother and didn't have matching credentials. Of course the Confucian vision of ideal wife is at odds with the modern wife image, which was imported into Korea from Meiji Japan at the end of the nineteenth century. Shinsaimdang's symbolic status today owes more to the imported modern wife image than to the traditional Confucian outstanding wife image.

Thoughts of My Mother *(hanshi)*

Home is a thousand *li* away
across studded mountain peaks;
even in dreams I can't get there.
Full moon on the lake at Hansŏng Pavilion;
wind fresh off the sea at Kyŏngp'o;
white cranes light on the sand and fly away again;
fisher boats come and go across the water.
When will I walk the Kangnŭng Road again?
I wish I were sitting at my mother's knee,
making rainbow baby jackets.

Shinsaimdang (1512–1559)

HŎ NANSŎRHŎN (1563–1589)

Hŏ Nansŏrhŏn belonged to one of the most distinguished literary families in Chosŏn. Unhappy in marriage, she expressed her loneliness and frustration in her poems. In the tradition of Chosŏn *yangban* women, she burned all her poems before her death. Her brother, Hŏ Kyun, working from letters and memory, compiled the first edition of her poems, which was published in China. Charges of plagiarism have been levelled against her, but such charges are difficult to substantiate in view of the fact that her brother edited the volume. Two of her best poems, regarded as too risqué to be printed in the front of the volume, are relegated to an appendix at the end.

To My Lord Reading in His Study *(hanshi)*

In pairs the sparrows fly the angle under the eaves;
falling leaves plop on my silk robe.
From the bridal I see as far as the eye can see: sick at heart,
for though all is green, my Kangnam love does not return.

Picking Lotus Seeds *(hanshi)*

The long lake was autumn fresh, the water blue as jade;
I tied my boat deep within the lotus lushness.
I saw my love across the water; I tossed him lotus seeds.
Half the day I spent in shame, afraid I might have been seen.

Hŏ Nansŏrhŏn (1563-1589)

Interesting poems to have been written by a woman who didn't get on with her husband!

YI OKPONG (?–1592)

Yi Okpong, the illegitimate daughter of a *yangban*, was an excellent *hanshi* poet. Her poems are filled with the loneliness of the concubine, a status inevitably imposed on her by her parentage.

The Heart of a Lonely Woman *(hanshi)*

A lifetime of parting's bitterness breeds sickness in the body,
unalleviable with wine, untreatable with medicine.
Tears flow under the bedclothes like water under ice.
Night and day the river flows; no one ever knows.

The Sorrow of Parting *(hanshi)*

Tomorrow night when my love is gone,
let the night be as short as it wants;

but tonight when my love is here
let it be as long as it can be.
The cock crows, a new day dawns;
from my eyes flow idle tears.

Yi Okpong (?–1592)

YI MAECH'ANG (1573–1610)

Yi Maech'ang was one of Chosŏn's outstanding *kisaeng*. She was famed not so much for her physical beauty as for her skill in poetry and the *kŏmun'go*.

Autumn Thoughts *(hanshi)*

Last night there was a sharp frost;
wild geese complained in the autumn sky.
The wife, busy fulling her husband's clothes,
suddenly apprehensive, climbed the terrace.
Gone to the ends of the earth
and not a single letter!
Alone she leans on the high balustrade,
bound by the darkness of fear.

Yi Maech'ang (1573–1610)

Rhododendron

Sŏ Chŏngju's 'Rhododendron' is perhaps Korea's finest poem on the loneliness of the concubine's life:

A mountain
in each red petal

On the mountain
a concubine, sad, asleep

Outside her door
a brass chamber pot

Across the mountain
the sea at full tide

A seagull cries
for salt burned feet.

Sŏ Chŏngju (1915-2000)

CH'AE CHEGONG'S MOTHER

Not all Korea's noteworthy women were as unfortunate in marriage as Nansŏrhŏn. The mother of Ch'ae Chegong (1720–1799), a famous prime minister of Chosŏn, was one of the outstanding women of the Chosŏn dynasty. The story is told that her betrothed died a few days before the wedding. Custom decreed that she must let her hair down and begin mourning. She must join her betrothed's household and forego marriage completely. Her family bid her follow the time-honoured custom, but she refused adamantly. 'Why should I let my hair down,' she cried, 'and mourn a man whose face I've never seen?' Her household responded with the traditional lament, 'We're ruined, we're ruined.' Her father took to his bed and refused to eat or drink, whereupon she ran to the gates of the palace and blocked the palanquin of a minister of state. When the great man demanded to know why she was blocking his palanquin, she told him the whole story and asked him to bring her case to the king. 'Why, she asked, 'should I be forced to follow such an outrageous custom? Ask the king,' she said. 'You can give me his answer when you come back. I'll wait here.'

'Very good,' the great lord replied.' He didn't know what else to say. He had listened to the girl's story from beginning to end, his eyes trained on distant mountains; he could hardly believe his ears.

During the morning audience with the king, various matters were discussed. Eventually the minister brought up the subject of the girl at the palace gates. 'She sounds like an extraordinary girl,' the king said, 'and what she says makes sense. Make an exception so that she can get married.'

On the way out of the palace the minister of state informed the girl of the king's decision. She ran to her father's bedside. 'Are you going to defy the king's command?' she demanded. Her father, needless to say, relented and arranged another marriage for his formidable daughter. On her wedding day, once again she failed to follow the rules of propriety. She went from table to table, sampling all the dainties and delicacies. Her mother-in-law was appalled. We've brought a terrible example of humanity into our house, she thought. It's the end of all decorum. Ruin stared her in the face. But with the passage of time none of the mother-in-law's fears was realized. She discovered that her daughter-in-law was indeed a priceless jewel. The household prospered. The mother-in-law was profuse in her praise. In due time the daughter-in-law gave birth to a son who was destined to be prime minister under Chŏngjo. The prime minister's mother lost none of her sassiness with the passage of the years.

The Music of What Happens

Three countrywomen, basins
balanced on their heads, float
across the dyke between the paddies,
their passage the rhythm strummed
by an ancient Chinese poet
on a stringless lyre:
the essence of song,
the cadence of what endures,
the music of what happens.

LADY IMMORTAL STRIKES OUT BOLDLY: THE YEAR OF THE RAT

It was raining heavily. The *ajumŏni* struggled with her umbrella as she tried to get into the taxi. Finally she made it, rain dripping everywhere. The taxi driver looked in the rear mirror.

'You've lived in the US, *ajumŏni*,' he said.

'How do you know?' she parried. 'Are you a *chŏmjaengi* (fortune teller)?'

'Matter of fact, I am,' he answered. 'I'm right, am I not? You've lived in the US. When were you born?'

'Year of the rat.'

'Ah, 1960.'

'No, '48 actually, she said, purring now for being taken to be so young.

'How about your husband?'

''44.'

'Ah, year of the monkey. Rat and monkey, not great.'

'Everyone says rat and monkey get on fine together.'

The driver looked in the mirror again.

'Well, it's not really a great combination, but your face tells me your husband is a lucky man.'

'Why's that?'

'You share your blessings. You have a daughter, haven't you? She lives in America; you ought to live with her.'

'Why?'

'It would be good for her. She'd get all your blessings. Of course, it wouldn't do you a lot of good; your daughter would take all your good joss, but that's another story. Your eyebrows are very striking, you know. You have a face swimming in good fortune. If you hadn't married your present husband, you'd have been a very wealthy woman. Two husbands and lots of money.'

'What's so great about two husbands?'

'Well, it's better than being stuck with one all your life. Your husband should give thanks every day he wakes up,' he added.

'I think he does,' she said demurely.

They had reached the *ajumŏni's* destination in Miari. The fare was 4,800 wŏn. She gave the driver 10,000 wŏn. 'Keep the change,' she said. 'It's been a great pleasure being driven by you.'

'Thank you,' the driver said.

The driver was a very smart operator. At this rate of going, sweet-talking every *ajumŏni* in Seoul, he'd make double fare all day long. Imagine the husband's reaction that evening when his wife, as she inevitably would, told him about her exciting taxi driver. 'That's just great,' he'd say. 'You're on the town all day, enjoying yourself, being sweet-talked by taxi drivers, while I stay here on my own! And when you get back in the evening,

I'm supposed to say, "Thank you so much!" It's a very unfair world.'

For an Unidentified You

When I'm fast, fast asleep,
knock gently on my door.

When I turn in my sleep,
silently caress my breasts.

Then toe by toe
wake up all my sleeping cells.

And I'll get up
and teach you
how the stench of the void rises
from the red tape of human intercourse,
how the dark galleries of the blood
twist within the temple of culture,
how joy coils within single-minded abstinence,
how my roots wrap and wet you
with the sprung-from-death
sap of the sensual.
Yes, I'll get up
and teach you.

Ch'oe Sŭngja (1952–)

KIM TALLAE FROM TAEGU

In the 1940s a crazy woman called Kim Tallae from Taegu used to wander stark naked through the streets of Pusan. She was an institution in the city, so popular with police and citizenry that even casual passers-by rushed to see her perform. When she got on a tram, the seats near her – no matter how many passengers crowded aboard – were left vacant. And when she danced in the market, people lined up to watch. In the middle of the dance, if she spied something appetizing, she bounded across to where the item was on display and grabbed it. The owner of the stall would scream '*Aigume!*' and try to cover his merchandise with his arms, but he was never quick enough to stop her from getting her heart's desire. At the end of the performance, belly replete, she wiped her lips and disappeared.

Maybe she wasn't quite as crazy as she seemed. At least she kept herself fed.

Love

Love is
rooting out a fruit tree that doesn't bear fruit,
removing all the bugs from the clay around the rotting root,
then digging deep into loam moistened by sweaty hands
and planting the new seedling.

And on a night darker than the heart of a stone,
through the bitterness of wind and rain,
through the swallowing dark,
it is sitting through that dark, that night
guarding, protecting
until the bright dawn spreads
and the new seedling cuts through the sunlight
to come forth sprinkling light like water from a well.

Chŏn Ponggŏn (1928–1988)

ON THE SUBWAY

A well dressed *ajumŏni*, late fifties, got on the train at Hanshin Station. The man with her, presumably her husband, pointed to the seat reserved for senior citizens, pregnant women, and the infirm.

'Sit there,' he said.

At the next station an *ajŏsshi* got on. He was followed by an old man. The *ajŏsshi* had had a few drinks. He made a beeline for the *ajumŏni*.

'Get up, *ajumŏni*,' he said.

The *ajumŏni's* husband was a bit annoyed by a stranger speaking to his wife at all much less in this tone. She's a '*halmŏni*,' he said. 'Leave her alone.'

The *ajŏsshi*, completely unfazed, turned to the *ajumŏni*.

'What age are you, *ajumŏni? Todaech'e*, what age?' The *ajumŏni* was now smiling, happy to be taken for considerably younger than she was. 'Do I have to tell you my age?' she asked sweetly. 'I'm a granny,' she added.

'*Ani*,' he began. Now that '*ani*' word is really untranslatable. Suffice it to say that it contained a lot of personal frustration and disbelief and a painful history of looking at healthy young women occupying senior citizens' seats on subway cars. '*Ani*,' he said, 'What do you mean a granny; *todaech'e* what age are you?' Again the *todaech'e* for exasperated emphasis.

In the meantime, another *ajumŏni*, let's call her *ajumŏni* B, was telling her life story to *ajumŏni* A; a complete account of husband, children, in-laws, everything. *Ajumŏni* A had no idea why she was being favoured with all these confidences. She was obviously the kind of reserved woman who didn't talk to anyone on subway cars. Incredulity and amusement were written across her face. This was turning out to be a very strange day, but she had to admit she was enjoying herself. It wasn't every day she had the honour of having years carved off her age. Even her husband was amused at this stage. Upon reflection, he now liked the idea of being married to a young woman again.

The drunken *ajŏsshi* persisted. 'What age, *ajumŏni*?'

He had asked once too often. *Ajumŏni* B now took offence. After all she was recounting several life histories and she resented the untimely interruptions. '*Ani*,' she began. (Note that untranslatable '*ani*' word again; it often means trouble.)

'What's it to you what age she is,' she said tartly. 'Can't a woman sit down when she's tired?'

Ajumŏni B followed the initial volley with a scathing tirade, much of it quickly dipping to low form speech, which soon had the poor *ajŏsshi* spluttering, close to apoplexy.

The old man who had occasioned the altercation, fortunately, was as deaf as a beetle. He had no idea his existence had caused a major squabble. He smiled at everyone in the carriage, and everyone smiled at him. Needless to say, he was delighted when the lovely *ajumŏni* A rose from her seat and offered it to him. He refused three times as Confucian decorum demanded before gladly acceding.

The train pulled into the next station. The irate *ajŏsshi and* the doubly irate *ajumŏni* got off together as if no angry word had passed between them. The old man stayed on. He had never seen the *ajŏsshi* before in his life!

Three old men sitting opposite began a discussion on the rights and wrongs of the episode. True to the spirit of Confucian orthodoxy, they agreed that young people should give their seats to the elderly, and true to the spirit of modern democratic thinking, they agreed that women should sit down when they were tired.

Another *ajumŏni, Ajumŏni* C, we'll call her, addressed *Ajumŏni* A. 'Did you know that woman?' she asked. 'Never saw her before in my life,' *Ajumŏni* A answered.

'Why all the talk then?'

Ajumŏni A could offer no word of explanation.

Passing Map'o Market

No Shinsaimdang this lady! Dressed in flowing hanbok she raised a fluent hand to smite with his own cucumber an errant vending man.

What sin had provoked such towering rage? Frosted greens, inflated prices, infernal cheek?

What matter! The lesson was clear: the cucumber in her hand mushed forever the myth that woman is something less than man.

Years from Now

Should you come to me
years from now,
I shall say: I have forgotten.

Should you scold me,
I shall say: after much longing I have forgotten.

Should you persist in scolding me,
I shall say: for lack of trust I have forgotten.

Not yesterday, not today
but years from now
I shall say: I have forgotten.

Kim Sowŏl (1902–1934)

13

TALES OF THE IMMORTALS

Among the Immortals

These I list in the pantheon:
Chŏng Mongju, back to front on his horse;
Tanjong, the boy king, going toward the stars;
Yu Kwan, hands up umbrellaed in the rain;
Kim Shisŭp floating verses downstream;
Wŏlmyŏng, the monk, piping down
the lady on the moon;
Yi Sunshin fighting death's crazy swoon.

What's in a Name?

Myŏngnimŏsu, literally the gargler from the house of Myŏngnim,
was prime minister in Koguryŏ (230–254).

My name is nothing special:
it simply means the good gargler.
In the morning I wash in the stream,
fill my mouth with water,
spew it high in the sky
and greet the rising sun
with a flash of laughing teeth.
People liked this,
so they called me the gargler.
In Chinese it is written *myong-nim-ŏ-su,*

the gargler from the house of Myŏngnim.
I have no other exceptional skill
– once, though, I was prime minister.

Sŏ Chŏngju (1915–2000)

The King's Pride

Chidaero of Shilla's thingamajig – if you allow for a little fictive embellishment – was a foot and a half long, posing a major worry to the realm, for neither in mountain, nor field, nor by the sea, nor sequestered on any remote island was a girl to be found capable of withstanding the king's pride. Lo! one winter's day under an old withered tree – this too with a little fictive embellishment – a dung patty big as an hourglass drum was found. It had been made with such zest and whoopee that though two mongrels tug o' warred and devoured the prize, a sufficiency remained to attest to its magnificent original size. Who had left this giant patty? The question was asked in every corner of every village until finally a diminutive little girl came forward. 'The one you seek lives over there,' she said. 'Wasn't there a stream beside the patty,' she added, 'a lovely little stream? Well, the girl you want took her washing there, and when she had washed more than a hundred pieces, she went into the woods and that's what she made.'

The king paired with the patty maker and they produced an heir of the thought making capabilities of King Pophŭng who was indeed beautifully, beautifully made.

(Based on a Sŏ Chŏngju poem)

Kwŏn Kim

In the time of King Kongyang of Koryŏ, Kwŏn Kim from Hoeyang had a tummy so round that it became a symbol of solidity and trust to his wife. When Kwŏn Kim was attacked by a tiger, his wife stuck her bum against the jamb of the gate, wrapped her arms around her husband's tummy and refused to budge. The tiger was forced to flee. Kwŏn Kim, sadly, died next day of his injuries. Afterwards, on nights when Kwŏn Kim's wife found it impossible to sleep, she gently hugged the round tummy of a green celadon jar.

(Based on a Sŏ Chŏngju poem)

HOW CHŎNG MONGJU DIED

Chŏng Mongju (1337–1392), one of the great romantics of old Korea, was a loyal Koryŏ retainer, synonymous in Korean hearts with courage and fidelity. Yi Pangwŏn, the son of Yi Sŏnggye, the founder of the Chosŏn dynasty, and a central figure in the intrigue to set up the new dynasty, gave a banquet for key political figures in order to gauge their loyalty. His poem to Chŏng Mongju offered friendship and an alliance. Chŏng's answer is legendary, as is his courage in the face of death. First, Yi Pangwŏn's invitation:

What about living this way *(shijo)*

What about living this way,
what about living that way?
What about arrowroot vines intertwining on Mansusan?
Intertwined,
we could spend a hundred years in joy.

Chŏng Mongju replied:

Tanshim ka – Song of a red-blooded heart *(shijo)*

Though my body die and die again,
though it die a hundred deaths,
my skeleton turn to dust, my soul exist or no,
what could change
the red-blooded, undivided loyalty of this heart toward My
    Lord?

Chŏng Mongju knew that his days were numbered. He went to a friend's house with the intention of getting filthy drunk. The lovely Korean idiom is *tŏrŏpgye* (dirty) drunk. Sŏ Chŏngju tells the story:

> He went among the flowers,
> calling again and again for wine,
> which he drank in great double draughts:
> he drank it all, he drank it alone.
> And when the wine mood came
> and his shoulders dipped in the dance,
> he told his secretary to withdraw
> and he walked with teetering steps
> to Straight Bamboo Bridge
> where he was struck by the waiting iron club
> that sent him to his death.

Tourists in Kaesong note that the bridge where Chŏng Mongju met his fate is flecked with the blood of the martyr.

Yi Sŏnggye's Heaven

When Yi Sŏnggye, the founding king of Chosŏn, shot that arrow at his son, T'aejong, who was leaning against the tent pole, and when he saw the arrow miss its mark and lodge in the pole, he cried, 'It is the will of Heaven.' And when it was T'aejong's turn to grace the royal presence and offer a cup of wine, and the old king saw his wily son send another in his stead, he took out the murderous bar hidden in his sleeve and cried in a tone of resignation, 'This too is the will of Heaven.' Thus it was only with the greatest difficulty that T'aejong's right of succession was recognized. Yi Songgye's idea of the 'will of Heaven' has a flavour all its own.

(Sŏ Chŏngju 1915–2000)

DOGS FIGHTING IN MUDDY FIELDS

Yi Sŏnggye, the founder of Chosŏn, asked Chŏng Tojŏn, his finest theorist in Neo-Confucian ideology, to describe the character traits of the people of the eight provinces. Chŏng Tojŏn warmed to his task:

Seoul: Beauties reflected in a mirror
Ch'ungch'ŏng: Clear wind and bright moon
Chŏlla: Willows shaking in the wind
Kyŏngsang: Loyal as pine and bamboo
Kangwŏn: Old Buddhas under a rock
Hwanghae: Stones thrown into spring waves
P'yŏng'an: Tigers in mountain forests

That left Yi Sŏnggye's home province, Hamgyŏng. Chŏng Tojŏn hesitated. The king commanded him to speak forthwith. Very reluctantly, Chŏng Tojŏn said:

Hamgyŏng: Dogs fighting in muddy fields
The king was not pleased.
Chŏng Tojŏn made a second attempt.
Hamgyŏng: Oxen plowing stony fields.
Yi Sŏnggye smiled.

Sejong and His Two Brothers

While Prince Yangnyŏng was still officially crown prince in virtue of being T'aejong's first born son, the opinion was mooted that his claim to the throne should be voided because he was such a wastrel; whereupon his younger brother, Hyoryŏng, believing that the right of succession was now his, proceeded to behave impeccably and to devote himself to study. Yangnyŏng swung a kick at Hyoryŏng as he passed him one day. 'You miserable wretch,' he cried, 'Ch'ungnyŏng is the next king. Any fool should know that.'

Such was Hyoryŏng's fury that he sped like an arrow to a mountain top temple where he raged all day with both fists on the drum that hung in the pavilion decking the main gate, till the skin of the drum became a ghost with mugwort crazy hair.

It seems to me that this was more than enough proof of Hyoryŏng's qualifications for kingship. Things did not work out so.

The third son, Ch'ungnyŏng, who stayed quiet throughout the affair, became king, Sejong by name, proving that in these situations not doing anything is best of all.

Sŏ Chŏngju (1915–2000)

THE NAMING OF SHIKSADONG

When Yi Sŏnggye deposed King Kongyang, the last monarch of Koryŏ, the deposed king and his queen fled by night to a hermitage and hid there.

In fear of General Yi Sŏnggye, the monks moved the royal couple to a village which had a lotus pond surrounded by heavy thickets – present day Shiksadong – and they brought food every day to the royal couple.

One day the king and queen left their shoes side by side on the bank of the pond and drowned themselves.

Smile of the Ever-ready

The honourable Yu Kwan,
prime minister to Sejong,
lived in such poverty
that his roof leaked.
Whereupon he cupped his hands
into an umbrella to stop the flood
and called his wife with loud peals of laughter.
'A house without this umbrella
would be truly sad, you must agree?'
To which his wife replied:
'A house without a good hand-umbrella
might borrow your glorious laughter peals
and use them instead.'

Sŏ Chŏngju (1915–2000)

DEAD AS LIVING

Yi Sunshin (1545–1598) was the famous Korean admiral who invented the turtle ship and defeated numerically superior

Japanese forces in a series of naval battles during the Hideyoshi Wars. The admiral meditates on the lonely responsibilities of the commander-in-chief. Some doubt has been cast on the authorship of the poem, but in the hearts of the Korean people, it will always be associated with the redoubtable admiral.

The moon is bright tonight. I sit alone (shijo)

The moon is bright tonight. I sit alone
in the lookout on Hansan Island,
my great-sword slung at my side, my spirit deeply troubled.
From somewhere
the shrill note of a pipe cuts into my heart.

Sŏ Chŏngju tells the story of the admiral's last moments:

Admiral Yi Sunshin, while personally beating the drum that encouraged his troops in battle, was stricken by an arrow fired from the bow of a Japanese sniper, and as he lay close to death, he left these final words:

'You must not reveal that I am dead.
Stand in line, screen my dead body and fight.'
What a marvellous picture of a man in death continuing
forever his undying livingness. As if the final tum-tum-tum of
the drum went on and on and on in eternal reverberation.

The Colour White

Professors will explain the colour white in terms of social rank, the expense of importing dyes and so on, but Sŏ Chŏngju gives a much richer explanation in 'The Story of Korean White Clothes.'

Clothes are women's work. The first clothes for our people were made by the first woman of our people, the bear girl, Tan'gun's mother. After giving birth to our first king, Tan'gun, she set about making the baby's clothes, consulting with her husband

Hwan'ung as she went along. Hwan'ung said, 'Please, not a colour that elicits groans of shame. Look,' he said, 'for a colour that doesn't bawl and cry, look for one that always smiles with grace and dignity. Remember you had to endure the bitter taste of mugwort and the pungent taste of garlic before your belly rounded and you gave birth to the baby who is to wear these clothes.' Hwan'ung's wife, the bear woman, smiled like a white gourd flower and said: 'Well then, black, red, blue, and yellow won't do. I believe it'll have to be white.' Whereupon Hwan'ung said, 'White is good. After all, the sky is white too. It just seems blue by day and black by night because it is so far away.'

Sŏ Chŏngju (1915–2000)

The Toe of the Pŏsŏn and Komushin

You may be wondering about the curve in the toe of Korean traditional thick socks (*pŏsŏn*), or why rubber shoes (*komushin*) curve at the toe, or why roof lines in Korea differ from those in Japan and China.

The story goes that when Tan'gun's father and mother were discussing the clothes the baby should wear, a pair of cranes flew into sight and perched, necks stretched, side by side, on the gracefully extended branch of an old pine tree. Tan'gun's mother watched the birds dance their bobbing dance and fly off again into the sky. She noted the elegant curve of their wings, graceful and dignified in flight. Now that's the curve for the toes of the baby's *pŏsŏn* socks, she thought. And that's how the curved toe began. Subsequently, the lovely curve of the wings of two cranes flying with supreme grace though the unbounded sky was taken from the *pŏsŏn* and applied to the old wooden clogs our ancestors wore. Sometime later this design was applied with fluid elegance to the twin eaves of our old tile roofs. And afterwards the Chinese and the Japanese came, saw and imitated.

Sŏ Chŏngju (1915–2000)

THE FORGOTTEN IMMORTAL, JAMES SCARTH GALE

James Scarth Gale (1863–1937), linguist, historian, translator, commentator, Korea's more than Lafcadio Hearne, was the first great interpreter of the Korean mind to the English-speaking world. What distinguished Gale from Hearne was that he was much more than essay writer and commentator; Gale was a scholar and his language skills far outshone those of Hearne. His fluency in Korean was said to be remarkable; he wrote extensively in the language. He helped write the first grammar and the first dictionary. He wrote the first history and he translated widely. *Kuunmong* (The Nine Cloud Dream), Chosŏn's great symbolic novel, was perhaps his greatest translation achievement, but he also translated *hanshi, shijo, kasa* and contemporary vernacular literature. Gale also worked tirelessly to translate the bible into Korean. He had several secretaries who presumably did a lot of the work. Some of his contemporaries did not take kindly to his free translation style. I have seen his English prose criticized but never his Korean prose, which in itself is an interesting comment on Korean innate kindness and foreign natural meanness. He always said: translate paragraphs not phrases and lines. It is such good advice, at odds, of course, with the literal academic approach to translation that prevails in Korea to this day, inevitably so since most translators work into their second language. Gale's way, however, is much more likely to produce a work of literature.

Gale was no armchair scholar. Numerous times he travelled the length and breadth of the peninsula, invariably by pony, sharing food and lodgings with Koreans wherever he went. This was his way to experience culture at the deepest level. His stories on inns, fleas, vicious ponies and fun encounters on the road make hilarious reading. These sketches, however, sometimes strike a patronizing note, what I call the colonial missionary tone, as if he were constantly amused by the antics of the natives, an attitude and an idiom that is a bit off-putting today. You find the same tone in Allen's *Things Korean*. This may be part of the reason Gale was branded as pro-Japanese – *ch'inil* – the ultimate badge of contempt and dishonour in Korea. It was such an unwarranted slur on a man who loved every inch of Korea and whose greatest sin was that he shared the view of many of his fellow missionaries that Japan was necessary for Korea's industrial development.

Have you ever wondered why Sunday in Korean should be sun-shining-day and Monday moon-shining day and why the names of the rest of the days of the week come from the five elements? Gale explained it in an article in 'Korea Magazine', June 1918, pp. 253–255. Note his distinctive Romanization style.

In the year 1573 the Ming Government of China gave a special name to the reign of Sin-jong Mal-lyuk (Universal Calendar). Why such a name? The writers doubtless chose it simply as a suitable combination for good luck not dreaming that in nine years' time it would find a peculiar fulfilment in the arrival of Matteo Ricci, the Catholic Father who came bringing what was to be the Universal Calendar (1582 AD) of the world, and Western astronomical knowledge. China had evidently known the five planets from far distant ages and had them named long before the Christian era, Mercury, the Water Star (Soo-sung); Venus, the Metal Star (Keum-sung); Mars, the Fire Star (Wha-sung); Jupiter, the Wood Star (Mok-sung); and Saturn the Earth Star (T'o-sung). Thus it came about that the five Roman-Greek divinities had the names of the Five Elements apportioned to them. Later in the forming of the names of the days of the week this order was followed. Our Christian forefathers, it seems, had no special names for these and for lack of better fell into the habit of using the same names as their non-Christian country-men taken from the divinities of the old Germanic peoples. They called the first day Sunday which has now become translated Il yo il Sun-shining-day; Monday, Wul-yo-il, Moon-shining-day; Tuesday, from Tiw, the Scandinavian God of War, corresponding to Mars, Wha-yo-il (fire-shining-day), Fire being Mars' symbol.

We see the name Mars still in the French name mardi. Wednesday, or Woden's Day, Woden being the God of storms, corresponding to Mercury, was named Soo-yo-il, Water being the symbol decided on for Mercury. This name still is seen in the French mercredi. Thursday, or Thor's Day, Thor being equal to Jupiter, whose symbol is Wood, was named Mok-yo-il, Wood-shining-day. Friday or Freya's Day, she being the corresponding divinity to Venus, was called Keum-yo-il Metal-shining-day. Saturday still retains its old Roman-Greek name Saturn's Day, and was T'o-yo-il, Earth-shining-day. Hence it comes that we get our names in the following order il, wul, wha, soo, mok, keum, t'o.

Do you know them? If not, learn them. The Christians today, in the outlying country districts, say ye-pai-il, ye-pai-i, ye-pai-sam, just as the Christians did in the early days of the church, but assuredly, as the early Christians had to discard these as unsatisfactory, so it will come to pass here and we shall have il-yo-il, wul-yo-il, etc. used just as our names are with us.

It is not necessary to add that these names as decided on by the astronomers of the Mings made their way to Japan, and from Japan Proper they now make their way to Korea. (J. S. Gale)

FIDDLING IMMORTAL STRIKES A MAGIC NOTE

There were two brothers in Hamgyŏng Province, unusual men in that both were singularly un-Confucian in everything they did. The elder brother got a guitar in a deal of which the details are not clear except that he would never have had enough money to pay for the instrument. Inside three days the untutored younger brother was able to knock a tune out of it, much to the delight not to say surprise of the older brother. The younger brother, however, was interested in the violin not the guitar, so he availed of the first opportunity to take the guitar to an instrument store and swap it for a violin. The elder brother asked, 'Where's my guitar?' to which the younger brother replied, 'It changed into a fiddle.'

The younger brother took up the violin and soon was adept at the current crop of popular *kayo* or Japanese songs. In the meantime the Korean War broke out. In advance of the war, however, the younger brother came south. The war found him in Pusan, which was full of American camps and American soldiers. Musicians were at a premium. The young fiddler was in constant demand. Unfortunately the only Western tune he could play was 'When Irish Eyes Are Smiling.' Once he was booked to play a gig with his band and a team of dancers. Of course, he had no dancers and not much of a band, but he went anyway because he needed the money. After ten variations of 'When Irish Eyes Are Smiling,' the GIs were getting restless. They all had carbines and pistols, and every song request was accompanied by a volley of shots through the ceiling. The fiddler was scared out of his wits. He felt he could be shot at any moment. So with native guile, he approached a sergeant who had his head buried in his hands. 'You'll be my manager,' he said. It didn't occur to him to ask the sergeant why he had his head in his hands. Nor did it occur to him that it could be because of the awful music and the lack of dancing girls. A little later he came back to the sergeant and said, 'Give us our money.' The sergeant looked at him with total disdain. 'Get lost, you crooked *guk*. You can neither play, sing or dance,' he said, sticking his revolver in the fiddler's belly. The fiddler took to his heels.

The fiddler took no offence at the blatantly racist insult. He was quick to point out that after these gigs his pockets were always full of dollars. Stinginess was not a GI vice.

Plum Blossom *(hanshi)*

The white flower blooms under an icy sky;
the citrine fruit plumps out in fine rain.
A brother's entire life I see before me;
comes so early, lingers so late.

Kang Hŭian (1417–1464)

IMMORTAL COMES TO DUBLIN

Sŏ Chŏngju came to Dublin in 1995 for the launch of *Poems of a Wanderer*, a selected poems volume published by Dedalus. I found the great man sitting with his wife behind two pints of Guinness in Jury's Hotel in Ballsbridge, a picture of contentment. He loved Ireland. Richard Ryan, poet and diplomat, had introduced him to Ireland and to Irish poetry. He fell in love with both. In fact he wrote two remarkable poems on his Irish experience, one on the loves of W. B. Yeats and the other on the love life of a young Irish aristocrat. With his corncrake laugh and infectious sense of humour, he was a totally engaging man. On the night of the book launch, he took Ireland's literary world by storm. Brendan Kennelly, a prominent Irish poet, professor and raconteur, introduced the book in his own inimitable way. Sŏ Chŏngju stood up to reply. I had been approached earlier to translate. I asked him what he was going to say. He said he wouldn't know until he stood up. That was too much for me. I knew from experience that no translator in the world was equipped for the task. A kind Korean lady who was culturally aware and prominent in media circles was asked to do the honours. Sŏ Chŏngju was quickly into his favourite speech topic, the transmigration of souls. I groaned inwardly. The translator's efforts got shorter and shorter until she finally blurted, 'To tell you the truth, I haven't a notion what the great man is talking about, which promptly brought the house down. Brendan Kennelly had another appointment and had been getting progressively restless as Sŏ Chŏngju's speech lengthened. Suddenly, Sŏ Chŏngju's wife, sitting directly behind her husband, tapped him gently on the ankle with her stick. He stopped in mid-sentence. '*Kirŏ*? Too long?' he asked and she nodded. 'Well, he said, *mach'ijimo!*' There was no need to translate. Everyone understood. The mood was magic. Sŏ Chŏngju had won the heart of everyone in the room, including Brendan Kennelly, who was now able to beat a hasty retreat. Seamus Heaney's Nobel Prize was announced that night. We didn't even make a line in the Irish papers next morning. Sŏ Chŏngju remained completely unperturbed by the lack of fuss and he was enormously gracious in congratulating the young Irish poet.

Next day we went to the Joyce Tower in Sandycove. I can still see Sŏ Chŏngju going up the circular iron staircase, with his beloved wife in front, both feeling their way with canes. And when inevitably they got stuck, he said to his wife with an irrepressible giggle, 'Reverse, love. Reverse!'

Sŏ Chŏngju was eighty at the time. I introduced him to my sister-in-law's dad, who was ninety-two. I told Sŏ Chŏngju that our *harabŏji* (granddad) had the right by seniority to use low form language to the celebrated poet. Sŏ Chŏngju was a bit taken aback, but he said nothing. Our sprightly ninety-two year old was still playing golf, still going to bridge tournaments, still living a full active life. Sŏ Chŏngju looked at him in total amazement and said, 'You are a fairy.' He used the word in the sense of an Immortal. They were both too old to understand the modern implications of 'fairy.' In fact Sŏ Chŏngju's Japanese style pronunciation sounded more like 'You are a hairy.' Not that any of this mattered. This was a magical meeting of minds, two old men communing in the heart. I know they didn't understand a single word they said to each other that evening in Greystones' finest Chinese emporium. Our *harabŏji* was having the first Chinese meal of his long life and enjoying the food and conviviality enormously. By the time the meal ended Sŏ Chŏngju was talking fluent English and had invited me and my entire family to stay with him forever in his house in Kangnam. He was that kind of man. Next year I visited him in Kangnam with David McCann. We failed to get in. He had forgotten about the appointment and retired early!

Resting at *Shihu Inn* (hanshi)

Excessive thirst is an old complaint.
Muggy summer's day; I set out again on a long journey.
With a pot of tea I try an experiment in taste;
it's like frozen snow going down my throat.
I rest again in the pine pavilion;
already I feel autumn in every bone.

The lad can't understand me at all;
he thinks it weird I delay so long.
My disposition has always been broad and liberal:
when I get to a place, I stay as long as I want;
when I meet an obstruction, immediately I stop;
when I ride a river, I float.
What's the harm in staying here?
What's in it for me if I go there?
There's a lot of space between sky and earth;
my life has tranquility.

Yi Kyubo (1168–1241)

THE IMMORTAL KU SANG

It is said that when the whole world was looking for Park Chunghee during the week that preceded his famous or infamous coup in 1961 and failing to locate him, he was with Ku Sang. And after the coup when Park offered Ku Sang a ranking position, Ku Sang is said to have declined saying 'I'm a poet not an official.' It's the kind of thing that, true or false, warms the heart. Ku Sang's unique blend of playfulness, sensuality, and acute social vision, expressed itself in poems that deplored injustice, the abuse of civil rights, and the poet's own weakness in living up to his ideals. He constantly reminded us that the miracle of the Han was stained by the memory of shame. Shame has been at the heart of Korea's modern experience: the shame of a conquered nation; the shame of civil war and the atrocities civil war invites; the shame of subservience to a succession of dictatorial regimes; and the shame of being silent for years in the face of murder, torture and the denial of the most basic civil rights. Ku Sang faced up to this legacy of shame in a way that demanded courage, dignity and a profound moral sense. It is due to men like him that Korea today has been able to rise like the phoenix and deal with the past. I am deeply grateful for having known this fine man. May he rest in peace.

Shame

Between the bars and netting wire
of Changgyŏng Gardens' Zoo
I peer, in search of an animal
that knows shame.

Keeper, I cry!
Is there no presage of shame
in the monkey's
red hole?

What of the bear's paw,
incessantly licked,
the whiskers of the seal,
the female parrot's beak,
do they betray no harbinger of shame?

I've come to the zoo in search of a
shame
long atrophied
in the people of this city.

Korean poetry is rarely so self-critical.

Ku Sang (1919–2004)

The Immortal Cardinal Kim Suhwan

Dust of snow,
a wind that chills to the bone,
pinched mourning faces,
collars raised, hats pulled low,
the shiver of death everywhere.
Cardinal Kim Suhwan
is lowered to his final resting place.

He brought forth simplicity,
a water simplicity that quickened

every root it touched.
He brought forth patience,
a medicament patience that salved
the wounds of the poor.
He brought forth compassion,
a loving compassion that embraced the world.
Simplicity, patience, compassion,
these three:
timber for a master carpenter,
clay for a master potter,
the hub of a master priest's wheel.
'If you bring forth what is inside,
what you bring forth will save.'

Gentle into that Good Night – for Sr. Zita

I think of Dylan Thomas when I recall
her wasted face. Death is no great leveller;
cancer is. Consummation; diminution. Do not go
gentle into that good night, the poet cried.
My heart is with him, but this woman,
signing for her head to be moved to better
see a friend, spoke more clearly than any poet
that there is more than one way to mock death.

14

AT THE CULTURAL COALFACE: IMMERSION, SUBMERSION? – TAKE YOUR PICK

LET THERE BE LIGHT

IT WAS ONE OF THOSE FRESH, pleasant, late autumn days in Kangwŏn Province with just a hint of frost, the air so clean you could taste it. The parish priest, out for a morning stroll, felt invigorated by the crisp blow. Anxious as always to spread a bit of largess around, his one-man entourage advanced in semi-regal progress: he bowed to everyone he met, and everyone who met him bowed back. There were smiles and greetings all around. Good will to all people was in the air, on the tongue and entwined around the bending backs. Public relations was the agenda, an item of the highest priority to the parish priest.

Largess was a universal quality, to be dispensed in large quantities at all times... even when there was question of that most deadly of offences, encroachment. The foreigner always felt himself to be a prime target for encroachment, and every parish priest worth his salt held himself alert for any possibility of the dreaded offence. The world was full of people trying to encroach, but the successful parish priest could smell the kimch'i pot of encroachment before the lid was taken off. After all, protection of church boundaries, physical and spiritual, was his sacred trust.

Against this background, it should come as no surprise that on this particular morning when the parish priest turned the final corner home and noticed activity under an electric pole behind the church, he was alert immediately to the possibility of encroachment. He moved in the appropriate direction, but with neither change of pace nor expression. Everything was done with due seasonal rhythm.

'Morning, men.'

'Good morning, *shinbunim*.'

'Nice day, men.'

'Yes, indeed, *shinbunim*. Soon be winter though. Gets very dark in winter, shinbunim, very dark indeed.'

'Ah, yes, I know, I know.'

There was a brief pause after the seasonal greetings had been exchanged. It was important to hang loose, the parish priest knew, but the double dark reference was echoing through his head. His antenna was up. He did not like what he had heard. There could be encroachment here. Some investigation would be required. He began again, casually, tentatively.

'And what's the job here, men?' he asked.

'We're putting in a light, *shinbunim*.'

'Yes, I can see that,' the parish priest said. 'It's my pole too, I see,' he added.

'That's right, *shinbunim*, your pole, your light.'

'And what sort of light is it?' the parish priest asked, stalling for time.

'It's a special light, *shinbunim*, has to be switched off every morning and on every night.'

'Oh, I see, and who's going to do that, may I ask?

'Why, you, *shinbunim*, it's your pole and your light.'

There was another pause. The parish priest was not pleased with the way the conversation was going. The spokesman for the work party was a move ahead every time. And there were matters here of grave concern, matters of face, matters of money. They were talking encroachment. The face could not be discussed, but the money and the encroachment sure as hell could.

'And who's going to pay for this light?'

'Ah, no need to worry about that, *shinbunim*, it's a special light, hardly uses any electricity at all, *shinbunim*.'

That was the straw that broke the camel's back. The parish priest's inner alarm system went to red alert. Lights that cost nothing. Everything costs here, everything!

'Ah, but I do worry, men, I do. You'll have to take it down.'

'You're joking, *shinbunim*? We've done a lot of work here, and it's all for you. Lights up the church at night. Security, you know. You can't mean us to take it down.'

The parish priest was in a bind. Making the work party take down the light could have a bad effect on public relations. He would have to bear in mind the largess principle. But this was encroachment, encroachment that was going to cost money! Something more than largess would be needed here. This called for an age-old missionary yardstick, namely, low-down cunning, with the mind of the church, of course. The parish priest puckered his forehead and pursed his lips. All externals pointed to a supreme effort at understanding, accommodation, community awareness.

A minute passed in silence while the parish priest racked his brains for a solution. He decided to shift the blame delicately to shoulders broader than his own.

'I'd like to help,' he said, 'but I'd have to ask the parish council, and the parish council,' he continued, 'would have to ask the bishop, and the bishop would have to ask the pope in Rome. It could be six months to a year before we know.'

A master stroke, and everyone knew it. Not for nothing had the parish priest spent his decade in the orient.

The work party knew when they were beaten. There was some muttering about understanding and cooperation, and a lot of general shuffling, of the variety commonly experienced in Chinese restaurants when there are twenty waiters dashing hectically around but no food or drink coming. Eventually the light was removed, reluctantly it must be said, but removed nevertheless. The work party moved to the house of an unsuspecting neighbour, who bought the official line on need, convenience and price, hook, line, and sinker.

He'll be paying for it for the rest of his life, the parish priest thought, with an indulgent smile. Better him than me.

This old sick heart (shijo)

This old sick heart
I gave to the chrysanthemum;
My skein of worries I gave to the dark grape,
And to one long song
I gave the white hair that streams beneath my ears.

(Kim Sujang 1690 -?)

THE CIRCUS COMES TO TOWN
Samch'ŏk Festival. August 1972.

It was hot and sticky. The parish priest was badly in need of entertainment. He had been overcooked continuously for the last two months and was desperate for any kind of diversion. Although interested in the festival, he was not overly enthused. He had been to festivals before; he knew they were rather predictable. Then he noticed on the festival programme that the circus was coming to town; one of the highlights, in fact, of the festival calendar. Now that, the parish priest said to himself, might be a way of spending an evening. He had never been to a circus. He checked again. The first performance was today.

As was his wont, the parish priest sent out runners to ascertain how preparations for the circus were proceeding. News arrived that the big top was in place but that there had been a slight mishap earlier in the day. Seemingly when the elephant, the centrepiece of the show, was being unloaded from the boat to the pier, the ropes broke and the ageing elephant dropped into the water below the harbor wall. There was consternation – a series of *aigumes, ottokanies* and *k'unil nattas* – followed by flurries of excited consultation and anxious toing and froing. Much of the evening's entertainment depended on the gentle beast with the long trunk. Ingenuity and pride won the day. An elaborate truss was quickly assembled and a much cooler elephant was recovered from the water. To the delight of the townspeople, especially the children, the elephant although slightly lame was deemed fit enough to parade through the streets of the town, an essential part of the strategy for drawing a crowd.

The circus was scheduled to start at 5.00 in the afternoon. With time to spare, the parish priest headed for the fair green where the big top was pitched. He had seen bigger tents overlooking the sea in Kilkee, but he made no comment. He was amazed to find that despite the diminutive nature of the big top there was still a wide choice of seating, priced from ten won to five hundred. What the hell, he said, I'll splurge. He handed over his five hundred won and found himself sitting on a raised dais in what was purportedly the royal circle. With no Chŏnju Yi sshi in evidence, the parish priest took the centre position and parked himself on the cushions.

The crowd began to spill into the tent. Soon every seat was taken. The excitement was tangible. The ring master made a point of coming over to the foreigner and addressing him in English. The townspeople were visibly impressed. The ring master enquired in English if the foreign dignitary had ever been to a circus. The foreigner assured him in Korean that this was his first experience. The crowd was even more impressed. The 'ask in one language and answer in another gambit' was a trick the foreigner had learned from ten years in the orient. Whenever he asked someone a question in his best Korean, the answer always came in broken English. He reversed the stratagem with a chuckle. The ringmaster had made face; he didn't mind what language the foreigner used. The parish priest had made face by offsetting the ring master's English with his Korean. Everyone was happy.

The ring master moved back to the centre of the ring, perhaps ten paces away. He welcomed all the citizens of Samch'ŏk; he welcomed especially the mayor, the county chief, assorted *yangban* dignitaries from *ŭp*, *myŏn* and *ri*, the managing-director of the cement factory, and of course the lone foreigner. The mayor made a short speech, which covered the weather, the season, the political climate, Pak Chunghee's love of the people, the price of cement, the well-being of the citizens of the town, and of course the details of the town festival. To a crescendo of approval he noted that the finest circus in the land had bestowed a great honour on Samch'ŏk by deigning to come to the town as the highlight of the festival.

The lights dimmed and the show began. There was a flurry in the corner of the tent. The flap was raised and an assortment of monkeys, clowns and dogs burst into the ring to a background of the loudest, most awful music the parish priest had ever heard. The monkeys and dogs were so close to him he thought he would end up with monkeys and dogs on his lap. The elephant was next into the ring. Dressed up in horsehair hat and traditional garb, it walked somewhat gingerly as a result of the mishap in the harbour. The elephant circled the tiny ring again and again, with repeats of standing on its front legs, and standing on its back legs, punctuated by an occasional stop and gesture with its trunk to the delighted audience. The clowns raced in and out of the ring, and in and out among the crowd, raising shrieks of delight. The tight rope act was next; the clowns performed on the rope at an elevation of about ten feet from the circus floor. A series of fluid exchanges was followed by some close mid-air misses and simulated falls, all of which brought *oohs, aahs, omanahs* and loud applause from the audience. It was at this point that the parish priest became aware something was wrong. He felt a growing discomfort in his lower extremities, a medley of irritants first on the calves of his legs, then on his thighs and – goddamnit – rising. He knew immediately he was playing host to the flea family of the assorted dogs and monkeys in the ring. This was an emergency. The flea invasion coupled with the return of the unfortunate elephant for another performance left the parish priest in no doubt as to what he should do. He lunged from his seat, plunged through the nearest opening in the big top and took off for home like a scalded cat. He had to race-run-walk as the fleas prevented him – in conscience – from taking a taxi. He got to the house, roared for the housekeeper, stripped off, rushed into the shower, screeched when the cold jet hit him. The fleas were presumably equally shocked. He was appalled by the peach-mugwort jungle on his calves and thighs and even higher in the secret foliage. He reached for the tin of DDT, a relic of gouge times, doused all the inflamed parts of his anatomy and any other part he could reach. When he came out, he was still shaking his head. He astonished his housekeeper by dousing his discarded clothes liberally with DDT and then instructing her to burn them. 'Goddamn circus,' he muttered as he took down the bottle of Captain Q.

DECADE-IN-THE-ORIENT MEN

Two stalwart *decade-in-the-orient-men* were preparing the candidates for baptism. A rickety granny presented herself for examination.

Did she know enough to be baptized?

The examiners escorted her into the yard to the statue of the Virgin. The inquisition began.

'Who's that, halmŏni?'

There was a long pause before the halmŏni haltingly began, 'Well,' she said, 'if it's not Peter, it must be Paul!'

One inquisitor eyed the other. Two out of three, they agreed. Not bad. Pass!

A Word for the Wise

What a joy this man,
a catechist who speaks Latin.
'Stercora, Thomas, ubi?'
'Ubique, Father,
ubique's fine.'

EPISCOPAL CLOUT

'The parish priest is a bloody clown,' the bishop muttered. 'That woman is teaching birth control and abortion and God knows what all misfortune, and he doesn't know a damn thing about it. I'll have to handle it myself. Will you drive me up to Omuri, Paddy?' the bishop asked one of his priests who had come into the Bishop's House on business.

'Certainly, bishop. When do you want to go?'

'Now, Paddy, now!'

The bishop was very angry, so angry that very little was said during the two hour drive to Omuri, except for an occasional muttered 'bloody clown.' Eventually the jeep swung into Omuri. The bishop sprang out.

'I don't know where she lives,' the bishop said. 'We'll have to look for her.'

Without more ado the bishop shot into the nearest alleyway and accosted the first woman he met.

'Kim Chŏngsuk,' he said. 'Kim Chŏngsuk!'

The woman looked at the strange, corpulent, foreign figure – the incarnation of a fire breathing dragon. More than a little frightened, she took to her heels: discretion seemed the better part of valour.

'What's wrong with her,' Paddy?' the bishop asked.

'Don't know, bishop,' Paddy replied.

'We'll try a real estate office, Paddy,' the bishop said.

'OK, bishop,' Paddy replied.

As luck would have it, the real estate office manager knew Kim Chŏngsuk well, and he was able to direct the two foreigners to a house about four lanes away. After some more excitement, they succeeded in locating the house in question.

'Leave this to me, Paddy,' the bishop said.

Paddy had had no contrary intentions from the word go.

The bishop rang the bell and banged the gate in one deft movement, a skill he had acquired through many years of residence in an alien culture. A nice looking lady in her early forties answered the frantic ring-knock. The bishop sized his adversary up.

'Are you Kim Chŏngsuk?' he said, so excited by the gravity of his mission that he forgot the seasonal references normal in Korean civilized conversation.

'Yes. Why?'
'Are you a social worker?'
'Yes. Why?'
'Do you teach birth control?'
'Of course, that's why I'm here.'
'And abortion?'
'Yes.'
'You're fired.'
'Fired? You can't fire me.'
'I just did.'
'But you can't fire me.'
'Why not?'
'I don't work for you.'
'Aren't you Kim Chŏngsuk?
'Yes.'
'Aren't you a social worker?'
'Yes.'
'I'm firing you.'
'You can't. I don't work for you. I work for the government. You can't fire me.'

'Oh,' the bishop said, stunned. 'Oh,' he repeated, groping for words. But,' the bishop said, 'you shouldn't be teaching those things no matter who you're working for.'

'And who are you?' the lady asked.
'I'm the bishop.'
'Bishop?' she said. 'What's a bishop?'
'Ah, Jasus, let's get to hell out of here, Paddy.'
'Yes, bishop.'

'Bloody clown, bloody clown,' the bishop kept muttering all the way back to the jeep.

Outside the Confessional

'For your penance, *halmŏni*, three Hail Marys.'
'What?'
'Three Hail Marys for your penance!'

'I can't hear you, Father.'
'Three Hail Marys!'
'What?'
'Ah, go on, go on, I'll say the bloody thing myself.'

GREETINGS

The parish priest was in the hospital to see one of his parishioners. He was feeling fairly sorry for himself, his head still throbbing from the night before. If anyone deserves to be in hospital, he thought, it's me. He bumped into a nun on the corridor.

'Nice to see you, Father. Happy New Year! How are you?'

The parish priest was in no mood for small talk.

'Terrible,' he said.

'Oh! What's wrong?'

'Hangover.'

'Oh! What were you drinking?'

'Martinis.'

'Never heard of them. What do they taste like?'

He thought for a moment.

'Sanctifying grace!' he said.

THE FORTUNE TELLER

The fortune teller had a nice perch in the laneway leading to the church. The wall behind blocked the wind and he had built a little awning to protect the books of his trade which were arrayed on two little stools. The third stool he sat on himself. Fervent *ajumas* on their way home after mass – when they thought no one was looking – checked important matters such as dates for weddings or taking a trip. The parish priest, a man with two decades experience of East Asian affairs, was wise enough to know when it behoved him not to know such things and when to avail himself of the services on offer. A kindly man, he always gave the fortune teller the high form.

'Good morning, Mr Kim. Have you had your rice?'

'Yes, thank you, *shinbunim*. Lovely day and how are you?'

'Fine, thank you. Is it a good day for things in general?'

'Depends on what you have in mind, *shinbunim*.'

'I was thinking of planting a few trees.'

The fortune teller looked up the books. An enquiry from the foreign priest brought a measure of gravitas to his enterprise. It took a few minutes.

'Not so good this morning, *shinbunim*,' he said, 'but anytime after three will be fine.'

When the parish priest got home, he called the cook. 'We'll plant the camellia today,' he said. 'The fortune teller says it's auspicious after three.'

'How much did you give him, *shinbunim*?' the cook asked.

'A thousand wŏn,' he replied.

'*Shinbunim*, you can't get anything worthwhile nowadays for a thousand wŏn!'

Episcopal Solicitude

'And is the parish united?'

'You can sing that, bishop. They're all united against me.'

'And what are you doing for the poor of the parish?'

'I give them the high form, bishop.'

Ch'usŏk: The Harvest Moon Festival

Celebrated Chusŏk with barrels of potent brew.
Weary revellers straddled the warm ŏndŏl floor.
Dawn shivered in; the snores rose a decibel:
too late the portent for those asleep downstream.

THE ONE TRUE CHURCH

The parish priest had his own ideas on Church and community. He announced early on that there was only one church in the area and that it was the Catholic Church of which he was head. This was not openly contested, but old and young worshippers chose to proceed with caution.

The parish priest organized a retreat for the young, a category which included late teens to early and late twenties, in an effort to lift the community out of what he saw as a bout of the doldrums. He figured that he ought to include those contemplating revolt as well as those who had tried revolt and failed. The barber was seen as a key man among those who favoured revolution. The parish priest invited him to come to church and see for himself. The barber liked the foreigner's custom. It gave his salon a certain oomph, so much so that to show his appreciation, he hung a cross in a prominent place on the wall.
The retreat day came, but to the parish priest's utter disgust the barber didn't show. To check on the poor man's health, the parish priest called around to the salon, only to find the barber doing his hair cutting thing with no religious thoughts or empathy for Church gatherings. The parish priest was a little upset. He got himself a chair, climbed up on it, whipped the barber's cross from the wall and headed out the door at speed. The startled barber was stuck to the floor for a fateful moment, then headed off in hot pursuit. The parish priest made it back to the rectory ahead of the barber and bolted the door. The outraged barber kicked in the door but the parish priest sensing the urgency of the situation was already gone out the back heading in full flight for the Old Folks Home, where he took refuge among the grannies until the barber's rage abated.
They say the cross never hung again on the barber's wall.

Written on the Upper Storey of Yosŏng Posthouse *(hanshi)*

When the mood comes, I order a carriage;
when I feel tired, I rest.
A thousand thanks to heaven and earth
for freeing me for such leisure.
I feel sorry for the white haired official
who works the station;
he's cast an entire life
between the hooves of a horse.

Yi Kyubo (1168–1241)

THE PAIN OF IT ALL

The foundress of the Seaton Sisters had been canonized, an event that inspired a huge party in Kangjin. The fathers came from far and wide. They entered into the spirit of the occasion by eating mountains of food and washing it down with barrels of drink. A very auspicious occasion, suitably celebrated, everyone agreed – at least until the evening time when the early pukers began to come to light, followed some time later by a troupe of lads who came down with what Korean describes as motor cycle runs. Many were laid low with one or both symptoms. Those that weren't felt a certain moral superiority, which encouraged them to visit the sick, partly to assuage the suffering of the unfortunate, and partly to exacerbate the situation with a wry sense of fun.

'How are you, Pat?'

'Terrible, terrible,' Pat groaned, running his hand through his hair, a picture of unadulterated misery.

'God save us from sisters,' he said. 'They cause a lot of misfortune in the world.'

'Begor, Pat, you may think you're bad, but you should see Mick next door. He's in a terrible state.'

'Ho, ho!' Pat cried, visibly pleased to hear of the misfortune of someone else. 'Ho, ho,' he cried again. 'That's terrible, terrible. And what are his symptoms?'

'Well, you're just puking, Pat; Mick is puking like a race horse and he has the galloping runs on top of that. He's shit from head to toe.'

'Ho, ho,' Pat cried, 'The poor man, that's terrible.'

The assuager moved next door, thoroughly enjoying himself now.

'How are you, Mick?'

'Bad, bad, bad, very bad,' Mick said. 'It was the oysters. I knew I shouldn't. Ah bad, bad.'

'Begor, Mick, you may think you're bad, but you should see Pat next door. He's in a terrible state.'

'Ha, ha,' Mick cried, delighted to hear that someone was worse then himself. 'Ha, ha,' he repeated, 'the poor man. How is he?'

'Well, you're just puking, Mick; Pat is puking like a race horse and he has the galloping runs on top of that. He's shit from head to toe.'

'Ha, ha, that's terrible.'

Later visitors noted that both patients were much better. Was it Heine that immortalized delectatio in the misfortune of a friend?

AT THE BISHOP'S TABLE

'See here, I've been getting reports of dancing in the parish!'
'Arrah just a bit of waltzing, bishop.'
'Ah, waltzing, is it,
sure that's hardly dancing at all.'

'Now, now, Thomas, if you don't buck up, you could find yourself out of that fine cathedral parish and abroad in an out-station!'
'And what would be wrong with that, My Lord?'

'Could you fellows help me? I've been wondering: is there any difference between a tearoom, a beerhall and a whorehouse?'
'The price, bishop!'

Association of Images

Things linked with bikes:
bad language,
the definitive wobble,
twelve crates on the carrier,
leg contortions,
pigs going to market,
ladders at zebra crossings,
chaos,
broken glass,
stroke.

THE PARISH PRIEST BAMBOOZLES THE LOCAL GENDARMERIE

In Kangwŏn Province in the old days, the priest in the town, especially if he was a foreigner, required some watching. A plainclothesman was always assigned to note all his movements; he wrote down carefully when the priest left the compound, when he returned, and presumably whom he visited. If he left the town in his jeep, the time was duly noted, as was the time of his return. Of what possible interest this was to anyone remains a mystery. We always presumed our phones were tapped, though it would have taken a genius to decode our messages. We used Irish and Irish-English; the erudite even used Latin. Konglish, however, was the lingua Franca and it was totally impenetrable to the local folks. We went for a *nolo,* which meant to go somewhere on a fun outing; we were *mianhaeyo,* which meant we were sorry or indebted, we were *hwaga nasŏ,* which meant angry; we were *nŭjŏ,* which meant late; we were out of *ton,* which meant broke. The NFG designator on a parishioner's file meant no f'ing good. We had a language that no policeman could decode. Of course, this may be the reason the police were always so worried about our *sasang,* meaning ideology or philosophy of life.

There was a timid knock. The housekeeper opened the door and admitted two uncomfortable looking policemen in plain clothes. The parish priest welcomed them, sat them down and ordered coffee, all the while wondering what the visit was about. One of the pair was his regular tail; the second man was new. These were fractious times; church and government were in sandpaper relations over human rights. Park Chunghee's purported *yushin* reform, which would in effect give him the presidency for life, was a huge bone of contention. One or two priests had been deported for their involvement in human rights demonstrations, but for the most part the pressure was more subtle, a sort of diplomatic pressure exerted primarily by the Immigration Office, and secondarily by the police and whoever was in charge of tapping phones. Foreigners dreaded going to the Immigration Office. The officials were cold, unfriendly, and you just never knew what document they were going to ask for next. You arrived each time armed with passport, residence permit, seal, and a multitude of statements and guarantees, some of which had to be notarized. Inevitably there were delays. If you were on the list of parlous persons, you were sent home to bring further documentation. By the time you picked up your residence permit, it was time to apply again. The drill was to exert a constant squeeze. And believe me, it worked!

The parish priest had been at most of the local prayer meetings and some of the demonstrations in Seoul and locally, but he suspected that his main sin had been one of association with those who were perceived to be trouble-makers rather than any personal goof he might have made himself. He talked affably about the weather, the town, the tourist season, business, anything in fact that would keep the two policemen away from the errand that had brought them in the first place.

It took a good thirty minutes for one of the policemen to get around to introducing the dreaded topic of why they were here. And when he did so, it was with a cough of embarrassment.

'*Shinbunim*,' he said, we have a request to make.'

'Oh,' said the parish priest, 'a request for me. Always glad to oblige. Whatever can it be?'

'We want you to fill in a form, *shinbunim*.'

'A form, is it? That's no problem at all. I've filled in hundreds of them. The immigration people have a room full of my forms. I often wonder what they do with them, because they're always the same forms. And are you working for immigration now?' he added sweetly.

'This isn't for immigration, *shinbunim*.'

'So who's it for?'

There was an embarrassed silence followed by a tentative reply.

'This is for internal security.'

'Internal security. Now that's a sobering thought. I've never heard of a priest filling in a form for internal security before. What's the form all about?'

'It's about *sasang*.'

'*Sasang*,' the parish priest said. 'What's *sasang*? I never heard of that before. Do the parishioners need it?'

'No,' *shinbunim*, it's not the parishioners' *sasang* that's the problem. We know that already. It's your *sasang*, *shinbunim*, that we're interested in.'

'My *sasang*? Now I'm totally confused. You'll have to explain.'

'Well *sasang* is what you think.'

'What I think? Do the police want to know what I think?'

'Well, it's not that exactly.'

'What is it, then?'

'It's your philosophy.'

'Ah, my philosophy, is it? Ah, that's easy. Why didn't you say so? I'm a scholastic. I follow Thomas Aquinas.'

'Thomas who?

'Aquinas.'

'Was he Marxist, or socialist?'

'You must be kidding. Aquinas was Aristotelian.'

'Oh! What's that?'

'Well, you'd have to begin with Plato and do all the rounds of Greek philosophy to understand the term Aristotelian. It would take months of explanation. Give us the form there and I'll sign the *sasang* as scholastic. Will that do?

'Ah, never mind the *sasang* bit, *shinbunim*. We'll fill that in ourselves. Fill in the rest of the form.'

The parish priest quickly filled in the form: name, address, home address, title, employer, port of entry, date of entry, date of expected departure. He'd done it a million times. He liked the employer question best. Invariably he giggled and wrote the pope's name. He thanked the police for their care in always looking after him, and their broadness of disposition in dealing so well with his many gaps in understanding. And as he thanked them, he moved them gently in the direction of the doorway. Many bows on both sides were followed by much shaking of hands and a final goodbye.

The parish priest closed the door. Saved again by low-down cunning, he thought with a grin!

Seoul Cabby Objects

'More tests!' the Celt moaned,
unaware that he had an audience.
'I'm sick of bloody tests,
of endless trekking to hospitals!'
The cry of the Celt
was interpreted as song.
The taxi driver turned around.
'No singing, please,'
he said, 'in my car.'

LADY OF PERPETUAL SUCCOUR

It was a strange name for a temple, I suppose, no doubt influenced by local devotion to Maitreya. Perhaps some sick child had been made whole through the intercession of the Goddess of Mercy.

The monks were at table.

'What gobshite put the statue facing the wrong way?' a very young monk asked.

There was a stunned silence at the temple table. The neophyte had obviously not yet learned the wisdom of custody of the tongue at temple luncheon gatherings.

'Pass the salt, please,' the head monk said in a mortified voice.

They got through the lunch without the anticipated explosion. On the way out the oldest monk in the group addressed the neophyte. 'Could I have a word with you, young man?'

'Certainly,' the neophyte said.

'You know,' the old monk began, 'When I was head monk here many years ago, I put up that statue.'

'I didn't know,' the young monk said. 'I'm very sorry.'

'I know you didn't know. That's why I'm telling you. Come out into the yard.'

The two men went outside and stood beside the statue.

'What do you see?' the old man asked.

'Where?' said the neophyte.

'Over there.'

'Where?'

'Ah, out the gate, man,' the old monk said testily.

'I don't see anything.'

'Ah, across the road, look, man!'

'I don't see anything.'

'Ah, use your eyes, man. Can't you see it's a whorehouse. I couldn't have her looking in the door of a whorehouse. That's why I put the statue where it is,' the old monk said triumphantly. 'I couldn't have her looking at a whorehouse,' he repeated.

'Indeed you couldn't,' the neophyte said. 'Indeed you couldn't.'

'You see now why the statue is where it is.'

'I do, I do.'

'Good. Well, don't make a stupid goddamn comment like that again.'

'I won't, I won't. Thank you for telling me.

Marriage Tribunal

But was the marriage consummated, *halmŏni?*

Oh, it was, bishop, it was.

How do you know, *halmŏni?*

I was there, bishop, I was there.

POSHINT'ANG

The bishop of Wŏnju, known affectionately to his priests as Danny Chi, was getting out of jail. His incarceration for opposition to Park Chunghee's *yushin* constitution had been a *cause célèbre*. Many of his priests had grown beards to express their solidarity and support. Now the great man was getting out, and a suitable bash had been organized to honour the occasion. The party was in the bishop's house. *Hŭng* was in the air. Much *soju* was consumed. Someone said the occasion called for *poshint'ang* (soup that fortifies the body), a particular favourite at clerical gatherings. On such an auspicious occasion, nothing could be denied the guests. The executioner was dispatched to the back yard and the bishop's beloved Chindo dog was summarily executed. The meat was delicious, everyone agreed, the soup tantalizingly good. You need a good dog for good dog meat, the assembly of clerics proclaimed. Eventually the revelling petered out and everyone went to bed but not before several more barrels of *soju* had been consumed.

The bishop was first up in the morning. He was feeling a bit groggy but anything was better than being in jail. As was his custom he made his way out to the yard to talk to his dog. Consternation. The dog was nowhere in sight. Staff were summoned forthwith.

'Where's the dog?' the bishop growled.

'My Lord, you ate the dog last night!'

Tears rolled down the episcopal cheeks.

Poem of Flower Stone Pavilion *(hanshi)*

Already the last of autumn is in the woodland pavilion;
a poet's thoughts are without end.
Distant mountains touch the sky with blue;
frosted leaves redden toward the sun.
The mountain spews out a lonely rounded moon;
the river is replete with ten thousand *li* of wind.
Wild geese crowd the sky; whither are they bound,
their cries cut off, caught in evening cloud?

Yi Yulgok (1536–1584)

NO BONES

'No bones,' the parish priest said. 'No bones.'

He put down the phone, sat back in his chair and continued the conversation as if he had just said the most normal thing in the world. Butcher, graveyard robber, crematorium executive – who or what was being refused? No one knew, but there wasn't a man in the room who would not have killed to find out.

A slip of the tongue by one of the sisters solved the mystery. The parish priest, a man of some eloquence, had perfected the art of preaching four sermons in one, but his elongated masterpieces were a source of great confusion to the sisters who craved guidance through his labyrinth of the word: they wanted the bones of his sermon in advance. 'No bones, no bones,' was his answer. Only the initiated knew that there were no *a priori* bones: the bones were born in delivery.

Early Morning Aggravation

Never keep the phone in your sitting room.
Knock at the door: parish priest in long johns.
Thanks be to God, the housekeeper's in.
'Put on your trousers, *shinbunim*, you've a visitor.'
Oh Jesus, what will the people think!

'Ah, come in, come in. What's wrong?'
'I had a dream, *shinbunim*, a dream.'
'I'm sorry, I don't believe in dreams.'
'Neither do I, *shinbunim!* But I dreamt
I bought a statue of the Virgin.
I brought it home and made a tabernacle.
When I woke in the night,
the light that shone from it
lit everything for ten *li* around.
How much are they, *shinbunim*?'
Oh Jesus, this is what the people think.

PRIESTS NOT QUITE FOREVER

Men had started leaving the priesthood. There had been three or four in quick succession. Shock waves were rocking the

Columban Richter scale. A mass visitation was decreed by the Superior General. The abbot, an affectionate title for our regional superior at the time, was very ill at ease in this most necessary of duties. He set out on a trial run taking the vice-abbot with him, a known wag.

Their first stop was a man of unimpeachable propriety. There was a long introductory chat about the weather and Korean politics. The interviewee was much more *au fait* with these matters than the inquisitors. After the third long pause, the inquisitors broke the ice.

'You know why we've come, Tommy?'

'Well, to tell you the truth, I have no idea,' Tommy said. 'I presumed ye were a bit lonesome in Seoul and came out for a chat.'

Tommy knew better than most that four hours in a jeep was a long haul for a chat, but he had no intention of making their intrusion any easier than necessary.

'Men have been leaving, Tommy. We're very concerned.'

'Well, ye can rest easy, lads. I'm not thinking of anything like that at the moment.'

'Ah, we know that Tommy. It's the example we're worried about.'

'The example?'

'It's Stella, your cook? She's the problem'

'Ah, Stella, is it. You're worried about my Stella?'

Stella was in her sixties, big as a house, the plainest woman in the province and the worst cook.

'Gentlemen,' Tommy said with a smile. 'Stella's star would have to shine considerably brighter before there's likely to be any trouble here.'

Invitation

An orchid on the balcony;
a bonsai tree on the table inside –
the pot is ugly but who cares? –
Marian Anderson singing

the St. Matthew Passion;
a volume of Yang Wanli in my hand.
I sit here savouring the moment.
Won't you come and visit?
If you bring the cheese,
I can promise poetry talk
and a bottle of St. Estephe!

15

NINE PRIEST IMMORTALS

Burying Mike Bransfield

Tears, the whimper-rumbling kind
that straddle the Korean volcano of the heart,
eddied through the church, building to an awful
moment. Would the eruption come? No,
ritual carried the day: incense, Holy Water and
malssŭms – a lot of *malssŭms* –
lulled us into everlasting rest in the
buxom bosom of the Lord!
And then, a voice, croaky
and foreign, cut the platitudes.
We've lost a brother, it said;
we lost him a long time ago;
we lost him to the Korean people.
For long we didn't understand.
But we've come, we've seen, we understand.
And we have our peace!

Passing (In memory of Sean Quinn)

Standing on that plateau, close to the sky,
as Big Sean joined his dust to a foreign kind,
I felt weighted to the ground,
too oppressed to cry.

But the sudden intercalation in the Korean service
of a Gaelic prayer – bás gan bás – bridged
half a world and eons of time;
tears circled my eyes.

Mystery

When big Sean died, a man from Pusan said:
I remember him well,
he spoke good Chinese.
Sean's Korean was hands
and the back of his nose;
his English was eyes and ripples all over.
But whatever the mysteries
of his language skills,
you knew it when he was and wasn't pleased.

Good Friday: After a Poem by an Old Master
(In memory of Phil Crosbie)

The day he left
spring roots stirred
in the town where he spent his life.
Holy Week in Hongch'ŏn,
crystal clean, not a mote.
At the perfect time
a subtle fragrance rode the evening breeze.
The flower lives.
For those of us who served with him
the broken bread remains forever.

Purest Celadon (In Memory of Hub Hayward)

We mourn the passing
of one of the last of the greats,
a misshapen pot aesthetically,
but fired at a temperature

that moulded man, message and Church
into a vessel of singular grace.
Purest celadon,
fashioned from first Columban clay,
his memory assuages the pain of his going.
'I work for God,' he said,
'not for any secular power.'
He smelled of pineapples and crème de cacao.
Even in death his name evokes a smile.

February 2008 (In Memory of Wally Nugent)

How we laughed all those years ago
when supper in the market left him green
and he announced solemnly, 'Lads,
I think I have the jaundice!'
We laughed at the incongruity of any bug
being able to beat the centre back's defence!
But God's ways are inscrutable.
Sickness bowed his branches early to the ground.
The slow, inexorable draining of the sap
was painful beyond all telling.
In Korea where the battle began
we weep for the felling of another tree
that purified our air and gave shade in summer heat.
The trees that remain are mostly skeletal shapes,
preyed on by forest vulnerabilities.

Farewell to Jack Roche

He went with a sigh
no heavier than a feather.
He sank without fear
into the deep shadow.
He lacks nothing;
he is at peace.

The inner emptiness,
the sense of loss
are ours not his.
The one remaining task
is for the *ajŏsshi*
who guards the pearly gates to ask,
'Where you go?'
I feel sure he'll answer,
'Ŭijŏngbu. I'm going home.'

Death Song (Grieving for Noel Ryan) – After a poem
by a Koryŏ monk

Seventy years have passed;
now all is consummated.
The road home is smooth;
there will be no more pain.
Your faith and the love of your friends
is all you carry, but it is enough.
For our part memory assuages,
a medicament that cannot be bought
for a thousand pieces of gold.

Granite Man (In Memory of Tommy Comerford)

He thought to end his days, he said,
in a Mongolian village.
We smiled at the indomitable will
of a granite man,
though those of us who knew him
were aware that the no bones king
rarely said exactly what was in his mind.
To rest in the Mongolian plains
would be unthinkable.
Body and soul he belonged with TQ and the boys
in that exclusive plot behind the cathedral in Ch'unch'ŏn.

'And what would be wrong with that,
My Lord?'

It has not been easy to watch
the red embers fade to grey,
the oil in the wise virgin's lamp run out.
Yet the wasting years have been perversely ennobling.
As in John Paul's endgame,
decrepitude flowered, not just in the man himself
but also in those around him.

A moon in the Columban sky,
he lit up the weave of what we've tried to be.
I thought to write a beautiful poem
about the moon sinking slowly into the Styx,
and the symbolic coins for the boatman
laid on a friend's eyes. Words fail me.
The wind tonight is cold; it blows
a gelid note across a gelid river.
Clouds screen the moon;
raindrops splatter the window.

A Cold Eye (In memory of Aidan Murray)

'Cast a cold eye on life and death.'
Yeats' master line rings plaintive.
Murr had no lust for life, no fear of death.
He took what was given,
gladly and without care,
and he went in the end
like the wind leaving the lotus,
'Sorry,
not utterly sorry,

just sorry enough for parting,
not utter parting,
but parting with the promise
of meeting again
in the next life.'

16

SEEKING THE WAY

Looking for the cow – Shim'ujang – (modern shijo)

THE IDEA OF LOOKING FOR A COW that hasn't been lost delights all those who search after truth. Han Yong'un's house was known as *Shim'ujang*, literally search-cow-house. Looking for the cow means searching for enlightenment. Most readers will be familiar with the ten panel screen depicting the theme. The cow gradually changes colour until it becomes white and finally disappears. The boy also disappears.

Han Yong'un's house was on the mountain behind the residence of the Governor-General but facing the other way so that the patriot monk wouldn't have the daily necessity of looking at national disgrace. His poem sums up the contradictions inherent in the search for transcendence.

> No cow's been lost;
> It's silly to look.
> Were it really lost,
> would it be finders keepers?
> Better not look at all;
> that way I won't lose it again.

Han Yong'un (1879–1944)

All My Life

All my life I've sought the Way,
not, I must admit, with much success.

Merton was once my master,
then Yi Kyubo, then Sŏ Chŏngju.
I've known most of Korea's modern literary greats
and one or two of Ireland's.
Super egos and pettiness,
twin art maladies
dulled their burnish.

Kyeshim-sa *(Open the Heart Temple)*

Kyeshim-sa (open the heart temple), a delightful temple in
North Ch'ungch'ŏng Province, is built with twisted pillars and
beams that create an extraordinary harmony. I formulated some
lovely theories on the art intentions of the builders that were
beautifully blown away by the monk's simple explanation: there
were no straight trees when the temple was being built.

Open the heart,
empty the heart!
You open the heart
presumably to see what's inside;
you empty it of what you opened it to see.
Then what?
I try some nice temple speculations:
endless art possibilities on the gothic twists
of pillars and beams.
The monk explains: trees didn't grow straight here,
and it was too far to bring straight timber in.
Good man, Kevin, wrong again!
The monk says that finding the heart
is what his life is all about.
That's why I read poetry, I thought,
grow orchids, stagger
through my rickety qigong routine.
All my life I've gotten it wrong;
I've taken on board what I should have chucked out;
chucked out what I should have taken on board.

Open the heart, Kevin;
empty the heart, Kevin!
Ah bol..!

Savouring the Moment

Sunday morning; the forsythia
about to pop out a bell-tip yellow world.
Two Immortals sit sideways on their tiny bench;
wine cups down, harps – or whatever
those instruments are – down too.
Savour time,
every sense electric alive –
pre-thought, pre-feeling.
I slide in between the two figures,
ask about tea,
and joy and knowing.
Glittering eyes say
Savour!
Eyes all voice, ears all fragrance.
Abstractions shackle!
Know in the belly, not the head.
That's all the joy there is.

Chang'andong Chest

In old Korea cabinet makers did not use rulers. That's why the
drawer on the left in an old cabinet usually cannot be swapped
with the one on the right. And that's why when you paper a
room, the last sheet will be way off the line; old Korea does not
have straight lines or square spaces.

I know many who rant and rave
about angles and squares
on building projects;
no ruler, no plumb line,
no straight-edge.

It's the same story papering rooms;
never a straight wall, never a right line.

I have an antique chest from Chang'andong –
three *ajumŏnis* told me to throw it out,
to get something new and nice instead –
a perfectly mazed harmony
of mismatched lines and crookedness,
inscape of Korean loveliness.

Evening: Self-Portrait

The poet Cho Byunghwa vowed not to build his house in this world.

I've cast off in life what may be cast off;
I've cast off in life what may not be cast off,
and here I am just as you see me.

Have you seen mountains fly? I certainly didn't as a young man, but the passage of the years has brought me closer to the perspective of Chŏng Chisang.

Summer Clouds *(hanshi)*

Sunny day: floating clouds form peaks
in the heart of the sky.
A monk at the sight wonders if there's a temple there.
A crane looking on regrets the absence of pine.
A flash of lightning is the woodsman's axe;
a peal of thunder is the bell of the hidden temple.
Who said mountains don't move?
In the wind that rises with the fading light they fly!

Chŏng Chisang (?–1135)

I've never tied up in riverside bamboo, but when a poet talks about shivering leaves voicing his cares, I think I know what he's talking about.

Night Rain on the Xiaoxiang *(hanshi)*

A stretch of blue water divides autumn shores;
the wind blows a fine rain on my homing boat.
Night comes; I tie up in riverside bamboo.
Each shivering leaf voices all my cares.

Yi Illo (1152–1220)

ANTIDOTE TO AVARICE

I have a Chinese doohickey I picked up for a punt in a curio shop in Dalkey: a boatman sits on a bamboo raft, hands up, head cocked, as if reciting a poem. The paddle is almost ornamental, balanced precariously on a precariously balanced basket, while the boatman's bum, I surmise, were the situation real, would repose in the wet; an irrelevancy, of course, here. Two herons provide the social ambience, one balanced on the foot of the precariously balanced paddle, the other balanced on the top of the precariously balanced basket, delighting, it appears, to play a part in the seesaw ride. I smile when I look at it: I suppose the punt was too much, but money can't define the pleasure it gives me. Should some fool offer me a small fortune for it, I hope I would have the grace to refuse.

Is a Little Learning a Dangerous Thing?

I'm learning the little things now:
how the ring of the phone
beeps the pulse; how wonderful it is
to be, without the blind compulsion of having to do.
Monks call it the joy of inaction;
Koreans call it *hŭng*.
When the fish of imagination nibbles the line,
be it God, Yi Kyubo, a friend, a glass of wine,
the Matthew Passion, a poem, whatever…
shoulders sway in an ageless ritual dance.
Now old age has a new joy in its caverns of loss:

I savour moments more; notice how mountains
run on cloudy days when I never noticed before;
hear the silences inside
when once all I heard was noise.
My God, betrayal of betrayals!
If I'm not careful, I could
turn orthodoxy on its ear
and end up a happy man
in this vale of tears!

17

FOR THOSE OF US WITH LESS THAN IMMORTAL STATUS

Spring Rain

Hardly a day goes by that I don't recall
the Song poet's lament for seventy years
of listening without understanding
to the patter of spring rain in the river.
I listen on, still hoping for the flash
of that elusive harmonics of the heart.

SILENCE

In discussing the human heart, the monk Wŏlha said it is a place neither hot nor cold, a place where there are no worries or misgivings; no thoughts or feelings; no right, wrong, ugly, or beautiful; no time, space, attachment, or argument; nothing physical or material.

What could possibly fill that immense nothingness?
Silence?
The story is never entirely in the words.

Speaking My Mind in Sickness (hanshi)

The world has many flavours;
but I'm the same old me.
Caught between heaven and earth,

my body is a caricature.
It's midday in my mountain retreat;
quiet, not much afoot.
I lie here with the thousand books
in my belly drying in the sun.

Kim Shisŭp (1435–1493)

RUFFLED FEATHERS

The painters came today: feathers were ruffled on both sides in what proved a keenly fought game. A roly-poly *ajumŏni* lay on the bell and served the first ball. I went to the door.

'Is the bell broken, *ajumŏni?*' I asked.

'No, it's working fine,' she said, stepping inside me with her brush and can, as if going into her own house and not into mine.

Love-15.

She didn't say who she was, nice day, by your leave, or why she had come. I suppose she presumed I knew, which I did, but it would have been nice if she'd said 'Hello' and I'd said 'Come in.'

The old talk-decorative high form, ripe rice stalks bowing to the ground days are gone, I thought with a sigh.

'*Ajŏsshi*,' she asked, 'are you going to paint the dust shute?'

'I'm not painting anything,' I replied, a bit annoyed. 'You're the painter here!'

'Well, I have to know whether you want it painted or not. Can't you make up your mind?'

'Paint it,' I said.

I sat down again, aware I had lost another point.

Love-30.

Soon the *ajumŏni was* back.

'I can't paint that door,' she said.

'Why not?' I asked.

'There's nothing to keep it open,' she said.

I crossed to the door, pulled out the string behind and tied it on the knob.

'There are ways out of any impasse, *ajumŏni*,' I said, returning to my chair with the beginnings of a smile.

15–30, I thought smugly, I'm back in the game.

The doorbell rang again. This time it was an *ajŏsshi*. He looked at me in some surprise and obviously felt beholden to make some remark.

'*Pilyo opso*, paint,' he said, with a few dismissive waves of his hand as if scattering chickens from under his feet. He meant, I presume, he didn't need me: I gave him the benefit of the doubt, at the same time recalling all that non-person stuff I'd read about in Cranes's book.

'15–40,' I growled.

A second *ajŏsshi* popped his head in.

'Have you nothing to prop open the door,' he asked. 'We can't paint it like this.'

'You've already painted three hundred doors in the building. What did you do till now?' I enquired with considered condescension.

That's more like it, I thought: 30–40, getting a little of the old confidence back.

My query elicited no response except that he looked at me a little crossly. He solved his dilemma by press-ganging a reluctant passing *ajumŏni*.

Some minutes passed. I drew myself up to my full height, and in my best Korean, form just high enough, I asked, 'When are you going to paint the balcony?'

I knew immediately I had made a fatal mistake.

'We're not painting the balcony. You missed your chance. Apply in the front office if you want it painted now,' he said, shaking his finger sternly in my face as if giving out to me for peeing on the carpet.

'Don't do that, *ajŏsshi*,' I said. 'That sort of gesture is offensive. Where I come from you only do that to a dog.' He looked at me, a long, lingering, angry look. He slammed the door in my face.

Game, set and match. So much for cultural accommodation, I thought. Blew it again!

Autumn night falls on the river *(shijo)*

Autumn night falls on the river;
The water grows chill.
I cast a line, but the fish do not bite.
Loaded only with
insensible moonlight, I row back an empty boat.

Prince Wŏlsan (1454–1488)

ILSAN *YANGBAN* FAILS THE IMMORTALS' EXAM

A *yangban* travelling on the Ilsan railway – taking the subway was beneath his dignity and against his better judgment – happened to sit beside a young woman and her baby. The baby kept rubbing his dirty shoes on the *yangban's* trousers. The *yangban* tried to bring the matter to the mother's attention by a discreet fit of coughing and a very obvious display of brushing, but the young woman didn't seem to notice. The baby rubbed his dirty shoes on the *yangban's* trousers all the way to Kyŏngbok Palace Station. The *yangban* rebuked himself for getting annoyed at the small indiscretion of an innocent child. At the same time he began to justify his anger in terms of righteous indignation, a psychological phenomenon that has been expropriated by the cap and whistle brigade and is becoming more prevalent in Korea as the years go by. The mother is still wet behind the ears, he thought. And she hasn't an ounce of cultural sense. How did her mother rear her?

'Madam,' he said, 'Why don't you take off the baby's shoes?'

'No need,' she said, 'they're perfectly all right.'

'Madam,' the *yangban* said, 'They may be all right for you, but they're not all right for me.'

The woman's face got red as a carrot and she quickly slipped off the baby's shoes.

What can you say? The woman was embarrassed and annoyed. And when the *yangban* saw the effect of his words, he was filled with remorse.

He had failed the Immortals' exam.

A night of wind and snow (shijo)

A night of wind and snow:
I face a plum tree in my mountain home.
I smile at it; it smiles at me.
Well we might,
for the plum is me and I am it.

Song T'a (sixteenth century)

AT THE CLOSING OF KWANDAERI

At the closing of the American base in Kwandaeri not only was the barman ordered out from behind the bar, not only did one man's head fall on the counter from the sheer weight of what he was saying, not only was a road found home that no one ever found again, but a granny looking for the last rites for the third time that week was told by the parish priest that he was a more deserving case than she.

Belch and a Half

Would you believe that one almighty belch
brought an East Coast landrover
to a screeching halt?
The irate driver was heard to cry:
'Damn it,
the transmission's on the ground!'

NO IMMORTALS IN PUSAN

At the beginning of the Korean War, the North Koreans took Seoul and then swept south. Pusan, the temporary capital, was soon flooded with refugees from Seoul and the Kyŏnggi area, and this fuelled an incremental increase in the patrons of Pusan's bathhouses. This was great for the owners, but a problem arose when the new patrons refused to leave at closing time. When the bathhouse staff tackled them and asked why they wouldn't go home, they had no hesitation in saying, 'We are poverty stricken refugees with neither temple nor home to go to. What are we supposed to do on a cold night like this? So we intend to spend the night in the hot water. You'll have to throw the water out anyway, so just think of yourselves as giving a little charity.' This was the harikari of audacity. The hearts of the people of Pusan hardened. Soon the word got around that the refugees were ruining the bathhouses and Seoul people had to be careful because the hint of a Seoul accent could get them refused admission. Wealthy Seoul people used their gold and jewelry to buy rice and secure lodgings in tiny rooms. Making a living became harder. Refugees soon ousted the locals and assumed the reins of power. Northerners with their aggressive personalities hogged all the commercial rights in big arenas like the international market. Rolling stones replaced the native pebbles. The people of Pusan stuck out their tongues at the 38th Midgets, their name for the Northerners, who were notorious for their unyielding, aggressive attitudes. From the people of Seoul they learned how to eat onions and whale meat, which prompted them to write a popular song, 'Seoul-*naegi, tamanegi*.' The song puns on the Japanese word for onion (*tamanegi*) and the popular term for upstart Seoulites, Seoul-*negi*.

Sunrise

I've never been much of a sunrise man,
in the sense of a get up and look man.
All my poetry life I've fought against
the concept in favour of the fact,
but that's not how I was trained.
I was fitted early to a concept machine,
a kebab of Aristotle and Thomas Aquinas:
sun and sunrise for me were symbolic things.
Lately I've begun to think in Chinese terms,
of a sun struggling to get out of bed,

creaking above the east horizon, sweating
to get rainbow colours right.
My God,
no wonder it sits down to rest
first chance it gets!
What I need is a tree!

RIYAKHA

I'm not sure that our ex-pat population is familiar with that
transport vehicle from the past known as the *riyakha*. *Riyakha* is
the Korean pronunciation of a Japanese language import from
English – rear car – which describes the ubiquitous wheel-
barrow-handcart-transport vehicle supreme invariably parked
smack in the middle of cluttered alleys, in a manner, you might
think, calculated to block the greatest number of cars and trip
the greatest number of feet. Not so: transcendence is at work
here; the driver's staff is pointed at the clouds. Beyond trivialities
of time and tide, impervious to the world of time and space, the
driver is for a moment what every Korean aspires to be – the
only man in the world.

My Kingdom for a Phone

The phone is on the blink:
All four apartment buildings
in a communications blackout
the likes of which has not been seen
in Tapshimni since Tan'gun
ruled the land of Han.
Ajumŏnis line up, four deep,
to use the public phones, fists full of coins
to facilitate innumerable calls,
enunciations in shrill tones –
the voices carry to Shinsŏldong –
of a terrible burden:
WE CAN'T PHONE!

I am reminded of the iron wisdom
of an old confrère, now beyond
communication, who in less affluent times
was wont to view with sandpaper distaste
the legions of parishioners
beguiled by the parish phone.
'Do you know what I do?'
he would say
in his granite way.
'I keep my hat on my phone.'

THINGS ARE NOT LIKE THEY USED TO BE

You know what Korean poetry doesn't give me anymore; it doesn't give me the sense of Seoul apartment life Ku Sang style: the sexy flowers of his Mammoth Apartments, the nubile, kiss-bitten women pushing reluctant men out to work. Ku Sang had it, Sŏ Chŏngju had it. But it's gone. Today's poet crop deals with abstractions: they don't give the democratic affront of the apartment speaker system announcing without apology imminent electrical outs, or good value in garlic or oil; they don't echo the cries of *ajŏsshis* selling scabbard fish and other unmentionables in the back yard; or the fruit vendors offering cheap fruit procured cost price in East Gate Market; or the *ajumas* in shabby pants, light years from the glories of Myŏngdong fashion, selling anything that will make a few bob.

Why is Korean poetry so divorced from lived lives, so utterly abstract, so far from Yeats' ragshop of the heart? Why does it marginalize feeling in a land where Zen used to be what everything is about?

Whoever has the answers will be our next great poet.

Spring

Late March;
Cleartown veranda
just before the light;

orchids within, faint
forsythia tips without,
the first of spring
yellow belling the slate light,
while the magnolia behind,
ghostlike, guards
the remnants of the night.
It's not as if the scene
will charm Seoul birds into song.
They haven't sung for years,
if indeed they ever did,
but it's mine to see and feel.
Equally well I know
it's not mine to keep!

READING THE PAPER

The foreigner was riding Line 1 on the subway, the
Chŏngyangni Line, which is noted for high rates of sexual
harassment, not that this is in any way relevant to my tale. On
the other side of the carriage an older Korean was reading his
newspaper, the *Chungang ilbo*. The foreigner was delighted to
be able to make this out; it marked a sort of cultural break-
through to be able to recognize the *Chungang ilbo* from the
other side of the aisle. He was even more delighted when he
saw that the back page of the paper had a huge photograph of
the Giant's Causeway, which was only ten miles from where
he had grown up.

'Are you reading my paper?' the Korean asked.

'Oh, sorry, no!' the flustered foreigner replied.

'It's all right,' the Korean gentleman said. 'I'm pleased. It means
you know some Korean. Come over here and sit beside me. Do
you know Ireland? I've always wanted to go there. I'm told the
Irish are like the Koreans.' He glanced at the photograph of the
causeway. 'What an extraordinary place,' he said. It looks like the
Immortals made it. I really have to go there before I die.'

The foreigner was embarrassed. He had never been at the causeway himself, even though he was born ten miles away. Perhaps the wisdom of the great Samuel Johnson had seeped down through the generations: Johnson once noted that the causeway was worth seeing but not worth going to see. However, this situation demanded a long account of the magic of the place, which he duly provided. The Korean gentleman was delighted to have met someone who knew the causeway intimately; the foreigner was chuffed to find someone interested in his home acreage.

Next time the foreigner was at home, he made a point of taking the pilgrimage.

What a Man!

In the old days
he wouldn't go to bed:
'Might miss something,' he would say.
Five times around the zodiac
and the tune hadn't changed:
'There's a lot to be done,' he would claim.
It took a Dublin don only a minute
to put the bricks in place:
'Were you a hurler,' says he.
'Aye,' came the nervous reply,
'I swung a stick in my time.'
'I knew it,' says the don,
'your eye is never off the ball.'

MOVING HOUSE

Yi Hwang (T'oegye) wrote 'Moving House' when at the age of fifty he moved to the study of his dreams, Hansŏam (Cool Nest Hermitage).

This is a remote place; visitors seldom come;
deep mountain folds where the sun sets easily.

Life here I know is poor,
but it's better than having the body rule the heart.

Returning to the mountains was the ideal of the scholar-official. He could now separate himself from the turmoil of public life and concentrate on learning and personal cultivation. The Chinese poet Tao Yuanming (365–427) wrote a poem in which he said that his heart was the slave of his body during his official career. 'Moving House' was Yi Hwang's response. In retirement, he hoped, the heart would rule the body.

Unfortunately, I haven't found moving house or retirement quite the cultural experience that Yi Hwang talks about. Maybe it would have been different if I had moved after I retired, but my early experiences of moving were so bad that I swore I wouldn't move again unless planted in a box. I knew already from my Columban confreres that moving could be traumatic, because the departing incumbent sometimes insisted on stripping the house of all household appurtenances, often leaving the new man without a cup or a saucer. I remember a colleague running frantically after an overloaded jeep as it drove out of the church yard., 'That's my beer!' he screamed at the top of his lungs. The departing parish priest came to a gingerly stop and restored the case of beer to its frothing owner. 'The cook made a mistake,' he said apologetically. The cook made a lot of mistakes. Of course, my friend had to drink his beer from the bottle because when he went into the house he discovered that all the cups and glasses were on the jeep. So when I took over a *chŏnsae* (key money) apartment from a Korean *ajumŏni* in T'apsimni, I was prepared for some pain. First of all, the keys were supposed to be handed over at ten in the morning. The *ajumŏni* wasn't nearly ready. Two hours later I spied her taking down the curtain rings. I was a bit annoyed. The curtain rings were worth 1,000 wŏn at most, but I'd have to go to East Gate Market to get new ones.

'Why don't you take the paper off the walls, *ajumŏni*,' I said, careful to keep the form suitably low.

'Ah no, no, no, *sŏnsaengnim*,' she said with a smile. 'The paper isn't mine. The previous owner put that up.'
There are times when cultural accommodation can break your heart. Ireland's finest sarcasm, born of the seed of Swift, Joyce, and Yeats is a paper tiger.

Rosslare Birds

I dug up the flower patch today;
spent two hours watching the birds.
A blackbird made two jumps up the wall
like a salmon going up the falls
but with none of the grace.
Got a snail on its second foray,
left the other one, obviously not worth the effort.
Half an hour later a robin made two sorties,
failed and abandoned the quest
as if it didn't really care.
I wondered was it subterfuge.
As Frost would say, birds are not wall savvy;
they cannot fly up there;
they approach their task like thieving cats.
There were five snails on that wall last night.
I left them there, reluctant
to do anything that might impair a life.
I mightn't have bothered.
In the morning there were two;
and now there's only one.
3.30 in the afternoon;
the last one is gone;
I missed its demise.
Presumably the robin changed its mind.
It's hard to imagine the law of the jungle
in my miniscule flower patch,
but that's the way it is.

18

LEARNING KOREAN

I'M RELUCTANT TO TREAT the topic of learning Korean because I don't know what to say that won't sound trite. In the 1960s, there was a school of thought that viewed efforts by foreigners to learn Korean as fundamentally silly. James Wade was the group's major general. Wade was an icon in cultural matters. A big-framed, handsome man, he was a noted music teacher and composer, and an all round man of letters, He had a column in the Korea Times – Scouting the City – which was eagerly awaited every Saturday by the ex-pat community. I loved his column even if I didn't agree with his views on learning Korean, but to be fair, his attitude to the language was based on the difficulty of getting anywhere unless you were willing to live with a Korean family, which would have been very difficult in Wade's time, and attend a full-time language institute, which would have been even more difficult since such institutes did not exist until the end of the 1950s. The Korean Language Institute of Yonsei University (KLI) was founded in 1959 and it claims to be the first of its kind in the country. Columbans ahead of me attended language classes in Seoul National University, but I'm not sure if there was a formal language school there at the time.

It's widely agreed that Korean is a very difficult language for a Westerner to learn. I put in the Westerner proviso deliberately because in my school days Japanese students learned in six months what it took us two years to learn. And my teacher told me she taught two Indian students in the 1960s who learned much faster than any Japanese student in her experience. No one is sure why East Asians learn Korean so easily and we find it so difficult. We complain about the particles *nŭn/ka, ŭl/rŭl,* and we gripe about honorifics and the irregular verbs. None of these is the root of the problem. Getting the particles right facilitates using nice Korean, but the particles were never a barrier to communication, not any more than confusing the definite and indefinite articles in English interferes with communication. I remember Kim Tonguk, scholar, gentleman, and professor of classical Korean literature in Yonsei, talking about the difficulty foreigners have in using the personal pronouns correctly and me interjecting that I had no problem at all while in point of fact using the wrong pronoun. He graciously refrained from commenting on my ignorance. However, while using the wrong pronoun infringes on decorum, it does not impede communication. If you stay away from *nanŭn* and *naega* and stick to *chŏnŭn* and *chaega* when talking to people who are older than you or outrank you, you will avoid trouble.

After forty years of study, I'm still grappling with the Korean language. I'm tired of listening to stories of foreigners who speak perfect Korean. Perhaps there are one or two: usually they were born here and grew up speaking Korean. If you listen closely to conversations in English or Korean, you'll be surprised how many English speakers use halting English and how many Koreans speak halting Korean. English speakers pepper what they say with eh, like, you know, don't you know, I suppose, maybe, say, by the way and so on. Koreans use cha (자), kŭrŏm(그럼), kŭrŏnikka (그러니까), chŏgijŏ (저기저), kŭ (그), itjanayo (있잖아요) and that darling Cholla word kŏshigi (거시기); malhajamyŏn (말하자면) and yek'ŏndae (예컨대) are fillers for the more erudite. If you want to test your language proficiency, summarize a story. You will be amazed how poorly you do in English or Korean. If you want to gauge the next grade of your language proficiency, take ten minutes to prepare a summary. If you don't pass this time, language proficiency is not one of your undoubted many attainments. If you speak fluent English, you will – in time – usually speak fluent Korean, but unless you read widely, the range of your competence will be limited. I knew a man who could crack up Koreans with his funny stories in Korean. His vocabulary, however, was very limited though he could use what he had with professional expertise. Koreans understood him perfectly. 'You're so fluent!' someone said. 'What's fluent?' he asked. I have known many foreigners who were wonderful at chit chatting in Korean, but take them out of familiar territory and they were lost. An eminent Korean bishop talked halting English, but once he got onto his favourite bandwagon, the plight of miners in north east Kangwŏn Province, he waxed eloquent. An Irish priest being interrogated by the Korean CIA in their feared Namsan Compound during the Catholic Church-Pak Chunghee *yushin* standoff in the 1970s, answered all the interrogators' questions with the lovely *kŭlseyo* word, which means anything from nothing to almost nothing. When his interrogators asked, 'What do you mean by *kŭlseyo?*' he replied, 'Exactly what you mean by *kŭlseyo.*' During a moment of silence, generated presumably by the exasperation of the interrogators, he stood up and said, 'Well, I'm a busy man, I'll be on my way.' The story goes that he was half way across the compound before they hauled him back.

As far as learning Korean is concerned, the bottom line is this: if you're an English-speaking foreigner and you begin your study of Korean in your mid-twenties – as most do – mastering Korean will be a life-long battle. If you drop your sights a little and are content to learn enough to talk with your friends and get around comfortably, you can easily join the thousands who have achieved this standard. The short road is to stay with a Korean family and attend a regular course at a language school, preferably four hours a day, five days a week, but this is not everyone's cup of tea. If you are considerably over thirty when you start, the chances are you will never speak fluent Korean, but there's no need to fall into the slough of despond. You too

can learn enough to talk with your friends, get around comfortably and make your stay in Korea very pleasurable. In all
language performance, the rule is: the better you prepare, the
more fluent you sound.

I have noticed that Koreans rarely use Korean dictionaries. I
asked a good friend, and he said, 'I seldom come across a word
I don't know.' I constantly come across English words I don't
know. I need a dictionary to read the London Review of Books
or anything else of a semi-learned nature. I can't read Pound,
Eliot or Heaney without a dictionary. Pound always said, don't
blame the writer for your ignorance, buy a good dictionary!
In Korea this is easier said than done. The quality of Korean
dictionaries remains poor; they are not much better today than
they were forty years ago. There seems to be no process for
refining and updating definitions. Adjectives, adverbs, colours,
feelings, sensations, trees and flowers pose particular difficulty.
If you try to read anything pre-1900, you will constantly meet
words that are not in the dictionary. If you buy one of those
fancy electronic dictionaries, you will find that English-Korean
is the best section, Korean-English is poor, and English-Eng-
lish is appalling – inexcusably so because all that's needed is a
decent computer chip. The 2007 edition of Korean Word has a
translation facility; point the cursor at the Korean word and the
English translation pops up. It's a wonderful facility except that
half the time the word you seek is not in the program's dictionary. The language of Chosŏn is quite different from the language of the twentieth century, and the language of the first half
of the twentieth century is quite different from the language of
the second half. Any translator knows that post-Korean War fiction goes into English much easier than the pre-war idiom. And
in the last twenty years a new idiom is developing, influenced
by the PC and the world of new technology. In Dublin I get
about thirty percent of what my teenager grandniece says when
she talks fast, which she usually does. I suspect older Koreans are
having the same problem with the younger generations here.
Recently I began to read Sŏ Chŏngju again after an interval of

ten years. I'm astonished by the idiom: it is totally different to what poets are writing today. I'm surprised that college students understand him.

In the old days most Korean language students were missionaries. That has changed. Most students today are Korean-Chinese trying to better themselves in life, or Korean-American kids reestablishing roots, or young people of a wide range of nationalities broadening their experience. Often they stay with Korean families, and their language skills reflect this. TV programmes regularly feature young Korean-speaking foreigners. I'm amazed how good some of them are. The secret is obviously to start in time and live in a Korean speaking environment. Our living environment was utterly English – we talked nothing but English at home – and this militated against ever learning the language properly.

Pronunciation is a real problem. The row about Busan and Pusan, Daegu and Taegu is because the actual sound is between B and P, and D and T, but closer to B and D in a Korean speaker's ear and closer to P and T in an English speaker's ear. In the last hundred years the pronunciation of our second city has gone from Fusan, to Pusan, to Busan, quite extraordinary in a language that has no 'f' sound. I concluded that Fusan is a Japanese name (like Fujisan), but my Korean friends say this is not so. Pusan, of course, is much more comfortable to an English speaker; it looks better and sounds more natural. You can never take the bus out of Busan, just as you can't take the dog out of dogripmun. Romanization is an example of how Korea's culture excludes. It ought to be a tool to help foreigners read signs and get safely to their destinations. Instead it is a tool for linguistics scholars to publish their research in learned journals. Korean romanization doesn't care about aesthetics; nor does it care about the difficulties foreigners have in living here. The result is the adoption of a system that looks ugly and sounds ugly. It has seriously impeded the introduction of Korean culture, especially literature, to the outside world. Literature and ugliness are uncomfortable bedfellows. Travellers in the airports of Europe ask about flights to In–che–on (three syllables). In the terminal in Kangnam foreigners look for the bus to Che-on-ju (three syllables). The language is being mangled, but no one seems to notice or care.

You can learn to read *han'gŭl* in a few hours. It is the key to success or failure in your language studies. If you can't spell, you can't pronounce. If you don't know whether the sound is 오 or 어; ㅈ, ㅉ, or ㅊ; ㅂ, ㅃ, or ㅍ: ㄷ, ㄸ, or ㅌ: ㄱ or ㄲ, ㅅ or ㅆ, you cannot pronounce the sound correctly. Most foreigners call Chonggak Station Ch'ŏnggak, refer to Ch'unch'ŏn as Chŏnchŏn, Tongdaemun as Tŏngdaemun and so on. So the sooner you learn to spell, the quicker you'll learn the language. But you won't learn to spell unless you read and write a lot, and foreign students of Korean rarely do either. Read, read, read; listen, listen, listen! Read books and newspapers; listen to the spoken language and to radio and TV. With radio and TV you don't have to worry about what you are going to answer, so you can give comprehension your total attention. The main difficulty in listening to radio and TV news broadcasts is that the language is not the language of the street. It is a specialized language, largely *hanmun* dependent. You will notice that your TV screen provides summary captions in addition to the spoken text. Which is more difficult is a moot point. The captions are invariably pure *hanmun* but excellent training for reading the newspaper. Watch your Korean friends, especially if they are older: they read the captions rather than listen to the newscast. You have to be very quick to read them. And remember, every new news item has a new vocabulary.

In 1964, I began to attend the Korean Language Institute in Yonsei University. KLI had been in operation for a number of years, but priests were being accepted as students for the first time. There were twenty-three of us Columbans, all at various stages of expertise, from raw recruits like myself to men with four or five years experience but little formal training. Two *hapsŭngs* and a jeep took us back and forth to the school every day. There were seven in our group, all newcomers, and because we had arrived in country late, we were formed into a class on our own. Class work was a hard grind: four hours a day of the repeat after me variety, *annyŏng hashimnikka, annyŏng hashimnikka*. But we were young, excited, enthusiastic, and our teacher was a dream. We struck up an immediate rapport and turned the class into a sort of grown-up kindergarten, causing a great deal of curiosity and not a little jealousy in the other groups about what could possibly be creating such hilarity in the dull grind of class work. We had many learning problems. The system was geared to a repeat-remember format, without grammatical explanations. We had been educated in a traditional system, which devoted much time to the intricacies of Irish grammar and the niceties of Latin and Greek grammar so that we found it impossible to pass by material we could not under-stand in the confident belief, as our teachers urged, that one day a great enlightenment would come. The rhythm of class was punctuated by lengthy grammatical asides, trying to straighten out the *ŭl/rŭl* particle in our accusative case terms, and *nŭn/ka* in nominative case terms. The particles baffled us. Just when it seemed we had finally got to grips with the problem, something would happen that put us back to square one. For example, a Korean would say, '*kŭ ch'aegŭn nan choahae.*' We understood in terms of subject and object particle. Terms of comparison were not within our scope. Of course, I realize now that we really needed faith, as the teacher kept telling us, and that Korean's *nŭn/ka* and *ŭl/rŭl* are as unexplainable as the definite and indef-inite article in English. In your own language you use the right form automatically; in a new language you seem to use the wrong form automatically, showing again man's natural perver-sity. I know nothing of the theoretical intricacies of linguistics, but this simple language phenomenon has always been enough to convince me that Chomsky was right when he said you do not learn a language, you grow in it. One of the curious things about the learning process was that most of us had blank spots, that is, areas in which we convinced ourselves we just couldn't learn the point at issue. Some kept on – and still do to this day

– using nominative particles to indicate direct objects. Hours of explaining a simple construction like 'I read the book' in terms of subject, verb and object were to no avail. Others could not distinguish between verbs of action and descriptive verbs, and this caused a lot of confusion in the use of the -e and -esŏ particles. Still more insisted on saying *hakkyo-ŭro* instead of *hakkyoro* and could not be convinced of their error. The wrong pattern seemed to bury itself in ten feet of ferro-concrete consciousness. My own bugbear was the passive and middle voices. It remains so to this day.

There's a vagueness in the Korean language that scholars have never addressed. Active verbs for the most part are straightforward; nouns are relatively easy too, except for the legion of abstract nouns coined by using the ubiquitous *hwa, sŏng* and *chŏk* characters. The big problems come with descriptive verbs, adjectives and adverbs. When I look up a word like *hojŏt hada,* for example, I seem to be looking at the world through a different lens. The dictionary definitions are hushed, still, deserted, lonely, solitary, desolate and so on. My friends tell me that none of these dictionary entries are adequate; *hojŏt hada,* they say, has an essential sweet, cosy note that the dictionaries never mention. And there's a world of difference between hushed and deserted, between still and desolate, between deserted and lonely. In addition, all these words carry enormous emotional baggage. The problem with the English synonyms for a word like *hojŏt hada* – and there are countless examples of such words – is lack of specificity. You solve some of the problem, of course, if you can give the *hanmun*; *hojŏt hada,* however, is pure Korean.

You won't hear a foreigner using *hojŏt hada* because, I believe, the range of meanings is too broad. Similarly, foreigners don't use the popular adverb *kwayŏn* (sure enough, as expected, as a matter of fact). I have vivid memories of teachers straining every nerve to explain *kwayŏn,* failing miserably every time and being at a total loss as to where the difficulty was in the first place. *Kuji* is another difficult adverb. The dictionary meanings of strongly, strictly, stubbornly and so on don't really explain the slight negativity that always accompanies the word. *Ojuk* (how, very, indeed) and *kojak* (at most, merely) are further examples of difficult adverbs. You won't hear *ojuk* until you are fairly good at Korean. Then when you begin to hear it, you will hear it a million times a day. Your Korean friends will tell you *ojuk* and *kojak* are very old words. They'll say they don't use them, but they do, especially *ojuk*. Dictionary meanings for *ojuk* – very, indeed, how – are not much help. 'You better believe it' or 'you betcha' are as near as I can get to it. *Kolguro* and *kosŭranhi* are common Korean adverbs never used by foreigners. *Kolguro* ranges in meaning from evenly, equally, uniformly, to impartially and indiscriminately – a very wide compass indeed; kosŭranhi ranges from completely to unchanged, again a compass much too wide for a foreigner to handle with comfort.

I've never heard a foreigner use *tŏrŏ*, which ranges in meaning from a little to occasionally to a few. Foreigners don't use *purŏ* (most wouldn't even know it's a slang form of the commonly used *ilburŏ*. Nor have I heard a foreigner use *chigŭshi*, which means anything from patiently to gently, or *chigŭt hada*, which means rather old in the sense of a bit decrepit, or *chigŭtchigŭt hada* meaning something between wearisome and tiresome. The range of meaning in these similar sounding terms explains some of the difficulty a foreigner has in learning Korean. A foreigner will never use *hayŏm ŏpta* or the adverbial form *hayŏm ŏpshi*. *Hayŏm ŏpnŭn* tears is a very common expression. The equivalent form in English for phrases like *hayŏm ŏpshi* – I suspect – is noun+less (endless, shapeless, hopeless, timeless, etc.). In English the noun term is clear – end, shape, hope, time – but when you ask what *hayŏm* is, no one seems to know. This is true also *of pujil ŏpshi, nŭtat ŏpshi, and nande ŏpshi*. You won't find an entry in your dictionary for *pujil, nŭtat, or nande*. *Tŏt ŏpshi* and *kŏch'im ŏpshi* are probably explainable in semantic terms, but if you ask your Korean friend what *tŏt* or *kŏch'im* is, you will probably meet a blank stare before *tŏt* is explained as a short interval of time and *kŏch'im* as an obstacle.

In the case of *hayŏm ŏpta*, meanings range from blankly, to purposelessly, to endlessly. To a Western sensibility there is an enormous difference between endless tears and idle tears (Tennyson style), but the distinction doesn't seem to bother Koreans at all. *Kum ttŭda*, a common expression for slow execution, is another example of a phrase where no one knows what *kum* means. *Payahŭro* is not part of the spoken language, but you see the word all over the place in older writing. Dictionary meanings range through truly, about to, in full swing, etc. I've looked it up a million times, but I'm still never sure what it means in a particular context. Dictionary definitions are impossibly vague and the examples used to illustrate usage are impossibly inadequate. *ŏgim ŏpta* and *pujil ŏpta* are examples of very simple Korean expressions that in a context can leave a foreigner unsure of the exact meaning. *ŏgim ŏpshi pomi onda* (spring comes without fail) always strikes me as very strange. *ŏgida* means to go against expectations, break the law, *pŏbŭl ogida,* for example, but to expect spring not to come is ridiculous. *Hada mothae, tutda mothae, and poda mothae* are all slightly different in every new context. You won't find foreigners using them. Look up *tambaek hada,* which is used both of food and personality. If you settle on bland as the basic meaning, you will always be just a little wrong. Look up *hŏt'al or hŏt'algam.* You'll find a range of meanings from physical collapse to despondency, but the dictionary will not give you the sense of nihil or inner emptiness that the *hŏ* character in *hŏt'al* invokes. There are many words built around the *ŏpsŭl mu* character, *mushim, mubang* and so on. I take my stance on these *mu* words from the feelings of the fisherman returning with no fish but with a boatload of *mushimhan* moonlight, which is supposed to be as near as you can get to enlightenment.

Occasionally you'll hear a foreigner use the *itgŏdŭnyo* pattern. Invariably it sounds wrong on foreign lips. When Sŏ Chŏngju was speaking informally, every second sentence ended in a gravelly *itgŏdŭn.* It sounded wonderful, but whenever I tried it, my Korean friends smiled. The smile was enough to tell me not to use it.

Foreigners don't use *morŭmjigi*. And they don't use *hamat'ŏmyon*, a word for which I have a particular affection because my electronic dictionary says it means 'as near as a toucher.' I have no idea what a toucher is. Your English dictionary presumably will not have an entry. In Ireland someone on the touch is trying to relieve you of your money. Of course a toucher could also be a first cousin of someone entering the halls of sexual abuse. 'As near as a toucher' shows the limitations of Korean dictionaries. *Manman* means full of, brimming with; *manman hada* means tender, soft, easily managed; *manman chianta* means not easy to deal with or difficult. It's the normal term used in sports to indicate a difficult or strong opponent. The negative is off-putting for a foreigner. Somehow we expect the word to mean weak or indifferent, the direct opposite of the actual meaning. Many foreigners will be familiar with the word *akki* for musical instrument and *akpo* for score, but who is prepared for *osŏnji* for the paper on which music is written even though – if you know a little *hanmun* – o-sŏn-ji (five-line paper) is eminently reasonable? Foreigners are often uncomfortable with words like *anssŭrŏpta*, *ssuksŭrŏpta* and *minmangsŭrŏpta*, perhaps because they are never sure who exactly is feeling bad – you or the other party. *Ansŭlp'ŭda* only adds to the confusion. And if you can figure why *anssŭrŏpta* has double s and *minmangsŭrŏpta* single s, you belong in the scholarship class. You won't get much help from dictionaries in trying to understand words like *yarŭthada* and *yamujida*. *Yarŭthada* ranges between mysterious and odd; *yamujida* is firm, strong, resilient. But what are we supposed to make of *yamujin ipsul* or *yamujin miso*! *Malttungmalttung* ranges in meaning in the dictionary from blank to wide-awake. What's a poor foreigner supposed to make of that?

Chinese characters were introduced early into Korea. 'Song of the Orioles', King Yuri's famous song, which was transcribed in Chinese, dates back to Koguryŏ. Kwanggaeto's monument (fourth century) is in Chinese, as is General Ŭlchi Mundŏk's poem to the Sui general, Yu Zhongwen, written in 612. Sŏl Ch'ong's *hyangch'al* system, a cumbersome tool to transcribe the vernacular with Chinese characters, dates from the seventh century. *Hunmin chŏngŭm* (Right sounds to educate the people) was created by Sejong and his scholars in 1446. The vernacular script was known as *ŏnmun*, vulgar language, and didn't gain acceptance until the rising tide of nationalism in the early decades of the twentieth century led young Korean intellectuals to see it as a vehicle for awakening national consciousness. The word *han'gŭl* describes the script not the language and so strictly speaking should not be used as a synonym for Korean.

Chinese was widely used in Koguryŏ, Paekche and Shilla. The tradition of the educated class writing classical Chinese poetry dates from Unified Shilla (668–935). Chinese was the cornerstone of a good education, and skill in poetry composition was a major indicator of a man's ability to serve his country well as a public servant; it was also a yardstick of personal cultivation.

We don't like to talk about it very much, but the downside of the dominance of Chinese in the bureaucracy and in Korean intellectual life until the end of the nineteenth century was that it inhibited the development of the Korean language. Very few educated Koreans read *hanmun* texts with real fluency nowadays, and yet the *hanmun* cliché is still a large part of the educated man's language armour. *Saja sŏngŏ*, four character Chinese idioms, dot the pages of the newspapers. The president starts the year with *saja sŏngŏ*. So does the mayor of Seoul and various other dignitaries. These dignitaries may be excellent *hanmun* scholars – though I must admit I'd be surprised. *Saja sŏngŏ* don't seem to be much of a problem for Koreans, but the foreigner is lost unless he knows the characters. *Hanmun*, of course, is decoration; it imparts a superficial gravitas, and gravitas subsumes substance. Go anywhere you like in Korea. You'll soon find that traditional *hanmun* gravitas is *de rigueur*, especially among professionals. Your doctor and dentist invariably use *hanmun* terms that are way outside the vocabulary range of most

Korean-speaking foreigners.You get *kongbok* for fasting, *pok'yong* for taking medication, *ch'wich'im* for going to bed and so on. There are a million such formal expressions. Doctors rarely talk Korean to a foreigner partly because of the need for gravitas but also because they presume, usually correctly, that foreigners won't understand the technical term.What they don't realize is that foreigners usually don't understand the English technical term either.

Admittedly, in the conduct of your daily life, this built-in Chinese formality is not a big deal. If you fancy your Korean, you can always buy a book on medical terminology.You'll have a small battle with the doctor to get him to talk to you in Korean, especially if you don't know him well, but if you are stubborn enough, you'll win in the end.The doctor won't like you for it, but eventually he'll give in. One way or the other, you get your teeth pulled and filled in *hanmun*, you get your appendix out in *hanmun*, and you eat your pills in *hanmun*. And that's only the first chapter of gravitas. Functions of every kind – weddings, funerals, opening and closing ceremonies, staff (faculty) meetings, and so on – employ a formal *hanmun* idiom not used in the normal run of daily life.You'll be told, for example, that the *parin* (hearse <bier> going to the cemetery) is at two o'clock, or the *hoeshik* (meal, dinner) is at 6.00 pm as if these expressions were the simplest in the world.The ordinary *put'ak* (request) becomes *ŭroe* so that instead of *kyojŏng put'akhamnida* (please edit), you get *kamsu ŭroehamnida*. In short, everything in Korea that calls for a bow is in *hanmun*. Koreans, of course, know the *hanmun* terms. Only the poor foreigner is in the dark. If you wonder sometimes about a line of employees outside a bank or department store bowing to prospective customers, or students lining up at the beginning of term to bow to teachers, look no further than gravitas for your answer. Look at the line of ranking professors at any formal school gathering. Look at the way they stand, the way they greet each other, the way they ignore outsiders and non-ranking colleagues – every pore radiates gravitas.There is no gravitas in *p'ansori*.

Hanmun has enriched Korea's language and literature but at enormous cost. It is the root cause of many of the problems in Korea's educational system, primarily because it drives a wedge in the cognitive processes between enunciating concepts and using the imagination. It also encourages superficiality. In Shilla and Koryŏ, poets like Hyeshim and Yi Kyubo, and in Chosŏn, poet-officials like Sŏ Kŏjŏng and monks like Kim Shisŭp were able to see through the characters to the underlying Zen. Nowadays, the characters are floral decoration. When people switch on the Chinese mode at meetings and functions, they are content with clichés in ornate *hanmun*; nothing of substance is said. You won't find passion here; the moon never rises.

One of the more interesting facets of learning Korean is the reverse effect that the learning process has on the way you use English. I knew one man who got into the most extraordinary habits of talking. He would say things like, 'Why you leave case with Mr Kim at Bando?' Another man never gave you a simple yes or no choice; he always said, 'Make up your mind, *ipshi* or *ŏpshi*.' Then there was the gentleman who when he was mildly displeased might call you a 'number ten dog's baby,' which was a gentle translation of a much stronger Korean expression. I remember once meeting an American sergeant in the snack bar of an army camp. He started a conversation in which he insisted everyone should learn Korean. I had been struggling with the language for about five years and I was interested in his experience. I asked him how long he had been here. He said about six months, but that six weeks had been more than enough to master the language. He offered to help me order whatever I wanted to eat. 'It's easy,' he said. 'Toxon means big and scoshi means small. So if you want a big tuna sandwich, you just ask for toxon toona sandwichi; if you want a small one, ask for scoshi toona sandwichi. Nothing to it. Of course, full sentences are a bit more difficult, he explained, but with a little experience, there's no great problem. For example,' he said, 'I'll be going to my hootch (quarters) right after I eat. How do I say that? Well, it goes something like this. Mianmy yobo more small scoshi cuta chogi.' I remember feeling that I had been wasting my time at language school when all you really needed was a bit of neck. The sergeant's sentence was part English – minanmy being me and my; yobo is a homemade Korean-English word meaning girlfriend, boyfriend (wife, lover) depending on the speaker; part Japanese – scoshi means small or short; and finally the bit of Korean – cuta chogi, that is, kada – go and chŏgi – over there.

One night at a movie in Camp Page in Ch'unch'ŏn, a soldier and his girl were watching a jungle movie when a leopard appeared on the screen.

'What that?' the girl asked.

'That's a caaaaaaaaaat,' the soldier said, dragging out the vowel.

'Toxon goddamn cat!' the girl said.

Finally there is the now classic remark of the soldier after a particularly gruelling Ch'usŏk (Harvest Moon Festival). He said: 'Goddamn the harvest moon festival, goddamn Miss Kim and goddamn her goddamn ttŏk!' Ttŏk are Korean rice-cakes, a Ch'usŏk delicacy, of which the soldier had presumably got an overdose. And the soldier added: 'And there's no such goddamn thing as good goddamn makkŏlli!'

Were the soldier to return today, he would have to admit that nowadays there is a profusion of excellent makkŏlli. I suppose the process of inculturation is invariably painful.

There are many amusing stories about howlers committed by foreigners in the course of learning Korean. One man told his parishioners to come out next Sunday paji opshi – without their trousers, whereas he meant to say ppajim opshi, which means without fail. A friend of mine was preparing to go home on his first leave and he wanted to get a picture of a bullock being shod because otherwise he figured no one in Ireland would believe him. He heard that there was a place where bullocks were shod in Ttŭksŏm and he set out to find it. He met a drover near Hanyang University.

'Do you know where the shin put'inŭndae is?' my friend asked in his best Korean. Shin meant shoe and put'ida he figured was the verb to put on or stick on. The drover was a bit surprised, but he answered in a respectful tone.

'Yes,' he said. 'I'm going there myself.'

'Well now. That's a coincidence,' my friend said. 'Do you mind if I go with you?'

'Not at all. But why are you so interested?'

'I want to take a photograph of it.'

'A photograph? What ever for?'

'They don't do it that way where I come from.'

'Is that a fact? And what way do they do it where you come from?'

It was a whole hour later before my friend discovered that *shin* is also the word for semen and the reason the drover was going to Ttŭksŏm was to have his cows serviced!

Another humorous incident tells of a man who saw a shirt he liked in a shop window. He went into the shop and asked the shopkeeper how much the shirt was worth. The owner told him it cost x thousand won. He said he would take it. The shopkeeper said he couldn't have it. He insisted he wanted it. The shopkeeper insisted he couldn't have it. After wrangling for half an hour, the foreigner finally had his way and left the shop with the shirt under his arm. Several weeks later he learned a new word, *soet'akso*, which means laundry. He had commandeered someone's shirt!

There are numerous stories involving confusion of similar sounding words like *ch'o* – candle and *ch'ŏ* – wife. Two fellows got a flat tyre near Samch'ŏk close to curfew time. They pulled up outside a farmer's house, which was showing a dim light. Not having any light themselves and having great difficulty trying to change the wheel, the two travellers went up to the house and knocked on the door. An aged grandfather came to the door. He was profoundly shocked to be greeted in Korean at his own front door by two foreigners. However, it was the message that really blew the old man's mind. The travellers thought they were asking for a candle, *ch'o*. In fact they were asking the old man for the loan of his wife, *ch'ŏ*! 'What business have you with my wife!' the old man roared.

Usan (umbrella) and *yusan* (abortion) are another dangerous pair. A man asked a nice lady one rainy day if she needed an abortion (*yusan*) when all he wanted to do was lend her an umbrella (*usan*). Another howler involved the confusion of *pural* – testicle with *puhwal* – resurrection. That Easter sermon will not be easily forgotten! Nor that famous sermon when confusion between the double *ss* and the single *s* sound led the preacher to announce that the sower went out to scatter the pee! One man told me how he noticed that Koreans often ended formal speeches with the words *isangimnida,* meaning that's all or that concludes what I have to say. He figured this was just what he needed to give his talks a little literary flavour. So from then on he always concluded his sermons with the verb form *isangham-nida,* which means 'it's strange' or 'how strange!'

I set out to examine the difficulty Westerners have in learning Korean. I'm afraid I haven't solved the problem. I am not a linguist. Most of my speculations have been based on my personal experience of learning Korean. No one I've ever asked has been able to shed much light on the subject. Most Koreans react by saying, 'Join the club, English isn't easy either.' It's a commonplace of language studies that 3,000 English words are enough to read Hemingway. I have no idea how much Korean you could read with 3,000 words, but I suspect not an awful lot because Korean employs an enormous vocabulary. You don't need this vocabulary to speak the language, but you need it to understand what's said to you and to read books and the print media. I know quite a few foreigners who speak excellent Korean, but they understand very little on TV or in the newspapers. French and German language programmes concentrate on the most commonly used 500 words. I have never seen a list of the most commonly used Korean words, but I'm assured that several lists have been compiled. I suspect there are considerable differences between the lists. And I've never heard of any formal study of the difficulties foreigners have in learning Korean. While it's unthinkable that such studies have not been done, the Korean language teachers I've asked have been unable to enlighten me. All I can tell you is that if such research has been done, it is veiled in extraordinary secrecy.

I believe the difficulty in learning Korean is primarily vocabulary related, firstly in terms of the sheer number of words in everyday use, secondly in terms of Western logic failing to grasp the nuances of a myriad Korean terms, what I have described earlier as seeing the world through a different lens, and thirdly in terms of how the particular language forum – street, pub, kitchen, class room, TV, newspaper and so on – controls vocabulary. Our Western syllogistic approach is miles from the Korean circular style of thinking. I often wonder if adverbs, in particular, have Buddhist underpinnings that cause foreigners problems. I think especially of adverbs that use the *hŏ, mu,* or *pu* character. The range of meanings in these Korean adverbial forms is often outside the parameters of our Western logic.

The area cries out for research by a first-rate Korean linguist. Chu Shigyŏng (1876–1914) and Ch'oe Hyŏnbae (1894–1970) were the early giants in the field of Korean grammar. Chu Shigyong invented the term han'gŭl and wrote the first grammar, *Kugŏ munbŏp* (1910). Ch'oe Hyŏnbae's *Urimalbon* was published in 1937. Notice that thirty years divide these seminal publication events. Even more interestingly, the first Korean dictionary (*hangŭl*) wasn't published until 1957. *Roget's Thesaurus* has a permanent place on my desk. Translation without it would be unthinkable. I have no idea if there is a Korean thesaurus, though I presume there must be. All I can say is that my friends never use one.

The road to mastery of Korean is long and hard. You may never get there, but you'll have a lot of fun trying and your life here will be enormously enriched. And remember: in acquiring language proficiency a bit of neck is worth its weight in gold. I wish you much good luck in your efforts.

AFTERWORD

THIS BOOK WOULD NOT BE COMPLETE without a note on North Korea. A trip to the Diamond Mountains reinforced the idea of the ugly arrayed alongside the beautiful, though the north's greatest ugliness was its utter lack of freedom.

Kŭmgang San: The Diamond Mountains

It's a pure land, but alien, aloof, contradictory;
no fish in its mountain waters,
no birds in its mountain air;
no tangible Buddha presence anywhere.
A green antiseptic beauty reigns,
encumbering the intruder,
tying the ox to its cart,
regulating Zen from the heart.

Samilp'o, where the hwarang sported
while the lake water laughed in the sun,
is holy ground now; idols are enshrined.
Joy would be indecorous; the water is forbidden to laugh.

Kim Shisŭp, mendicant monk, slipped from the woods:
'Find joy where you can,' he said; 'that's what counts!'
'Awe comes easy here,' I said; 'but joy is constrained.'
'There comes a time,' the good monk said,
'when you let the thousand books in your belly dry in the sun;
forget ideology; think mugwort thoughts.

Draw into the light to see what you're saying.
Go to Nine Dragon Falls; jade water slips from pool to pool.
There's been no rainy season this year; the flow is slack,
but there are other pulses there that will let you feel
the vitality that has sustained us for five thousand years.'
I took the monk at his word
and made the two hour trek to the falls.
I discovered the elusive pulse of joy
where I least expected it, in the cries of pleasure
of grannies gulping the elixir waters. Iron-couraged,
they had slid-scrambled for hours to make it here.
No surge of unfreedom would prevail
against this tide of redeeming *yin*.

Man makes lovely things; not here though;
there are no pavilions, no temples, no wind bells.
The denizens of the land are denied access;
no monks play *paduk* in the shade.
Man's legacy is concrete grey.
Moonlight sweeps the deck of the Kŭmgang ho;
'White Night' frost chills the heart.
Diamond beauty, I reflect, has been dearly bought.

Lovely Kŭmgang, a forty-year dream is fulfilled.
I'm glad to have made this pilgrimage;
I rejoice in the beauty I've seen,
shudder that it's barely allowed to breathe.
I will not return while the present insanity prevails.
I resent being herded like sheep through a gap,
watched by ice eyes under broad brimmed caps.
I want to sail up the coast by day,
not slink up under cover of dark!
And surely a single stamp in and out should suffice!
Grannies with sticks are unlikely spies.
I want to see men and women on the docks,
enjoy a cup of coffee in the town,

talk to the people about the drought.
I want evidence that the human spirit is intact.
Above all, I want to buy a simple book of poems
and know it won't be confiscated in the south.

BIBLIOGRAPHY

◙

Crane Paul. *Korean Patterns*. Seoul: RAS, 1978.

Dallet, Claude Charles, *Histoire de L'Eglise de Coree*. Paris: Librairie Victoire Palme, 1874. (A partial English translation is available.)

Hoyt, James. *Soaring Phoenixes and Prancing Dragons*. Seoul: Jimoondang, 2000.

Kim Chonggil. *The Darling Buds of May*. Seoul: Korea University Press, 1991.

Kim Hŭnggyu. *Understanding Korean Literature*, translated by Robert J. Fouser. New York: Sharpe, 1987.

Ledyard, Gari. *The Dutch Come to Korea*. Seoul: RAS, 1971.

Liu, James. *The Art of Chinese Poetry*. Chicago and London: The University of Chicago Press, 1966.

Mullany, Francis. *Symbolism in Korean Ink Brush Painting*. Folkestone: Global Oriental, 2006.

O'Rourke, Kevin. *Tilting the Jar, Spilling the Moon*. Dublin: Dedalus 1993.

O'Rourke, Kevin. *Poems of a Wanderer: Selected Poems of Sŏ Chŏngju*. Dublin: Dedalus, 1995.

O'Rourke, Kevin. *Looking for the Cow* (modern Korean poems). Dublin: Dedalus, 1999.

O'Rourke, Kevin. *Mirrored Minds: A Thousand Years of Korean Verse*. Seoul: Eastward Publication, 2001.

O'Rourke, Kevin. *The Book of Korean Shijo*. Cambridge: Harvard, 2002.

O'Rourke, Kevin. *A Hundred Love Poems from Old Korea*. Folkestone: Global Oriental, 2005.

O'Rourke, *Kevin, Selected Poems of Kim Sakkat*. Taegu: Keimyung University Press, 2012.

O'Rourke, Kevin. *Singing Like a Cricket, Hooting Like an Owl: Selected Poems of Yi Kyubo*. Ithaca: Cornell East Asia Series, 1995.

O'Rourke, Kevin. *The Book of Korean Poetry: Chosŏn Dynasty*. Singapore: Stallion Press, 2013.

O'Rourke, Kevin. *The Book of Korean Poetry: Songs of Shilla and Koryŏ*. Iowa City: Iowa University Press, 2006.

O'Rourke, Kevin. (Yi Munyŏl novella) *Our Twisted Hero*. Seoul: Minŭmsa 1989, NewYork: Hyperion 2002.

Rutt, Richard, Kim Chŏng-un. *Virtuous Women*. Seoul: Unesco, 1974.

Rutt, Richard. *History of the Korean People*. Seoul: RAS, 1972

INDEX

回